Medieval Saints in
Late Nineteenth Century
French Culture

Medieval Saints in Late Nineteenth Century French Culture

Eight Essays

Edited by
ELIZABETH EMERY *and*
LAURIE POSTLEWATE

McFarland & Company, Inc., Publishers
Jefferson, North Carolina, and London

LIBRARY OF CONGRESS CATALOGUING-IN-PUBLICATION DATA

Medieval saints in late nineteenth century French culture : eight
  essays / edited by Elizabeth Emery and Laurie Postlewate.
       p.   cm.
  Includes bibliographical references and index.

  ISBN 0-7864-1769-2 (softcover : 50# alkaline paper)

  1. French literature—19th century—History and citicism.
  2. Saints in literature.   I. Emery, Elizabeth (Elizabeth Nicole).
  II. Postlewate, Laurie, 1957- .
  PQ283.M4 2004
  840.9'38270092—dc22
                                                  2004004058

British Library cataloguing data are available

©2004 Elizabeth Emery and Laurie Postlewate. All rights reserved

*No part of this book may be reproduced or transmitted in any form
or by any means, electronic or mechanical, including photocopying
or recording, or by any information storage and retrieval system,
without permission in writing from the publisher.*

Cover photograph: S. Luc patron des artistes et ouvriers d'art. Painting from
Notre-Dame du Travail, Paris, France.

Manufactured in the United States of America

McFarland & Company, Inc., Publishers
  Box 611, Jefferson, North Carolina 28640
    www.mcfarlandpub.com

Contents

Introduction   *Elizabeth Emery*   1

PART ONE
SAINTS AS INSPIRATION FOR ART, LITERATURE AND MUSIC

1. "Sur un vitrail d'église": Structures and Sources in Flaubert's "Légende de Saint Julien l'Hospitalier"   **Rori Bloom**   13

2. When the Saints Go Marching In: Popular Performances of *La Tentation de Saint Antoine* and *Sainte Geneviève de Paris* at the Chat Noir Shadow Theater   **Madhuri Mukherjee**   25

PART TWO
THE "SCIENTIFIC" EXAMINATION OF SAINTS' VISIONS

3. Odilon Redon's *Temptation of Saint Anthony* Lithographs   **Barbara Larson**   47

4. *The Golden Legend* in the Fin de Siècle: Zola's *Le Rêve* and Its Reception   **Elizabeth Emery**   83

PART THREE
THE STRUGGLE TO RECONTEXTUALIZE HAGIOGRAPHY

5. *Translatio Lidwinae*: The Adaptation of Medieval Sources in Huysmans' *Sainte Lydwine de Schiedam*   **Laurie Postlewate**   119

6. Discourse on Method: Hippolyte Delehaye's *Légendes hagiographiques*   **C. J. T. Talar**   139

PART FOUR
HAGIOGRAPHY AND THE CULT OF THE NATION

7. Polychromatic Piety: Saints According to Anatole France
   Christina Ferree Chabrier   163

8. Unofficial and Secular Saint in Integral Nationalist Discourse: Maurice Barrès' Literary Jeanne d'Arc
   Carolyn Snipes-Hoyt   195

Conclusion   *Elizabeth Emery*   223

Select Bibliography of Secondary Sources   237
About the Contributors   243
Index   245

Introduction

Elizabeth Emery

Les primitifs en peinture, au théâtre les anciens mystères, voilà l'objectif d'une époque raffinée et compliquée jusqu'au bysantinisme, et déjà la jeunesse, écoeurée des vieilles rengaines de la routine et de l'école, se prend, dans un indicible malaise d'étouffement, à tendre des bras désespérés vers le catholicisme, vers tes ailes de pierre, ô folle cathédrale, et tes lentes sonneries, et tes clairs angélus, et ta croix haute et fière entre l'envol de tes tours. ... La cathédrale, l'enfance, la légende des saints, miraculeuse et fleurie, épelée sur les genoux de l'aïeule, la grand-messe où l'on nous conduisait le dimanche, la somnolence des vêpres entendues comme dans un rêve, et la fantasmagorie des fins encensoirs d'or montant dans les pierreries brazillantes des vitraux, et puis Pâques, et son ciel d'avril lumineux et léger, tout rempli d'envolées d'archanges en fusée, d'extatiques ascensions de saintes, les mains jointes, d'essors d'âmes toutes blanches et d'hymnes d'allégresse ardente et de pur amour![1]
—Jean Lorrain, "Les Costumes mystiques," 1891

At the end of the nineteenth century, legends, tales and mystery plays featuring saints captivated the French. As Jean Lorrain pointed out in an 1891 article for the popular weekly *Le Courrier Français*, the seemingly simple language of saints' lives, their valiant battles between good and evil, and the atmosphere of religious mysticism that infused them appealed to many, especially those involved in the visual and performing arts. He also noted that between 1890 and 1891, saints appeared all over Paris: the Chat Noir shadow play "Marche à l'étoile" (1890), Edmond d'Haraucourt's mystery play, La Passion (1890), and Maurice Bouchor's short plays (Tobie, 1889, Noël, 1890), which were performed with music at the Théâtre des Marionettes in the Galerie Vivienne. In literature, Jean Moréas's collection of poems, Le Pèlerin passionné, was serialized in L'Echo de Paris in 1891, while an illustrated edition of Emile Zola's 1888 novel Le Rêve was published in La Revue illustrée. In the late 1880s and early 1890s, artists appropriated the saints for popular culture.

Given France's loyalty to the Catholic Church (the country was known as the eldest daughter of the Church), it is not surprising that saints would be influential; indeed, one would expect it. What is surprising, however, is, as Lorrain pointed out, the extent to which "the young"—the artists and writers of the first "Republican generation" in France, a group exposed to a largely secular public school system—would favor saints and mystical tendencies.[2] Renewed interest in the saints and religious imagery would seem natural for periods such as the Restoration, in which the recently reestablished monarchy worked to reaffirm the nation's Catholic heritage, or the Second Empire, where Louis-Napoléon championed the Church. It is thus odd that the Third Republic (1870–1940), a regime that claimed to reinforce and institute the secular ideals of the French Revolution, would be the period to witness such popular interest in the saints. The motto of one of the Republic's early defenders, Léon Gambetta, was, after all, "Le cléricalisme, voici l'ennemi!" His followers imposed secular education, broke up congregations and established the formal separation of church and state (1905).

Pierre Larousse, author of the Grand dictionnaire universel du XIXe siècle, captures the skepticism of Republican attitudes toward religion in his dictionary entry for "saints." He characterizes saints' lives as violent and exotic fairy tales: "Aussi pauvres d'idées que de style, compilations de légendes souvent indécentes et toujours grotesques ... une succession de récits merveilleux à faire pâlir les Mille et une nuits."[3] Given this intellectual climate, why did so many agnostic writers, artists and historians choose to represent religious figures in their works? What was the attraction of such beliefs? What does the fascination with the saints say about this period, outwardly so dedicated to anticlerical movements?

Such questions about the paradoxical fascination with the saints during one of the most anticlerical periods of French history prompted this volume. These essays explore the popularity of saints from the 1850s to the 1920s, while appraising the role they played in literature, art, music, science, history and politics. In examining low and high culture—from children's literature, shadow plays and the popular press to literature, opera and theological studies—the volume reveals the prevalence of saints in fin-de-siècle France while analyzing their appeal. Although a number of articles and books have explored the importance that saints have played for individual authors or within specific fields, few have acknowledged the widespread interest in saints and religious imagery in Third Republic society as a whole, and none has examined their prevalence at all levels of society.[4] Michael Paul Driskel's seminal work *Representing Belief: Religion, Art, and Society in Nineteenth-Century France* is one of the few works to draw attention to the critical importance of religious themes in the art of the period.[5] Cristina Mazzoni's *Saint Hysteria: Neurosis, Mysticism, and Gender in European Culture* is similarly important for saints in the realm of science, psychology and gender studies.[6] In *Consuming the Past: The Medieval Revival in Fin-de-siècle France*, Elizabeth Emery and Laura Morowitz trace the ways in which interest in the saints occurred alongside general enthusiasm for all things medieval.[7] These studies all provide a valuable complement to this volume, which discusses art and science, but which also extends the study of saints to literature, music, history and politics. Saints' lives, which could be appropriated as legend, history or hagiography, allowed for a great deal of interpretorial flexibility: popularizing them as "tales" or biography invited one to isolate *vitae* from the religious context that had once inspired them, thus leaving them free to take on new forms.

Although not all saints lived during the Middle Ages, they are often associated with the medieval period because of its widespread cult of the saints. The numerous hagiographies (from the Greek *hagios*, holy, and *graphe*, writing) composed during the Middle Ages were not biographies in the modern sense, but rather attempts to represent saints as incarnations of the Church's values, as models of the Christian faith. As such, hagiographers were less concerned with historical accuracy than with recounting the particular moments of saints' lives that exemplified their virtues or their miraculous relationship with God.[8]

In the thirteenth century, Jacobus de Voragine's *Legenda Sanctorum* (*Readings on the Saints*), a compilation of saints' lives, was so beloved that it was nicknamed the *Légende dorée* or *Golden Legend*.[9] More than just an often copied manuscript, it was, as Sherry Reames has put it, "almost a cultural institution"; it is thought that only the Bible was more widely read and reproduced.[10] In the late Middle Ages, saints' lives were used not only to illustrate Christian virtues, but also to worship: Readings from *vitae* accompanied liturgical celebrations of saints' lives, and books of hours brought such celebration into the home; saints were represented in sculpture, stained glass and painting; and pilgrimages sprang up to venerate local saints, their relics and their miracles.[11] Although the great popularity of Voragine's text declined in the sixteenth and seventeenth centuries,[12] the lives of the saints remained popular in France; until late in the nineteenth century, it was not uncommon for rural families to own only one or two books, generally the Bible and a version of *La Vie de saints*.[13] The Société des Bollandistes, formed in the seventeenth century to publish volumes of saints' lives, established the *Acta Sanctorum* in 1643; this organization was instrumental in preserving texts dedicated to saints. Reformed at the beginning of the nineteenth century (1837), the group would renew historical studies of the saints in the fin de siècle through the establishment of new scholarly outlets: *Analecta Bollandiana* (1882) and *Subsidia Hagiographica* (1886).[14]

Popular images of the saints had long proliferated in France; in the Middle Ages wealthy patrons commissioned books of hours or reproductions of the lives of the saints, a practice that continued into the nineteenth century.[15] Early nineteenth-century developments in printing methods made it simple and inexpensive to reproduce images on a mass scale. Indeed, new technology coincided with France's post–Napoleonic return to Catholicism, thus creating an industry dedicated to producing pious images that were extremely popular as gifts.[16] These popular images were often of poor quality and portrayed simplistic images of the saints with raised eyes and hands lifted in prayer; they drew the ire of many artists, who harshly criticized these *bondieuseries* as commercial, kitschy, and bereft of artistic sentiment[17] (Fig. 0.1).

The pilgrimage movement that exploded in the second half of the nineteenth century made such images even more prevalent.[18] As organized pilgrimages brought millions of people to Lourdes and La Salette, recent sites of saintly apparitions, visitors purchased religious souvenirs and trinkets in huge volume. From statues of Bernadette and other saints to postcards, rosaries, votive candles and medallions, the production of religious souvenirs became a lucrative industry.[19]

In the fin de siècle, however, saints crossed from this largely religious context to avant-garde artistic circles, appearing not only in churches or at pilgrimage sites, but also in cabarets, Symbolist poems and plays. It is this phenomenon that lies at the center of this volume: Why would a generation raised on largely secular education and ideals turn to the saints as a source of inspiration? In the citation with which we began this introduction, Jean Lorrain links the widespread fascination for the saints to a variety of causes: a revival of interest in the medieval period, attraction to the mysticism and artistic trappings of religion and nostalgic memories of childhood religious experiences.[20] Indeed, for the first largely secular French generation, religious themes must have seemed exotic vestiges of the past.

All of these causes, however, were themselves prompted by another common complaint: dissatisfaction with the banality of the present. This sense of "stifling," as Lorrain calls it, or *spleen*, was widespread in artistic circles. In journalist Jules Huret's 1891 *Enquête sur l'évolution littéraire*, a series of interviews with leading literary figures published in *L'Echo de Paris*, nearly every writer interviewed complained about modern France.[21] From disgust with Naturalism and its overwhelming pessimism to distress over the ugliness of Republican art, they expressed fatigue and ennui with the routine of day-to-day life in fin-de-siècle France. As Lorrain put it, this period often compensated for its boredom by returning to the past for ideas.

The first section of this volume, "Saints as Inspiration for Art, Literature and Music," explores the tendency to seek artistic inspiration in models from the past. Rori Bloom and Madhuri Mukherjee examine the fascination that saints' lives exerted over writers and artists interested in exploring the relationships among different arts. Modeling their modern saints' lives on medieval or medieval-inspired representations of saints, Gustave Flaubert and Henri de Rivière took medieval art—hagiography, stained glass, painting and music—as a starting point for their own unique explorations of these legends in literature and the performing arts.

Such engagement with the exoticism of saintly figures coincided with the rise of scientific interest in *La Vie des saints*. Although Gustave Brunet had published an 1843 translation of Voragine's *La Légende dorée* (alleged to be the first published in the vernacular in 300 years), the text was not widely known in fin-de-siècle France. Alfred Maury's 1843 *Essai sur les légendes pieuses du moyen âge ou examen de ce qu'elles renferment de merveilleux, d'après les connaissances que fournissent de nos jours l'archéologie, la théologie, la philosophie, et la physiologie médicale*, one of the sources of Flaubert's tale, was much better known. Its insistence on scientific and positivist approaches to saints' lives influenced a generation of scientists, who reexamined saints' lives in the context of newly formed medical theories about visions and visionaries.[22] The second part of this volume, "The 'Scientific' Examination of Saints' Visions," examines the period's curiosity about medicalized studies of the saints.

Barbara Larson analyzes Odilon Redon's elaborate prints for Flaubert's *La Tentation de Saint Antoine*. While ostensibly based on medieval hagiography, this text and artistic responses to it exposed late nineteenth-century fears of sickness, contagion and madness. Paradoxically, it was author Emile Zola, renowned for his Naturalist studies of these very themes, who

Fig. O.1. Holy cards from late nineteenth- and early twentieth-century Paris.

popularized medieval saints' lives in the 1880s with his novel and opera *Le Rêve*. Elizabeth Emery's study of these works and their reception shows how Zola's glorification of *The Golden Legend* and his analysis of a young woman's spiritual education struck a chord with a variety of readers who interpreted the works according to very different conceptions of saints.

Popular and scientific appropriations of the previously sacred saints' lives set off a backlash in Catholic circles, thus leading to a movement to wrest them from "superficial" uses. The third section, "The Struggle to Recontextualize Hagiography," explores the tensions between secular and religious factions of society. In the period between 1870 and 1905 (the year in which the French finally separated church from state), tensions between believers and nonbelievers escalated. In this section, Laurie Postlewate traces J.-K. Huysmans' attempt to return to the practices of medieval hagiography in writing his "Life" of Saint Lydwine, while C. J. T. Talar analyzes hagiographical techniques debated by Bollandists at the turn of the century. Such writers attempted to recontextualize saints, to reinvest them with the exemplary functions and religious belief they originally served in the Church.

Saints became figures of predilection not only for the artistic avant-garde, for the medical establishment and for practicing Catholics, but also for those interested in the history of the French nation. The final section, "Hagiography and the Cult of the Nation," treats a different kind of sacred function for saints: They became figures representative of a valuable and disappearing common heritage. Christina Ferree Chabrier traces the anticlerical Anatole France's uncharacteristic fondness for the saints as a reflection of debates between reason and superstition, but also as nostalgia for a defunct way of life. Carolyn Snipes-Hoyt chronicles a different kind of appreciation for the past while studying the complex forces—among them religion, patriotism, misogyny and xenophobia—that led the French to canonize Joan of Arc, a medieval visionary turned national hero.

Though divided into thematic sections, these essays all share common elements: They reveal that throughout the fin-de-siècle period saints appeared in response to dissatisfaction with the present, to worries about the status of art, religion or morals, and to fears of sickness, contagion and foreign influence. Yet despite these commonalities, each representation of a saint was profoundly different. As in the Middle Ages, when saints' lives were valued less as biography than as examples of Christian faith, the nineteenth century took from these saints' stories what they needed for their immediate goals: local color, entertainment, scientific meditations, faith and patriotism, to name just a few. As a result, although representations of saints were influenced by medieval traditions, they were also profoundly anchored in the nineteenth century. Saints' lives echo many of the period's tensions: between art and commerce, faith and history, religious and secular beliefs, church and state. As nineteenth-century thinkers rediscovered the *vita*, their own practice of this medieval genre led to a reconsideration of its nature and application to modern society. Was it possible to write such a sacred narrative in the secular late nineteenth century? And if so, what form should it take? Was a saint's life legend, history or hagiography?

Notes

1. "Primitives in painting, old mystery plays at the theater, these are the objec- tives of an era refined and complicated to the hilt, and the young, sick from the

same old song of routine and school, are already caught up in an inexpressibly stifled state, reaching their arms desperately toward Catholicism, toward your wings of stone, oh wild cathedral, and your slow ringing, and your clear angelus, and your cross, high and proud between your soaring towers. ... The cathedral, childhood, the miraculous and flowering legend of saints sounded out on the knees of a grandparent, high mass where they led us on Sunday, the indolence of vespers heard as through a dream, and the phantasmagorical effect of delicate golden censers rising in the blazing gems of stained glass, and then Easter, and its luminous and light April sky, full of the rocket-like flights of archangels, of ecstatic ascensions of female saints, hands joined, of soaring pure white souls and ardent hymns of jubilation and pure love!" Jean Lorrain, "Les Costumes mystiques," *Le Courrier Français* (25 January 1891). Unless otherwise indicated, all translations from the French in this introduction are by Elizabeth Emery.

2. *Laïcité* or secular schooling was one of the most hotly debated issues of the 1870s and 1880s. As the Third Republic came into power, it passed laws requiring obligatory free secular primary education for the French. See Mona Ozouf, *L'Ecole, l'Eglise et la République 1871-1914* (Paris: Armand Colin, 1963). As Venita Datta has argued, many members of the "generation of 1890" attended secular *lycées* such as Henri IV, Louis-le-Grand or Condorcet, which helped foster literary and artistic relationships. *Birth of a National Icon: The Literary Avant-Garde and the Origins of the Intellectual in France* (Albany: State University of New York Press, 1999), 34-35.

3. "... as poor in ideas as in style, compilations of often indecent and always grotesque legends ... a series of magical stories that rival *A Thousand and One Nights*." He specifically mentions the *La Vie des saints* series by Father Ribadeneira (1599-1610). "Saints" in Vol. 14 of *Le grand dictionnaire encyclopédique du XIXe siècle* (Geneva: Slatkine Reprints, 1982), 55.

4. Many authors have studied Flaubert's "La Légende de Saint Julien l'Hospitalier" and *La Tentation de Saint Antoine* (see the essays of Rori Bloom, Madhuri Mukherjee and Barbara Larson contained in this volume), as they have Huysmans' *Sainte Lydwine de Schiedam* (see Laurie Postlewate's essay in this volume). Catherine Rosenbaum-Dondaine's catalog, *L'Image de piété en France, 1814-1914* (Paris: Musée-Galerie de la SEITA, 1984) is of critical importance for examining popular images of saints as are Richard Griffiths' and Frédéric Gugelot's studies of the Catholic revival of the time. Richard Griffiths, *The Reactionary Revolution: The Catholic Revival in French Literature 1870-1914* (London, Constable, 1966). Frédéric Gugelot, *La Conversion des intellectuels au Catholicisme en France 1885-1935* (Paris: CNRS Editions, 1998). These latter works focus primarily on the Catholic context.

5. University Park, PA: Pennsylvania State University Press, 1992. The chapter entitled "The Cultural Background" (19-58) is particularly important for understanding the ways in which popular Christian belief exploded with the advent of the Second Empire.

6. Ithaca, NY: Cornell University Press, 1996.

7. London: Ashgate Press, 2003.

8. For more about the medieval practice of hagiography, see René Aigrain, *L'hagiographie: ses sources, ses méthodes, son histoire* (Mayenne: Bloud & Gay, 1953) and Jacques Dubois and Jean-Loup Lemaitre, *Sources et méthodes de l'hagiographie médiévale* (Paris: Editions du Cerf, 1993). For a straightforward and concise definition of hagiography, see Thomas

Head, "Hagiography." In *Medieval France: An Encyclopedia*, ed. William Kibler and Grover Zinn (New York: Garland, 1995), 433-37.

9. See William Granger Ryan's preface to *The Golden Legend*. As he remarks, the book's original title heading read *"Incipit prologus super legenda sanctorum." The Golden Legend: Readings on the Saints*, 2 vols. (Princeton: Princeton University Press, 1993), I: xiii.

10. See Sherry L. Reames, *The Legenda Aurea: A Reexamination of its Paradoxical History* (Madison: University of Wisconsin Press, 1985), 3-4. She traces the manuscript and print legacy of the text, remarking that over 800 extant manuscripts contain part or all of the Latin text; this does not include the great number of translations into French, Spanish, Italian, English, German and other languages. As Robert F. Seybolt has shown, at least 156 editions of the *Legenda* were printed between 1470 and 1500 (and only 128 of the Bible). "Fifteenth-Century Editions of the *Legenda aurea.*" *Speculum* 21 (1946): 327-38 and "The *Legenda aurea*, Bible, and *Historia scholastica.*" *Speculum* 21 (1946): 339-42. Cited in Reames, 4.

11. For more about the medieval cult of the saints, see Steven Wilson, ed. *Saints and their Cults* (Cambridge: Cambridge University Press, 1983) and Jonathan Sumption, *Pilgrimage: An Image of Mediaeval Religion* (Totowa, NJ: Rowman and Littlefield, 1975).

12. See Reames, whose book evokes the numerous reasons behind the decline of interest in the *Golden Legend* in the Renaissance, especially the Reformation.

13. In George Sand's *François le Champi*, for example, the Blanchet family's only books are the *Bible* and an abridged *Vie de saints. François le Champi* (Paris: Livre de poche, 1983), 60.

14. See C. J. T. Talar's contribution to this volume. Perhaps the best definition of the Bollandists' mission comes from their own works. See, for example, Hippolyte Delehaye, *L'Oeuvre des Bollandistes à travers trois siècles: 1615-1915* (Bruxelles: Société des Bollandistes, 1959) and Paul Peeters, *L'Oeuvre des Bollandistes* (Bruxelles: Palais des Académies, 1961).

15. See Roger S. Wieck, *Painted Prayers: The Book of Hours in Medieval and Renaissance Art* (New York: George Braziller in conjunction with the Pierpont Morgan Library, 1997). Leslie Ross's *Text, Image, Message: Saints in Medieval Manuscript Illustrations* (Wesport, CN: Greenwood Press, 1994) situates saints within this context. For an extended history of manuscript illumination, see Sandra Hindman, Michael Camille, Nina Rowe, and Rowan Watson, *Manuscript Illumination in the Modern Age* (Evanston, IL: Mary and Leigh Block Museum of Art, 2001). Not all manuscript illumination treated saints, but the chapter on "Reproductions: Transmission of Manuscript Illumination in the Nineteenth Century" reveals how widespread were reproductions of books of hours, which provided readers with images of scenes from the Bible of the lives of saints.

16. An eBay search for "holy card" brings up innumerable examples of this type of image. For an extremely valuable and well-illustrated discussion of religious imagery and its dissemination, see Catherine Rosenbaum-Dondaine's catalog, *L'Image de piété en France, 1814-1914*. See also her article on the same topic, "Un siècle et demi de petite imagerie de piété (après 1814)," *Revue de la Bibliothèque nationale* 6 (1982). Other useful sources include Duchartre et Saulnier, *L'Imagerie parisienne de la rue Saint-Jacques* (Grund, 1944); Alain Vircondelet, *Le monde merveilleux des images pieuses* (Paris: Hermé, 1988); and J. Pirotte, "Les Images de dévotion, témoins de la mentalité d'une époque, 1840-1965," *Revue d'histoire de la spiritualité*, 1974.

17. See, for example, p. 329 of J.-K. Huysmans' *En Route*, where his protagonist lambasts this type of inexpensive commercial image. *En Route*, reprinted in *Le Roman de Durtal* (Paris: Barthillat, 1999). A similar movement occurred in more official painting circles. In his account of the 1875 Salon, for example, Zola mentions the fact that the religious painting on display here was purely commercial: "J'aurais aimé parler de la peinture religieuse, seulement ici nous nous trouvons en face du commerce pur et simple. Les églises neuves ont besoin d'images, les curés achètent des crucifixions et des saintes-vierges. Il en résulte une vaste industrie...." "Lettres de Paris" for the *Messager de l'Europe* (June 1875). Retranslated from Russian and reprinted in *Les Oeuvres complètes* (Paris: Cercle du livre précieux, 1968), 920–942.

18. For the history of the pilgrimage movement in late nineteenth-century France, see Thomas A. Kselman, *Miracles and Prophecies in Nineteenth-Century France* (New Brunswick, NJ: Rutgers University Press, 1983). Jean-Emmanuel Drochon's 1890 *Histoire illustrée des pèlerinages* (Paris: Plon, 1890) provides a clear view of the numerous pilgrimage sites in the 1890s and their value for believers. Ruth Harris, *Lourdes: Body and Spirit in the Secular Age* (New York: Viking, 1999) describes the events occurring at Lourdes.

19. Suzanne Kaufman explores the links between pilgrimage and industry in "Miracles, Medicine and the Spectacle of Lourdes: Popular Religion and Modernity in Fin-de-siècle France" (Ph.D. thesis, The State University of New Jersey, Rutgers, 1996). See also J.-K. Huysmans' *Les Foules de Lourdes* for a contemporary account of the dizzying number of objects for sale: "... des statues de vierges en plâtre, les yeux au ciel, vêtues de blanc et ceinturées de bleu; pas une boutique où il n'y ait des médailles, des cierges, des chapelets, des scapulaires, des brochures racontant des miracles ... des chromos de Bernadettes, en jupe rouge et tablier bleu, agenouillées, un cierge à la main, devant la Vierge, avec des statuettes de Lilliput et des médailles qui font songer à une monnaie de poupée, frappée à la grosse, dans des rebuts de cuivre ... c'est l'explosion de la bimbeloterie de luxe." *Les Foules de Lourdes*, François Angelier, ed. (Collection Golgotha. Grenoble: J. Millon, 1993), 79–80.

20. For more about these trends, see Elizabeth Emery and Laura Morowitz, *Consuming the Past: The Medieval Revival in Late Nineteenth-Century France* (London: Ashgate Press, 2003); Janine Dakyns, *The Middle Ages in French Literature: 1851–1900* (London: Oxford University Press, 1973); Richard Griffiths, *The Reactionary Revolution* and Frédéric Gugelot, *La Conversion des intellectuels au Catholicisme en France*.

21. This compilation has most recently been reprinted by Les Editions Thot (Vanves, 1984) and is also available in Gallica, the Bibliothèque Nationale's database of scanned texts (http://gallica.bnf.fr).

22. For more about the influence of Maury's work, see Jean-Louis Cabanès, "Rêver La Légende dorée," *Les Cahiers Naturalistes* 76 (2002): 25–47. This informative article appeared after this introduction was written.

PART ONE

SAINTS AS INSPIRATION
FOR ART, LITERATURE AND MUSIC

1

"Sur un vitrail d'église": Structures and Sources in Flaubert's "Légende de Saint Julien l'Hospitalier"

Rori Bloom

In considering the titles of Sartre's literary biographies, it seems that Gustave Flaubert has been short-changed. While Sartre calls his study of Jean Genet *Saint Genet, comédien et martyr*, his multi-volume work on Flaubert is entitled *L'Idiot de la famille*. If several of Flaubert's characters—from Charles Bovary to Saint Julien l'Hospitalier—do seem slightly idiotic (the saint is described twice in Flaubert's tale as "stupéfait"),[1] Flaubert seems nonetheless as worthy as Genet of Sartre's canonization. In fact, Flaubert's career reveals an obsession with saintliness. In addition to his full-length work, *La Tentation de Saint Antoine*, each of Flaubert's *Trois contes* is a story of sainthood. "Un coeur simple" recounts the life of Félicité, a devout Christian and modern-day martyr who sacrifices herself in the service of others. "La Légende de Saint Julien l'Hospitalier" tells the story of a medieval hermit.[2] Finally, "Hérodias" relates an episode in the life of the New Testament's first saint, John the Baptist. However, it is in the central story, the legend of Saint Julien, that Flaubert most closely follows a hagiographic model; the medieval setting of the tale is that of the period in which the writing of saints' lives so flourished and this mystical biography mimics in modern idiom the hagiographic form.[3]

Flaubert's "Légende de Saint Julien l'Hospitalier" is not a simple transcription of the tale from old into modern French, but rather a reworking of a variety of sources. The extremely complex relationship of Flaubert's tale to an "original" story is enacted within the text through its expansion beyond the hagiographic model, through its borrowings from other genres of medieval literature and through its intertextual allusions to competing Christian and pagan myths. Moreover, Flaubert's use of contemporary generic structures, specifically those of the nineteenth-century fantastic tale, further destabilizes the story and works to jeopardize the edifying end of the original hagiography. Finally, in reclaiming a work of visual art as his text's principal inspiration, Flaubert adds another structure to the series of sources, making his affinity to this story of saintliness not just spiritual but primarily formal and aesthetic. Through a series of mirrorings, echoes and repetitions, Flaubert thus draws on a variety of sources (modern, medieval and mythic) to illustrate a postmodern myth described by Jacques Derrida as "the myth of the simplicity of origin."[4] For despite its seeming simplicity, Flaubert's tale insists upon the complexity of its creation.

The first line of "La Légende de Saint Julien l'Hospitalier" has a childlike simplicity: "Le père et la mère de Julien habitaient un château, au milieu des bois, sur la pente d'une colline."[5] However, Flaubert's study of these parents and their child shows that this story of a family is anything but simple. In fact, one of the most striking additions that Flaubert makes to medieval versions of the story of Saint Julien (from the *Legenda Aurea* or another prose version from the thirteenth century) is the invention of additional episodes from the saint's childhood which, while minimally documented in the medieval hagiographies, count for at least half of Flaubert's.[6] Indeed, in "La Légende de Saint Julien l'Hospitalier" as in all of the *Trois contes*, families and especially children are extremely problematic. In the first story of this collection, "Un Coeur simple," Félicité is tormented by her childlessness despite all of the children who surround her (Virginie dies, Paul marries, and Victor goes off to sea). In "Hérodias," the adolescent Salome is the pathetic pawn used in the seduction of Herod and the murder of John the Baptist. Finally, Julien, murderer of his beloved parents, is perhaps the most troubled and troubling child of them all. Here, however, the study of the hero's childhood can be seen not just as a psychological study of character, but also as an incitement to study family resemblances as signs of literary relationships, to consider the violations of the family structure as models for the eventual transgressions of literary ones.

Initially, however, Flaubert makes clear the literary legacy of his text through his use of allusions to the medieval period in which this legend was first formed. The tale thus draws on various genres of medieval literature to create its atmosphere. The episode of Julien's involvement in a conflict between the Empereur d'Occitanie and an oriental caliph evokes the adventures of the *chanson de geste*, while passages describing the hero's early education detail the knightly skills so central to chivalric stories. Julien's encounter with the talking stag recalls the *Lais* of Marie de France, specifically the story of Guigemar where the same magical animal appears. This specific intertextuality has important generic implications as well, for Marie, too, is an author who has a very particular relationship to her story's sources. She writes in the preface to the *Lais*: "J'ai donc pensé aux lais que j'avais entendus. Je savais en toute certitude que ceux qui avaient commencé à les écrire et à les répandre avaient voulu perpétuer le souvenir des aventures qu'ils avaient entendues."[7] She is writing her stories not as originals or even as transcriptions from a central source but as reworkings of multiple models mediated by many tellers and mutated through the unstable transmission of an oral culture.

It is evident that Flaubert recognizes the importance of oral culture in the Middle Ages since in his own story he makes frequent allusions to the act of storytelling. Julien's father in his isolated château welcomes pilgrims and listens attentively to their adventures, and he whiles away the long winter nights exchanging stories of old battles with other retired soldiers. Julien's own exotic adventures form the foundation for popular legends about his military heroism, and when he becomes a criminal he will repeat his story to all who will listen in penance for his sins. Stories are thus repeated and most often unrecorded so that no single authentic source is preserved; only a multitude of different versions exist.

In fact, Julien's earliest adventures are closely modeled on the most canonical of originary stories; the world of his childhood is a natural paradise and Julien is like the first man of the Old Testament book of Genesis. Julien, hero of the hunt, sees himself "comme Adam au milieu du paradis, entre toutes les bêtes,"[8] or he envisions himself as Noah, calling the beasts to him "deux à deux, par rang de tailles, depuis les éléphants et les lions, jusqu'aux hermines et aux canards, comme le jour qu'elles entrèrent dans l'arche."[9] The hero's own birth is related like an episode from the life of a Biblical patriarch, as his arrival is the answer to his mother's prayers. "A force de prier Dieu il lui vint un fils,"[10] the narrator says, thus aligning Julien's mother with such supplicant matriarchs as Sarah and Hannah. Not only does Flaubert emphasize the sacred nature of his story with these references, but he adds a New Testament nuance by comparing the birth of Julien to that of Jesus so that the saint's life is an imitation of Christ's. Thus, Julien's mother receives a prophecy about the future of her son that strongly resembles Gabriel's annunciation to Mary. In Flaubert's version of the Julien legend, a phantom announces, "Réjouistoi, ô mère, ton fils sera un saint!"[11] Indeed, the family group of Julien and his two adoring parents, mirrored in the animal group he encounters in the woods ("un cerf, une biche et son faon")[12] reflect the triadic structure of the Holy Family.

However, this Biblical paradigm proves unstable as the stag speaks to Julien and predicts the destruction of this sacred family bond: "Maudit, maudit, maudit!—Un jour coeur féroce, tu assassineras ton père et ta mère."[13] This prefiguring of parricide is strongly Oedipal in its echoes and the Greek story competes with the Biblical myth as a fundamental source of the text's structure. Moreover, the modern use of the Oedipus story in the psychoanalytical explanation of the origins of sexuality seems prophetically present in Flaubert's text, which predates Freud by at least a generation.[14] Although Julien may not have direct designs on his mother, he does kill his father in a fit of sexual jealousy, mistaking his father for his wife's lover. If, as a child, Julien's conflicting feelings about his family are suppressed (he runs away from home at an early age to lead the harsh and celibate life of a soldier), his acts of violence belie the sexual nature of his repression. In his love of hunting, Julien expresses his repressed sexuality in the erotic pleasure he derives from the pursuit and capture of his prey: "Il se mit à l'étrangler [un pigeon] et les convulsions de l'oiseau faisaient battre son coeur, l'emplissaient d'une volupté sauvage et tumultueuse. Au dernier raidissement, il se sentit défaillir."[15] If Julien's Oedipal complex is never fully resolved, his lustful urges are ever present, and Jean Bellemin-Noël persuasively analyses the last passage of the text—the saint's union with Christ—as a heavily homoerotic one.[16] The Lord in the form of a leper tests the saint by demanding that Julien warm him with his naked body. As a reward for his obedience, their spirits are united and Julien's spiritual ecstasy is described in terms that seem to suggest embrace, erection and eventually orgasm: "Julien s'étala dessus complètement, bouche contre bouche, poitrine sur poitrine. Alors le Lépreux l'étreignit; et ses yeux tout à coup prirent une clarté d'étoiles; ses cheveux s'allongèrent comme les rais du soleil.... Cependant une abondance de délices, une joie surhumaine descendait comme une inondation dans l'âme de Julien pâmé."[17]

If the sexualization of the sacred text through the use of a pagan myth is already quite heretical, Flaubert also destabilizes the hagiographic form from within by rewriting the sacred story in the secular genre of the fantastic tale. The fairy tale world of the tale with its castles filled with medieval maidens and forest inhabited by talking animals cedes to the structure of the fantastic as practiced with such success in the nineteenth century. While Flaubert is not normally associated with fantastic literature, "La Légende de Saint Julien l'Hospitalier" marks the meeting of medieval hagiography with the modern form of the "conte fantastique." The story has elements of the marvelous, such as the abundance of the castle's feasts (the chickens are as big as sheep) or the incredible conditions faced by Julien at war (it is so hot that his soldiers' hair bursts into flame or so cold that their limbs fall off). However, what truly defines the story as a work of fantastic and not just legendary literature is the characteristic that Tzvetan Todorov has identified as the hallmark of the genre: the hesitation between belief and disbelief in the phenomena described.[18] Hesitation is essential in the construction of this fable about faith, for the faithful must know when they should or should not believe their eyes. Despite the detailed descriptions of certain scenes where Flaubert's realism allows us to imagine almost exactly the facade of a castle or the scene of a crime, the clairvoyance of the narration is problematic since scenes are not always presented as seen, but also as spiritual visions.

Normally, Flaubertian description is associated with the stable solidity of realism, and in fact Roland Barthes begins his essay "L'Effet de réel" with references to the detailed descriptions of the bourgeois interior of the first of the *Trois contes*, "Un Coeur simple." In "L'Effet de réel" Barthes writes, "la description réaliste évite de se laisser entraîner dans une activité fantasmatique."[19] Yet it seems that in "Saint Julien" the realist Flaubert is engaging in fantasy, for the world of the tale is not only the world of legends but the world of dreams. "Les pavés de la cour étaient nets,"[20] he writes in "Saint Julien," seeming to view things with unerring clarity, and yet in *L'Education sentimentale*, a text considered a masterpiece of realism, Flaubert alludes to a precision which has "toute la netteté d'une hallucination."[21] Vision is problematic in the "Légende de Saint Julien," where the reliability of the senses is constantly put into question when the natural and supernatural, the human and divine, come into contact, for if "Saint Julien" is structured by a series of religious visions, what then becomes of the realist reliance on sight as the source of observation and the arbiter of reality?

The characters of Flaubert's story are never sure if they are seeing or just dreaming, and thus even their waking world takes on a strangely dreamlike quality. Julien's mother thinks she sees a hermit at her bedside who predicts the birth of her son, but in the morning she hesitates to share her strange nocturnal vision with others, doubting whether it was a man or a spirit: "Songe ou réalité, cela devait être une communication du ciel,"[22] she decides. Her husband thinks that in the fog of the night he has seen a gypsy who also pronounces obscure prophecies about their son. The gypsy disappears in the morning mists, and the man decides that this mysterious apparition was the effect of his tired mind: "[Il] attribua cette vision à la fatigue de sa tête pour avoir peu dormi."[23] During his military campaigns, Julien marches through haunted countries, "des pays où il y avait tant de brouillard que l'on marchait environné de fantômes."[24] Indeed, the hero's entire life has been lived as if in some strange trance. The narrator compares the young Julien's success in hunting with the "facilité qu'on éprouve dans les rêves."[25] Later, when the dreamlike forest of his childhood turns into a haunted wood, Julien seems to sleep-walk through it as if in some terrible nightmare: "[La forêt] était embarrassée de lianes; il les coupait avec son sabre, quand une fouine glissa brusquement entre ses jambes, une panthère fit un bond par dessus son épaule, un serpent monta en spirale autour d'un frêne.... Julien se mit à courir; ils coururent. Le serpent sifflait, les bêtes puantes bavaient.... Ils semblaient méditer un plan de vengeance ... [Julien] marchait les bras tendus et les paupières closes comme un aveugle sans même avoir la force de crier grâce."[26]

The unreliability of the senses, the oscillation between reality and dream, is the prime condition for the fantastic which, according to Todorov, "occupe le temps de cette incertitude."[27] The tale is characterized by these moments of doubt. While Julien's parents are pious believers in God, they hesitate to accept the prophecies about their son. Although Julien believes the prophecy that he will kill his beloved parents, he does all he can to avoid it, cautiously calling out to any elderly people he meets to assure himself that they are not his predicted victims. Even when in a rage he does decide to murder, this act—however savage—is not completely impulsive. Julien, who in the darkened room cannot trust his sight, doubts his senses for a moment when he feels a beard against his face instead of his wife's smooth cheek: "Il se recula, croyant devenir fou. Mais il revint près du lit, et ses doigts, en palpant, rencontrèrent des cheveux, qui étaient très longs. Pour se convaincre de son erreur, il repassa lentement sa main sur l'oreiller."[28] Even after this decisive act, hesitation persists almost to the tale's end. Julien becomes a hermit ferryman and decides to sacrifice himself to others by rowing them across the waters of a dangerous river. When on a particularly stormy night he hears a call for help, he doubts his senses, hesitating before answering. The clarity of the voice seems impossible in the midst of a blowing gale, but after a third clear call and "une minute d'hésitation,"[29] Julien boards his boat. Rowing through the storm, he stops for a moment and then continues, propelled by the implicit importance of his mission. Unlike that other scene where the disciples doubt their Lord's power to bring their boat safely to shore, Julien believes; his hesitations dwindle each time the leper asks him for a service. When Julien, despite his poverty, looks for scraps to serve his guest, he is surprised to find wine in his empty urn and hesitates for a moment before handing it to the leper.

However, just as he is about to pause "le Lépreux avança le bras, et d'un trait vida toute la cruche."[30] Julien, too, is seized by the power of the divine presence and can only obey his orders, embracing the ulcerated body of the leper in a totally unquestioning act. In the end, the Christian myth problematizes hesitation in order to dispel it; the presence of the Lord brings doubt to an end.

If the hesitation of the *conte fantastique* is dispelled and displaced by the power of Christian faith, our faith in the tale is nonetheless profoundly shaken by its ending. Todorov has said that upon reading the end of any *conte fantastique* our subsequent readings of the tale can only be "meta-readings,"[31] as doubt has been dissipated and the reader's hesitation can no longer accompany that of the characters. Hagiography does not even entertain doubt upon the first reading, since with its evident finality in faith, this genre always concludes with the end of the hero's doubts and his indubitable profession of faith. However, if at the close of his story, Julien hesitates no more, the reader's faith in the text is shaken by its final line, which tells us that the story we have read is in fact not inspired by a literary but by a visual source: "Et voilà l'histoire de saint Julien-l'Hospitalier telle à peu près qu'on la trouve, sur un vitrail d'église, dans mon pays,"[32] announces the narrator moving us from a foreign to a familiar setting, from the Middle Ages to the present, from an often repeated and thus infinitely variable story to a fixed image on a church window. This ending is as startling as the sound of breaking glass. Until the last lines, the reader believes that he is reading a modern version of a medieval legend, but finally the author admits that the "Légende de Saint Julien" is a legend in another sense, for in French *légende* means not just legend but caption, and the story's subservience to its visual inspiration reduces it to the status of secondary literature. Thus any rereading of Flaubert's text can only be a fallen reading, a realization that the legend does not narrate the unfolding of adventures, but describes the painted personages of an immobile image.

If we reread it carefully, this story of hunts and battles and journeys and murders reduces itself to a series of silent tableaux. Life at the castle is quiet and strangely still: "On vivait en paix depuis si longtemps que la herse ne s'abaissait plus; les fossés étaient pleins d'herbes."[33] And despite the speed and movement of the hunting scenes, their evocation of animals—hares, ermine, deer—brings to mind the still images of medieval tapestries. The hunt's result is after all the immobilization of the animals, for after Julien's slaughter "tout fut immobile."[34] Even in his new home, the oriental palace of his bride, life is quiet and still: "il y avait partout ... un tel silence."[35] Julien himself is described as stunned into immobility, "stupéfait,"[36] when he first kills an animal, a white churchmouse, and later again when the stag predicts his fate. Dialogue is drowned in silence as Julien does not believe that he has actually heard a stag speak, just as his parents doubt their ears upon hearing prophecies about the fate of their son. Aside from these half-heard predictions there are few words spoken throughout the story since it is inspired not by a verbal but by a visual source—the stained-glass windows in the cathedral of Rouen.

The significance of the church windows as source is suggested from the start of the story with evocations of Gothic architecture on the tale's first page: "Les quatre tours aux angles avaient des toits pointus recouverts d'écailles de plomb.... Les pavés de la cour étaient nets comme le dallage d'une église. De longues gouttières, figurant de dragons la gueule en bas, crachaient l'eau des pluies vers la citerne;—et sur le bord des fenêtres, à tous les étages, dans un pot d'argile peinte, un basilic ou un héliotrope s'épanouissait."[37] Windows are evoked as well as Gothic gargoyles, and the paving stones of the castle keep resemble those of a church, even perhaps the one in which the narrator stands when looking at the windows depicting the life of Saint Julien. These allusions to the cathedral and its windows persist throughout the story in which Julien's father with his long beard is compared to "une statue d'église,"[38] and once dead he and his wife, "étendus sur le dos ... leurs visages d'une majestueuse douceur,"[39] remind us of sculptures on the sarcophagi in medieval churches. Later, when the leper calls out to Julien, his voice is compared to a "cloche d'église."[40] In addition, windows are mentioned several times, and the words *fenêtres* and *vitraux*[41] appear throughout the text before their central importance becomes clear in the text's last line.

In fact, specific passages of the story seem to evoke specific scenes represented by the Rouen *vitraux*, for Flaubert's descriptions in this tale reveal an almost painterly aesthetic that refers implicitly to their visual source. If in the end of the tale the windows of Julien's hermitage are "deux trous,"[42] evoking the transparency of vision of those who have seen the light, Flaubert's story emphasizes the mediation of his images by the images he has already seen. His tale is not the window of realism open onto the world, but the stained-glass window, artful and opaque. Flaubert's description of a "lac figé qui ressemblait à du plomb"[43] exchanges the transparent for the opaque and at the same time evokes the lead which lines the glass of stained-glass windows. In a more explicit evocation, Flaubert's description of the adult Julien is framed by a window, and its colors are as vibrant as those on a work of stained glass: "Vêtu de pourpre, il restait accoudé dans l'embrasure d'une fenêtre."[44] Characters are often framed in this way, like Julien's father, who looks through his window watching the snow, like Julien's wife, who stands with a lamp in the doorframe of the bedroom, and like Julien, whose own face is reflected in a still pool in a sort of double portrait in which he thinks he sees his father and finally recognizes himself. Finally, Flaubert's description of the murder scene is another allusion to the Rouen windows where the crime will be depicted. In the story, Julien's bedchamber is adorned with stained-glass windows, and as the sun comes up over the murder scene "le reflet écarlate du vitrail alors frappé par le soleil éclairait ces taches rouges et en jetait de plus nombreuses dans tout l'appartement."[45] This description in reds and whites—the white hair and skin of the cadavers, the white sheets of the bed, and the ivory crucifix suspended in the alcove spattered with the red of blood and the red light streaming in at the windows—is composed with as much care as the colored panes in the stained-glass source.

Despite the preponderance of such still images—the frozen lake or quiet pool—there is at the end of the story the violently rushing river Julien must cross. In Flaubert's tale the immobile image of the church window is met by the torrent of words the writer tries vainly to control. Like Julien's hounds who pull at their chains, trying to free themselves from captivity, Flaubert's words cannot help but move, moving us forward throughout the story and moving us in deeper ways. Perhaps this is because the images of the window, despite their fixity, are strangely vertiginous: At the limits of painting, they are almost alive. If, however, Flaubert was moved by the window, it seems that this inspiration was more aesthetic than religious, for Flaubert's interest in the Middle Ages is focused on the visual art of the period: church architecture, tapestries and most of all stained glass. Nonetheless, this resolution of the tale to a single source, the "vitrail d'église dans mon pays,"[46] oversimplifies a complex genesis. Flaubert not only looked at the Rouen images of Julien but at several other windows before composing his story. Not only this, but he had at hand his friend H. E. Langlois' description of the windows which provides a textual source that doubles the visual one.[47]

In multiplying the sources for his story, Flaubert prevents us from returning to its origin, encouraging nostalgia through his evocation of so many sources, but prohibiting us from identifying a single referent to which the others would be subservient. The text itself is a series of echoes that refer to each other in a sequence of perpetual unstable mirrorings. The stag brays as he prophecies Julien's crime and his cry is heard when Julien commits it. Julien's father's eye burns brightly even in death, and likewise the look of the leper sears Julien's soul. The animals look at the hunter with human emotion, while Julien kills with the indifference of a wild animal. In the final hunting scene where the prey foil the predator, the reversal is a sort of joke, for Flaubert writes of the wolf and wild boar who seem to be mocking the impotent hunter that "une ironie perçait dans leurs allures sournoises."[48] This irony in repetition is essentially Flaubertian. Christopher Prendergast has written that Flaubert constantly cites other novels in his own, thus decomposing the genre into which he inscribes his work.[49] In the *conte*, where the story cites stained glass, the author's irony is present despite the seriousness of his subject. The tale's seemingly straightforward presentation with its fairy-tale simple opening is undercut by the *chute* at the end, the fall from grace that reminds us of the story's postlapsarian nature. After all, Julien was never Adam naming the animals but a savage hunter slaying them. We have not been reading the spiritual story of his sainthood but rather a much-mediated description of a work of art that represents the saint's life. We are thus reminded that our access to the sacred is not, despite the seeming simplicity of the tale's language, direct and unmediated but rather always obscured by representations that inhibit our access to the divine presence. The window to God is not clear but colored, as the stained-glass images imply. And the last line of Flaubert's story, which transports the reader from a mythical past to a problematic present, reminds us that he is not a hagiographer but rather a modern artist interested in shaking the faith of his readers.

Notes

1. "Stupefied." Gustave Flaubert, *Trois Contes* (Paris: G. Charpentier, 1877), 102, 115. Unless otherwise noted, all translations in this chapter are by Rori Bloom.

2. Flaubert began work on Saint Julien in 1856, but the tale was only published as one of his *Trois Contes* in 1877.

3. Among the many studies of "La Légende de Saint Julien l'Hospitalier," of note is the recent book by Gérard Lehmann: *'La Légende de Saint Julien l'Hospitalier': Essai sur l'imaginaire flaubertien* (Odense: Odense University Press, 1999). Lehmann provides an extensive bibliography which I will not reproduce here, but besides the critical works I cite in this essay, two others may be of interest as pertains to Flaubert's use of structures and sources: Raymonde Debray-Genette, "'La Légende de Saint Julien l'Hospitalier': forme simple et forme savante" in *Essais sur Flaubert*, ed. Charles Carlut (Paris: Nizet, 1979) and Pierre-Marc De Biasi, "Le Palimpseste hagiographique. L'appropriation ludique des sources édifiantes dans la rédaction de 'La Légende de Saint Julien l'Hospitalier'" in *Revue des lettres modernes* (Paris: Minard, 1986), 777–81.

4. Jacques Derrida, *Of Grammatology*, Trans. G. C. Spivak (Baltimore: Johns Hopkins University Press, 1974), 92.

5. "Julien's father and mother lived in a castle, on a hillside, in the middle of the woods," 91.

6. B. F. Bart and R. F. Cook, *The Legendary Sources of Flaubert's "Saint Julien"* (Toronto: University of Toronto Press, 1977). Bart and Cook provide several of Flaubert's sources as appendices.

7. "I thought about the 'lais' that I had heard. I knew with certainty that

those who had begun to write them down and to circulate them wanted to preserve the memory of the adventures they had heard." Marie de France, *Lais* (Paris: Livre de Poche, 1990), 25.

8. "Like Adam in Paradise surrounded by all of the animals," 128.

9. "Two by two, in order of size, from the elephants and the lions to the ermine and the ducks, just like the day that they entered the ark," 128–29.

10. "After years of praying, she had a son," 95.

11. "Rejoice, o mother, your son will be a saint," 96.

12. "A stag, a doe and a fawn," 115.

13. "Three times damned!—One day, savage heart, you will murder your father and mother," 116–17.

14. For more on Flaubert and Oedipus, see William J. Berg, Michel Grimaud, and George Moskos, *Saint Oedipus: Psychocritical Approaches to Flaubert's Art* (Ithaca: Cornell University Press, 1982).

15. "He began to strangle [a pigeon] and the bird's convulsions made his heart beat faster, filling him with a wild and tumultuous pleasure. At its last spasm, he almost fainted," 103–04.

16. Jean Bellemin-Noël, *Le Quatrième Conte de Gustave Flaubert* (Paris: Pressses Universitaires de France, 1990), 77.

17. "Julien lay down on top of him, mouth against mouth, breast against breast. The leper embraced him; and all at once his eyes became as bright as stars; his hair as long as the rays of the sun.... At the same time an overwhelming pleasure, a superhuman joy flooded Julien's soul," 163.

18. Tzvetan Todorov, *Introduction à la littérature fantastique* (Paris: Seuil, 1970), Chapter 2.

19. "Realist description does not let itself slip into the realm of fantasy." Roland Barthes, "L'Effet de réel" in *Oeuvres complètes* (Paris: Seuil, 1993), 482.

20. "The paving stones of the courtyard were laid out with precision," 91.

21. "With all of the precision of a hallucination." Gustave Flaubert, *L'Education sentimentale* (Paris: Gallimard, 1989), 118.

22. "Dream or reality, it must have been a message from on high," 96.

23. "[He] attributed his vision to the fatigue he felt from not having slept," 98.

24. "Countries where the fog was so thick one walked surrounded by ghosts," 124.

25. "Ease one has in dreams," 113.

26. "[The forest] was thick with vines; he was cutting them with his saber when a weasel slid suddenly between his legs, a panther jumped over his shoulder, a snake spiraled around the trunk of an ash tree.... Julien began to run; and they ran, too. The snake hissed, the stinking animals foamed at the mouth.... They seemed to be meditating their vengeance.... [Julien] walked with his arms extended and his eyes closed like a blind man without even the strength to call for mercy," 138–41.

27. "Occupies the moment of this uncertainty." Todorov, 29.

28. "He stepped back, believing himself mad. But he returned to the bed, and his fingers, reaching out, met long hair. To convince himself of his error, he drew his hand once again slowly over the pillow," 143.

29. "A minute of hesitation," 158.

30. "The leper advanced an arm, and in one draught drained the whole vessel," 161.

31. Todorov, Chapter 3.

32. "And that is the story of Saint Julien l'Hospitalier more or less as one finds it on a stained-glass window in a church in my region," 164.

33. "The peace had lasted so long that the drawbridge could no longer be lowered; the moat was full of weeds," 92.

34. "Everything was immobile," 115.
35. "There was such silence everywhere," 127.
36. "Stupefied," 102.
37. "The four towers at the angles all had pointed roofs covered with lead tiles.... The paving stones of the court were laid out precisely, as they are in the floor of a church. Long gutters, shaped like dragons with their heads pointed downwards, spat rainwater into the cistern;—and on the windowsills of every floor, in painted clay pots, basil or heliotrope blossomed," 91–92.
38. "A statue in a church," 134.
39. "Lying on their backs ... their faces gentle yet majestic," 144.
40. "A church bell," 157.
41. Windows and stained-glass windows.
42. "Two holes."
43. "A frozen lake which looked like it was made of lead," 112.
44. "Dressed in purple, he stood with his elbows resting on the window sill," 128.
45. "The scarlet reflection of the stained-glass window as it was struck by the sun lit up the red stains and cast more red reflections throughout the apartment," 144–45.
46. "A stained-glass window in a church in my region," 164.
47. Bart and Cook, Chapter 4.
48. "A certain irony pierced through their sly expressions," 140–41.
49. Christopher Prendergast, *The Order of Mimesis: Balzac, Stendhal, Nerval, Flaubert* (Cambridge: Cambridge University Press, 1986), 190.

2

When the Saints Go Marching In: Popular Performances of *La Tentation de Saint Antoine* and *Sainte Geneviève de Paris* at the Chat Noir Shadow Theater

Madhuri Mukherjee

La Tentation de Saint Antoine (*The Temptation of Saint Anthony*) and *Sainte Geneviève de Paris* were two immensely popular shadow plays performed countless times at the Chat Noir cabaret in Paris, from 1887 to 1897. Based on the lives of two extremely beloved saints whose fame had risen to great heights during the medieval epoch, these plays may be considered yet another manifestation of the renewed interest in the medieval period which enthralled much of nineteenth-century France. Referring specifically to his experience watching one of the first performances of *La Tentation de Saint Antoine*, Jules Lemaître of the Académie Française, a well-known writer, journalist and theater critic of the time, wrote:

> Ce petit théâtre du Chat-Noir, rond comme la lune (cet astre des songes) et qui n'a pas deux coudées de diamètre, est une lucarne ouverte sur le monde surnaturel. ... C'est là que Henri Rivière a déroulé la légende des siècles et l'histoire des religions, a promené Saint Antoine par toutes les tentations de la chair et de l'esprit, et ramené le bon ermite, notre frère par l'inquiétude et la curiosité, au pied de la Croix rédemptrice.[1]

Referring to the Chat Noir's repertoire of shadow plays, Michel Herbert, an historian of Montmartre, qualified *Sainte Geneviève de Paris* as "... sa plus prodigieuse réussite."[2]

The objective of this essay is to relate the history of these two popular shadow theater productions and to examine how even the most avant-garde innovators of the time paid tribute to medieval themes and preoccupations, trying to recreate the atmosphere, aesthetic forms and experiences favored by medieval audiences. Before proceeding to an examination of these plays, however, it will be helpful to dwell briefly on some background information about the Chat Noir cabaret and about Henri Rivière, the genius who was responsible for designing and operating its famed Shadow Theater. It was thanks to Rivière, who created the shadows for the *Tentation de Saint-Antoine*, *Sainte Geneviève de Paris* and a host of other plays of biblical and religious inspiration, that a generation of nineteenth-century audiences was able to experience what watching a medieval mystery play might have been like, even as they simultaneously—and paradoxically—experienced the thrall of something akin to early silent motion pictures.

THE CHAT NOIR CABARET

Fin-de-siècle Paris' most famous artistic cabaret, the Chat Noir (1881–1897), was founded, flourished and closed down within the last two decades of the nineteenth century, while the medieval revival in France steadily pursued its course. The cabaret's founder and owner, Rodolphe Salis, capitalized on this interest by advertising his establishment in issues of *Le Chat Noir* journal as a "cabaret Louis XIII, fondé en 1114"![3] One of the factors that contributed greatly to the Chat Noir's success was the popularity enjoyed by its Shadow Theater. During the later years of the cabaret's existence, from 1887 onward, forty-three shadow plays were produced and performed by the various authors and artists who frequented the cabaret. Salis even took the Shadow Theater on tour to the provinces and when the closing down of the Chat Noir was imminent, he hoped to the end that the theater could be saved.[4]

Rodolphe Salis opened the Chat Noir cabaret in November 1881, in what used to be an old post office at 84, boulevard Rochechouart. A painter and writer himself, Salis rapidly attracted to his cabaret a coterie of aspiring and talented artists. This first Chat Noir was a small and rather modest establishment, consisting of only two rooms. In keeping with popular taste, Salis furnished his *hostellerie* in a pseudo-medieval fashion. As Jean

Pascal, another historian of Montmartre, describes it, "Des chaises rustiques, des bancs et des tables en bois massif, un vitrail enluminé, une haute cheminée, quelques armures anciennes, de luisantes pièces de dinanderie, constituaient l'établissement Louis XIII."[5] Within a month of the cabaret's opening, Salis had also founded the journal *Le Chat Noir*, in which the cabaret's habitués regularly published their works. Literary celebrities, such as Paul Verlaine and Villiers de l'Isle-Adam, also contributed to the journal. While it provided a forum of expression for aspiring writers, poets, artists and illustrators, the journal's principal mission was the unabashed and aggressive promotion of the Chat Noir cabaret, its proprietor and the literary and artistic enterprises of the people associated with it. When the cabaret's Shadow Theater was inaugurated, its productions were thus advertised in *Le Chat Noir*.

The two rooms of the first Chat Noir could barely hold thirty people, and the Parisian bourgeoisie was soon flocking to the cabaret in droves, entertained by the poetry, music, song and satirical skits and sketches its community of literary and artistic figures regularly staged. Barely three and a half years after its initial inauguration, the Chat Noir was ready to expand, and it moved into a luxurious, beautifully decorated, three storey building, located at 12, rue Laval (today, the rue Victor-Massé) in the heart of Montmartre. Lemaître described the new Chat Noir as an "... établissement composite qui est à la fois une brasserie, un restaurant, un cénacle littéraire, un atelier de peintre et un théâtre." [6] It was in this second Chat Noir, that Henri Rivière created and perfected the marvelous "Théâtre d'Ombres du Chat Noir"—the Chat Noir's Shadow Theater.

HENRI RIVIÈRE (1864–1951)

Henri Rivière, painter, book illustrator and printmaker, was one of the youngest of the Chat Noir habitués. Associated with the cabaret from its very beginnings, he remained loyal to Salis until the end. Aside from his reputation as a painter, skilled in the depiction of nature and of Symbolist subjects, Rivière has also earned an important place in theater history for the posters, program covers and decors he crafted for countless stage productions at the Chat Noir and elsewhere. The young painter was greatly attracted to Japanese art, which was gaining popularity in France (a movement known as *japonisme*), and was a serious collector of Japanese color wood-block prints, which he found particularly fascinating.[7] In addition to his artistic talents, moreover, Rivière was a great technical innovator, possessing a quick mind capable of inventing astonishing gadgets and machinery. This gift for technological innovation proved invaluable in devising solutions for the challenges posed by the unique shadow theater art form he was to popularize.

Chat Noir artists Henry Somm and George Auriol had built a little puppet theater, *le guignol du Chat Noir*, which stood in one of the rooms, the Salle des Fêtes, on the third floor of the second Chat Noir. Here, plays written by Chat Noir authors were performed in puppet theater adaptations. One evening, as the *chansonnier* Jules Jouy was entertaining a group of friends and visitors with a rendition of his popular satirical song "Les Sergots" (The Cops), Rivière stretched a piece of white cloth across the opening of the puppet theater. Placing cardboard silhouettes of policemen between a lamp and the back of the cloth, he moved their shadows across the makeshift screen, providing a visual accompaniment to Jouy's vocal histrionics. This shadow animation was enthusiastically applauded and wildly appreciated by those in attendance, who probably had no inkling they had just witnessed the pilot performance of an extraordinary form of entertainment, one that was going to augment the glory of the Chat Noir and fill its coffers.[8] Salis, the extremely astute *gentilhomme cabaratier*, however, was quick to recognize the enormous potential of Rivière's little demonstration. Usually rather parsimonious, paying his entertainers barely more than their beer and meals, he offered Rivière a salary of 300 francs a month, a generous budget and free rein to devise and construct a theater expressly for the performance of shadow plays. Such were the beginnings of the Chat Noir Shadow Theater.

THE CHAT NOIR SHADOW THEATER

Although the Chat Noir Shadow Theater appears to have been born almost by chance, out of a playful bit of whimsy by Rivière, its creation was actually the result of the convergence of several factors. At the outset, it is important to bear in mind that the genre itself was not invented by Rivière. Shadow theater, or *ombres chinoises* (Chinese shadows) as the form is often known, is an ancient traditional form of theater, its name in French calling attention to its Eastern origins.[9] However, until its popular success at the Chat Noir, shadow theater in the West had usually been, with a few notable exceptions, no more than an amateur household form of amusement.[10] In a major book on the subject, *Les Ombres chinoises de mon père* (1885), Paul Eudel describes the shadow plays that his father used to perform for his family in their living room.[11] Although not its inventor, Rivière's great merit in reviving this traditional form derives from the fact that

Fig. 2.1. Henri Rivière, *The Shadow Theater at the Chat Noir Cabaret*, c. 1888. Ink and gouache on paper. Jane Voorhees Zimmerli Art Museum, Rutgers, The State University of New Jersey. Mindy and Ramon Tublitz Purchase Fund. (Photograph by Victor Pustai.)

he transformed a humble form of family entertainment into a highly elaborate, aesthetically sophisticated public spectacle, adding color and perspective to what generally used to be a flat monochrome representation. Furthermore, where shadow play in the West traditionally involved individual puppeteers manipulating silhouettes and figures, or casting shadows of their own fingers, hands or arms to suggest the shapes of living creatures, Rivière's theater was a smoothly functioning, technically advanced, semi-mechanized production, requiring the collaboration of several stage hands. Of course, there was no dearth of eager assistants among the Chat Noir group.[12]

Rivière was a true creative genius. Under his direction, one of the walls of the Salle des Fêtes was broken down, and in this enlarged room a new shadow theater was built by the craftsman Isabey. The theater's first luminous screen measured approximately one square meter, and its gilded façade was elaborately decorated by Eugène Grasset. At a later point, this original screen was enlarged, and when the Chat Noir closed down, it measured 1 m 40 × 1 m 12. Cardboard, and later zinc, cut-outs, mounted on a wooden platform with rollers, were pulled across the back of the screen, an oxy-hydric lamp projecting their shadows onto the screen. The use of an open flame in preference to alternate sources of back lighting was of capital importance in the casting of dark and distinct shadows.[13] (Fig. 2.1).

The Chat Noir Shadow Theater was officially inaugurated in 1887 with the performance of three shadow plays, *L'Eléphant* by Henry Somm, *Un Crime en chemin de fer* by Lunel and Caran d'Ache's *1808* (an earlier version of his more famous shadow play, *L'Epopée*, glorifying the exploits of Napoleon Bonaparte). The short scatological tableau, *L'Eléphant*, which took barely half a minute to glide across the screen, was adopted as the opening number for all Chat Noir Shadow Theater performances. In the beginning, the shows were staged once every three weeks, but subsequently, the Shadow Theater performed every night except Sundays—the day the cabaret was closed. The first plays were entirely black and white. There were no light effects, with the exception, occasionally, of a blue sky to indicate night. Soon, however, by varying the distance at which the silhouettes were positioned behind the screen, Rivière obtained a range of hues. Silhouettes closest to the screen cast dark black shadows, while those a little farther back cast shadows in varying shades of grey, not only breaking the monotony of black and white, but also enhancing the show's three-dimensional effect. Not content to rest with this technical tour de force, Rivière began experimenting, first with colored paper, and later, with the projection of light through pieces of colored glass, eventually devising a way to cast colored shadows onto the screen. Thus, while the *Tentation*, performed in the first year of the Shadow Theater's operation, owed its colored shadows to colored paper glued directly onto the silhouettes, the full-color production of *Sainte Geneviève*, performed some five years later, employed much more complex machinery.[14]

Resident Chat Noir pianists, Albert Tinchant and later Charles de Sivry, provided live piano accompaniment for most Shadow Theater performances. Scores were specially composed by various musicians; sometimes, as in the case of the *Tentation*, original compositions were augmented with music, such as well-known operatic airs from celebrated composers, specially arranged to suit the tableaux. When required, drum rolls and the clashing of cymbals emanated from the wings, and many enthusiastic poets and artists, concealed backstage along with the chorus, provided other sound effects such as the murmur of voices or crowd noises. The effect of mist and smoke was also provided by the same affable assistants lying on the ground and puffing at large pipes for the occasion. Paul Jeanne recounts that lightning was simulated by setting aflame chemically treated pieces of paper, which were thrown into the air behind the luminous screen.[15]

He divides the productions of the Chat Noir Shadow Theater into two categories, the "répertoire Satirique et Humoristique" including, for example, *L'Eléphant, Le Voyage présidentiel, Flagrant Délit* and the "répertoire Lyrique," which includes plays adapted from biblical sources (*L'Enfant prodigue* and *La Marche à l'étoile*), from classical mythology (*Héro et Léandre*) and from hagiography (*La Tentation de Saint Antoine* and *Sainte Geneviève de Paris*). Roughly half of the forty-three plays were satirical, while the other half were lyrical.[16] The authors of the latter often added descriptive phrases to the plays' titles. For example, the play *l'Arche de Noë* (Noah's Ark) was described as an antediluvian fantasy, *l'Enfant Prodigue* (the Prodigal Son) as a Biblical parable and *la Marche à l'étoile* (The Procession to the Star) was billed, like *Sainte Geneviève*, as a mystery play.[17] These descriptions underscore the homage paid by nineteenth-century artists to religious, biblical and medieval sources of inspiration.

LA TENTATION DE SAINT ANTOINE

La Tentation de Saint Antoine, a play described by Lemaître as "... imposant, mirifique et considérable,"[18] was first performed at the Chat Noir on December 28, 1887. Following a series of humorous and satirical productions, it was the cabaret's first lyrical shadow play. As Barbara Larson points out in her essay in this volume, in the nineteenth century, dramatic evocations of the temptations flaunted before Anthony and unwaveringly rejected by him, were often enacted by troupes of ambulatory actors at various *fêtes foraines*, popular fairs across France. The trials of Anthony also fascinated many artists and authors, among them Gustave Flaubert.[19]

The Chat Noir's shadow play was largely based on Flaubert's work, which is itself a curious amalgamation of narrative prose and theatrical dialogues. To a lesser extent, the shadow *Tentation* also drew inspiration from the popular *fêtes foraines* performances. The major liberty taken by

Chat Noiristes with respect to these two sources was in setting the temptations assailing Saint Anthony against the backdrop of a modern Paris instead of situating them within the time and space of the saint's life. The play thus had an immediate, personal appeal to contemporary audiences.

The Chat Noir's production of the *Tentation* was originally announced in the June 26, 1886 issue of *Le Chat Noir* journal. The lapse of a year and a half between the initial conception and the inaugural performance suggests the complexity involved in its preparation and execution. For, indeed, it was a grandiose production. Described in the album of lithographs published to accompany the play as a "Féerie à grand spectacle, en 2 actes et 40 tableaux," the *Tentation* was also one of the longest plays in the Chat Noir shadow repertoire.

The silhouettes composing the forty tableaux that comprised its two acts were all meticulously drawn and painted by Rivière and a team of artists, among whom was Caran d'Ache. They were then carefully cut out in cardboard or in thin plates of zinc, using metal shears. Colored paper was glued to these silhouettes, which were then pierced with numerous holes, to create an effect similar to that of stained glass. The score for the production was written and arranged by Albert Tinchant and Georges Fragerolle, who also borrowed music from more famous composers, such as Wagner, Haydn and Gounod.[20]

The first act of the Chat Noir's shadow *Tentation* opened in the Egyptian desert. Against an arid background, the silhouette of Saint Anthony appeared, deeply immersed in prayer. To the left was a rock in which a mysterious eye suddenly opened and blinked three times: the first sign of the Devil at work. Anthony was so engrossed in prayer that a spider had had the time to weave a web anchored to the hermit's head. The Devil then made an abrupt entry and his haunt, the city of Paris in all its decadence, rose slowly and majestically on the horizon. In a series of tableaux that moved gradually and smoothly across the screen, every possible temptation was paraded before the hermit. These seductions included the pleasures of city life and the voluptuous satiation to be derived from giving in to various forms of greed. The pleasures of food, for example, were represented by a depiction of Les Halles, the cavernous old food market which stood in the heart of Paris (Fig. 2.2). The pleasures of wine were symbolized by a cortege led by Silenus and Bacchus, extending over two tableaux. These attractions were followed by the lure of money: A tableau depicting the pleasures of gambling was followed by the silhouette of the Golden Calf, in turn followed by a tableau depicting *la Bourse*, the stock market. Other ways the Devil sought to seduce Anthony were by showing him the great feats of science and industry in the form of majestic ships and powerful

2. Performances at the Chat Noir—*Madhuri Mukherjee* 33

Fig. 2.2. Henri Rivière, *La Gourmandise* from *La Tentation de Saint Antoine* (Paris: E. Plon, Nourrit et Cie, c. 1887). Stencil colored photo relief illustration. Jane Voorhees Zimmerli Art Museum, Rutgers, The State University of New Jersey. Norma B. Bartman Purchase Fund. (Photograph by Jack Abraham.)

locomotives. The Devil then tried to sway Anthony with metaphysical temptations, offering him a glimpse of the mysteries of the ocean, then swooping him up into the sky to seduce him with those of space. The three tableaux depicting the space odyssey of the Devil and Anthony required hundreds of holes to be pierced in the silhouettes to create the impression of a dark sky studded with multitudes of stars, with the occasional ringed planet circling by (Fig. 3.14).[21]

Roughly half of the shadow play's second act was taken up by tableaux depicting the cortege of the Queen of Sheba and her attempts to seduce the hermit with extravagant gifts culled from the farthest reaches of the Earth and with the legendary charms of her flesh. The act opened with the Queen's procession moving across the screen. Silhouettes of the numerous members of the Queen's entourage were visible in the foreground, the shadows cleverly crafted to give the impression that the procession was a long, sumptuous and colorful one. Flags and pennants that were just barely discernible in the first tableaux became steadily larger and more distinct as the cortege proceeded across the screen, and finally, the chariot bearing the Queen glided into view. This was the part of the play that borrowed most heavily from Flaubert's work. Rivière's visual creations were all accompanied by quotations taken directly from Flaubert's text. For example, the tableau of the Queen of Sheba alighting from her chariot and attempting to seduce Anthony with her voluptuous charms was accompanied by a passage from Flaubert's *Tentation*, which a *récitant*—Salis or an actor—would intone. Thus, while the audience's eyes were riveted on the Queen's comely silhouette resplendent on the screen in light and shade, the words Flaubert attributed to her would resonate in the Salle des Fêtes:

> Si tu posais ton doigt sur mon épaule, ce serait comme une traînée de feu dans tes veines. La possession de la moindre place de mon corps t'emplira d'une joie plus véhémente que la conquête d'un empire. Avance tes lèvres! Mes baisers ont le goût d'un fruit qui se fondrait dans ton coeur! Ah! Comme tu vas te perdre sous mes cheveux, humer ma poitrine, t'ébahir de mes membres, et brûlé par mes prunelles, entre mes bras, dans un tourbillon....
> *Antoine fait un signe de croix.*[22]

Following the tableau of the Queen of Sheba was a succession of scenes representing gods and deities of various faiths and mythologies from around the world. Scandinavian gods were represented by Odin and the Walkyries, appropriately accompanied by music from Wagner. Tableaux depicting Apollo, the Muses and Olympus were followed by a procession of Oriental deities. Egyptian gods gave way to Vishnu, creator of the universe according to Hinduism, succeeded by the Buddha, followed by Japanese gods, painted by Rivière.[23] The penultimate tableau returned spectators to the Egyptian desert, where Anthony resumed his interrupted prayer to the accompaniment of celestial music, Haydn's *Venite Adoremus*, sung by a children's choir assembled in the theater's wings.

The shadow *Tentation*'s final tableau depicted the apotheosis of Saint Anthony (Fig. 2.3). Having braved every conceivable temptation without weakening, the Saint was borne aloft into the sky by angels, to the accompaniment of music from Gounod's *Faust*. In describing this scene in his review, Lemaître points out that the angels are "... des anges du moyen âge, très longs, avec le bas de leurs robes étalé en cercle et faisant des plis compliqués." [24]

Rivière, in fact, may have drawn inspiration from popular medieval

Fig. 2.3. Henri Rivière, *Apothéose* from *La Tentation de Saint Antoine* (Paris: E. Plon, Nourrit et Cie, c. 1887). Stencil colored photo relief illustration, Jane Voorhees Zimmerli Art Museum, Rutgers, The State University of New Jersey. Norma B. Bartman Purchase Fund. (Photograph by Jack Abraham.)

pious images in the composition of some of his tableaux for the *Tentation*. The artist whose work is generally qualified as belonging to the symbolist tradition, who excelled in suggesting poetic, lyric and mysterious elements in the decors and programs he designed for Symbolist theater productions and in the illustrations he created to accompany the poetry of Symbolist writers, seems to have shown little restraint in his use of garish colors and realistic representation. In a general introduction to a catalogue of Rivière's works, François Fossier and his coauthors criticize Rivière's manner in certain tableaux of the *Tentation*, contrasting it with the artist's creations for *Sainte Geneviève* in which, according to them, Rivière "... retrouve son terrain d'élection, l'évocation de la nature."[25] Fossier et al. write, "... la gourmandise et la luxure qui viennent tenter Saint Antoine ... auraient fait rire une nonne. En dépit d'une débauche de couleurs et d'une incroyable quantité de personnages, ça n'était guère 'tentant.' Quant à la scène finale du paradis, un marchand d'images pieuses du quartier Saint-Sulpice en aurait fait son profit." [26] This critical judgment calls for two comments. First, like the "long" angels from the Middle Ages to which Lemaître alluded above, the "orgy of colors" and "unbelievable number of characters" may have been deliberately employed by Rivière, in imitation of a popular medieval style. Secondly, Fossier's remarks refer to Rivière's lithographs for the printed album of the *Tentation* and not to the actual shadows that were projected in the darkened cabaret. No doubt there was a world of difference between the effect created by a paper copy and that of luminous colored shadows being projected on screen during a live performance.

In this context, Lemaître's eyewitness account is illuminating. We have already seen, above, that he felt that the Chat Noir Shadow Theater offered audiences glimpses of the supernatural and that he observed how the angels painted by Rivière for the scene of Anthony's apotheosis resembled those in medieval depictions. Drawing another parallel between medieval art and the tableaux of the *Tentation*, Lemaître compares Rivière's exquisite shadows to the beauty of stained glass:

> Le tout donne une impression d'extrême splendeur, supérieure à celle des plus riches ballets de l'Eden-Théâtre. C'est l'éclat d'un vitrail incendié de lumière. Et la comparaison est absolument juste; car ces tableaux sont en effet composés comme des vitraux d'église, avec cette seule différence que les contours y sont determinés non par des nervures de plomb mais par les découpures du zinc, et que le verre y est remplacé par du papier de couleur que traverse la lumière oxhydrique.[27]

The successful recreation of the effect of medieval stained glass in the shadow theater medium that so impressed Lemaître at performances of the *Tentation*, was, as we are about to see, carried to even greater heights in the production of *Sainte Geneviève*.

Sainte Geneviève de Paris

Sainte Geneviève de Paris was performed for the first time at the Chat Noir Theater on January 6, 1893. Billed in its accompanying album as a "Mystère en 4 parties et 12 tableaux," [28] it was a much shorter production than the *Tentation*. However, more than five years had passed since the inauguration of shadow plays at the Chat Noir, and Rivière and his team had greatly refined their art. The incorporation of color had been perfected. No longer using pieces of colored paper to create multicolor effects on screen, Rivière had devised a system in which pieces of colored glass, which he baked and enameled himself, were mounted on rollers. An intricate piece of machinery controlled the angle and intensity of light passing through the glass onto the screen, enabling very sophisticated color effects to be achieved. Some plays required the operation of as many as 150 pieces of glass.[29]

Sainte Geneviève is the patron saint of the city of Paris. According to legend, Geneviève was born at Nanterre, near Paris, about 420 A.D.[30] She was the daughter of poor shepherds. From her earliest years, Geneviève revealed a passion for the religious life, devoting herself to prayer and worship. When she was nine years old, the bishops Rémy, Loup and Saint Germain of Auxerre halted at Nanterre on their way from Gaul to Britain, where they were headed to combat the Pelagian heresy. A great crowd flocked to the church to see them and to receive their blessing. Among the gathered multitude, Saint Germain distinguished the little shepherdess Geneviève. He addressed her, encouraging her to persevere in living a life of faith, virtue and chastity. Before continuing on his journey the next morning, Saint Germain is reported to have summoned Geneviève once more, to ascertain her commitment to a life of piety.

When Attila and the Huns were ravaging Gaul in 451 A.D., the citizens of Paris prepared to flee and to leave their city to the invaders. Geneviève prevailed on them to remain, to pray with her and to perform acts of penance. Attila and his hordes changed course and went off towards Orléans. Paris was spared and people saw this event as the miraculous result of Geneviève's prayers. A few years later, Paris was invaded and occupied by Mérovée and his army. During the siege, Geneviève became celebrated on account of her acts of charity and self sacrifice. It is believed that thanks to Geneviève's intercession on behalf of the citizens of Paris, Mérovée and his successors, Childéric and Clovis, displayed clemency toward the populace.

Sainte Geneviève died in 512 A.D. Numerous miracles, however, continued to be witnessed at her tomb. She is believed to have saved Paris from flooding in 834 A.D. In 1129, a terrible plague swept through the city and caused the deaths of over 14,000 people. The plague was suddenly arrested when a procession was organized in honor of the saint. Thus, Sainte Geneviève was extremely popular in medieval Paris and has since remained a most beloved figure in the popular imagination of Parisians.

Presumably adapted from various popular sources, the Chat Noir version of this beloved saint's life was written by Claudius Blanc and Léopold Dauphin. Its four parts were entitled "Aux Champs" (In the Fields), "A Nanterre" (At Nanterre), "Les Huns" (The Huns) and "A Paris" (At Paris). Each part consisted of three tableaux, marking the broad sections of the saint's life and her journey toward the apotheosis of the final scene. The roles of the principal characters were spoken by actors. An 1893 booklet accompanying the play indicates that an actor named Manoury gave voice to Saint Germain, the Bishop of Auxerre, another named Cadio narrated events and played the part of the *récitant*, while the role of Sainte Geneviève was recited and sung by Eva Michel. In addition to these main characters, there was also a chorus singing the parts of the peasant men and women, young girls and little children, celestial voices, angels and, of course, the Huns. Jeanne explains how Salis cleverly managed to get the choir of the Church of Notre-Dame-de-Lorette to perform the ensembles for the two plays *l'Enfant Prodigue* and *Sainte Geneviève*: "'C'est pour chanter les louanges du Très Haut' répondait Salis aux scrupules des curés de la paroisse." [31] For performances of *Sainte Geneviève*, the Chat Noir house pianist was also accompanied by a violinist. [32]

Henri Rivière's opening shadows for *Sainte Geneviève* were extremely lyrical, setting the tone for the entire mystery play. Here is a description of the first tableau depicting "Une route, près le bourg de Nanterre":

> Dissipant peu à peu les brouillards du matin, le soleil apparaît,
> à l'horizon, derrière les collines prochaines.
> Des paysans, leur faux sur l'épaule et conduisant de lourds chariots
> vides traînés par des boeufs, vont à la moisson: ils disent une
> mélopée rustique.
> Des femmes, portant des faucilles ou des paniers de vivres, les
> suivent : alertes et rieuses, elles saluent de leur chant matinal le
> retour du jour.[33]

It is not hard to imagine, in the darkened Salle des Fêtes, this early morning harvest procession slowly traversing the screen, while the live singers and chorus, accompanied by piano and violin, sing their parts. Henri Rivière's detailed and precise silhouettes cast sharp shadows on the screen, the steady brightening of the lamp creating the impression of the rising day and the slowly disappearing smoke simulating the vaporization of the morning fog.

As each tableau moved across the screen, the next one was inserted into the rollers and drawn, in turn, across the shadow theater's screen. When required, the curtain was lowered and raised between scenes. At the beginning of the play's second part, for example, the *récitant* spoke before a closed curtain, explaining the circumstances of the three bishops' visit to Nanterre and preparing the audience for the scene in which Saint Germain distinguished Geneviève.

Sainte Geneviève de Paris was performed at a time when the Chat Noir Theater had been artistically and technologically perfected by Rivière. Its creators had taken care to incorporate in the play's *mise en scène* elements which could fully exploit the theater's potential and completely dazzle the audience. Almost every tableau thus included some kind of special light and color effect. The first tableau, we have seen, required the gradual dissipation of morning mist and fog and the steady brightening of the scene as the sun rose. The second played with light and shade effects, as Geneviève watched her flock under vast, spreading trees outside her humble dwelling.[34] The third tableau involved delicate sunset hues: "Sur la cime des coteaux, les nuées se frangent d'or devant le soleil déclinant, le croissant de la lune s'argente et déjà les premières étoiles scintillent."[35] Yet, even as Geneviève is lost in prayer, kneeling before a roadside cross, the tranquility of the moonlight scene is replaced by sinister omens of the fate awaiting her land: "... des nuages couleur de sang éclipsent la lune : ils affectent de vagues formes de guerriers barbares armés de lances de feu."[36]

The fifth tableau simulates brilliant sunshine outside the church, whereas the sixth tableau transports us into its dark interior, where, above the altar, Geneviève sees a vision, a host of radiant and resplendent angels. Scenes involving the Huns are set against the backdrop of stormy skies, with great flashes of thunder and lightning. A subsequent tableau shows the town of Metz in flames, followed by a scene where, although the flames have died down, the ruins of the town are still smoldering and smoking in the ominous moonlight, a "clair de lune sinistre." The tenth tableau of *Sainte Geneviève* aimed to replicate a stained-glass window depicting Heaven: "Comme en un vitrail lumineux, apparaît le Paradis."[37] The eleventh tableau recreates the grey, close atmosphere of a snow fall, while the final tableau, the apotheosis of the saint, shows Geneviève rising on a cloud toward "la lumière éternelle," eternal light, above a faraway view of contemporary Paris.

Within the short duration of the play, there was thus a great range and variety of light and shade and color effects. The visual virtuosity was evenly matched by the musical component of the play, by the accompanying piano, violin and children's choir. The choir, too, was necessitated by the fact that the authors of the play composed lyrics for practically every character. The peasants sang morning and evening hymns as they went to and from the fields. Geneviève sang songs of praise to God in several tableaux. Saint Germain, the Bishop, expressed himself in song while hearing Geneviève's profession of faith and bestowing his benediction. Even the Huns sang, loudly and lustily, as they followed Attila, the Scourge of God, in his path of destruction. And as Geneviève rose above the earth, her ascension to Heaven was accompanied by a choir of angels. *Sainte Geneviève de Paris* may well be described as a shadow theater musical. As Steven Moore Whiting points out, "the piano-vocal score ... comprises no fewer than 109 pages of continuous music." [38] Combining such musical extravagance (let us not forget that *Sainte Geneviève* was a rather short play, comprising only twelve tableaux) and hitherto unseen, multicolor light and shade effects with the story of the life of a beloved saint, it was no wonder that this play was such a spectacular success.

Scholars such as Cate have pointed out that the audience watching a shadow play at the Chat Noir experienced a spectacle somewhat akin to that created by modern motion pictures.[39] The analogy is apt and particularly so with early silent movies, which were often accompanied by live piano or orchestra. In such a spectacle, the detailed, precise and painstaking work of the artist who created the silhouettes cannot be overemphasized, especially when one bears in mind that the shadows appearing on the luminous screen were magnified; they were many times larger than the actual cutouts, yet they needed to be absolutely sharp and distinct. As Jeanne remarks, "L'ombre ne supporte pas la médiocrité. Qu'elle soit décorative et lyrique, humouristique ou destinée à accompagner une belle oeuvre en vers ... elle doit atteindre à la perfection."[40]

Yet at the same time and despite the ultramodern (for that period) staging techniques of the Chat Noir Shadow Theater, accounts left by those present at these shows reveal that these spectators felt as if they had been present at the performance of a *mystère*, a mystery play. Part of this illusion, we have seen, has to do with the artists' success in recreating medieval forms and artistic styles—such as the effect of stained glass and popular pious images. Another significant factor contributing to this illusion was the very way in which the Chat Noir was arranged. As Elena Cueto-Asín very pertinently points out:

> The organization of the Chat Noir reproduced the essential coordinates of the public place prior to its privatization in the modern period which was exemplified by the medieval town square or plaza. This space was idealized as a center for literary and theatrical activities where the boundaries between spectacle and spectator were not fixed architecturally and the separation of the performing arts (theater, poetry and music) was nonexistent. ... The performance in the open plaza had to accommodate itself to the

rhythm and pace of the myriad of other activities that were going on simultaneously around it. It was a place where the full range of human social activities and interactions were joined with the creative endeavors of the artist.[41]

Thus, even as the shadow plays were performed at the Chat Noir, the multiple activities of the cabaret—drinking, eating, socializing, people-watching—went on simultaneously as in medieval times, for the Chat Noir, after all, was first and foremost a commercial establishment, the livelihood of its proprietor. Of course, it was also the most popular gathering place for the Parisian avant-garde. Therefore, we may say that although *La Tentation de Saint Antoine* and *Sainte Geneviève de Paris* were not staged on the *parvis* of an ancient cathedral, they were, in a sense, performed in a cathedral of sorts: the pseudo-medieval, darkened interior of nineteenth-century Paris' cathedral of the avant-garde: the Chat Noir.

Notes

1. "This little Chat Noir theater, round as the moon (the star of dreams) and barely two arm-lengths in diameter, is a skylight open to the supernatural world. ... It is here that Henri Rivère has unfolded the legend of centuries and the history of religions, confronted Saint Anthony with all the temptations of the flesh and of the spirit, and brought back the good hermit, our brother-in-arms in anxiety and curiosity, to the foot of the redemptive cross." Jules Lemaître, *Impressions de théâtre* (Cinquième série) (Paris: Société Française d'Imprimerie et de Librairie, 1891), 350. Unless otherwise noted, all translations in this chapter are by Madhuri Mukherjee.
2. "... It is [the Chat Noir's] most prodigious success." Michel Herbert, *La Chanson à Montmartre* (Paris: La Table Ronde, 1967), 164.
3. "A Louis XIII cabaret, founded in 1114!"
4. Mariel Oberthur, *Cafés and Cabarets of Montmartre* (Salt Lake City, UT: Gibbs M. Smith, 1984). Oberthur writes, "His [Salis's] only desire was to keep the shadow theater going and stage productions in France and abroad," 65.
5. "Rustic chairs, benches and solid wood tables, a stained-glass window, a tall fireplace, some antique armor, shining brass and copperware made up the Louis XIII establishment." Jean Pascal, "Les Chansons et poésies du Chat noir," *Les Chansonniers de Montmartre* 24 (25 June 1907), 2.
6. "... composite establishment, at once pub, restaurant, literary circle, painter's studio and theater." Jules Lemaître, *Impressions de théâtre* (Deuxième série) (Paris: Société Française d'Imprimerie et de Librairie, 1897), 322.
7. For information on Rivière and *japonisme*, see François Fossier et al., *Henri Rivière: Graveur et photographe* (Paris: Réunion des Musées Nationaux, 1988); Armond Fields, *Henri Rivière* (Salt Lake City UT: Peregrine Smith Books, 1983); Gabriel P. Weisberg et al., *Japonisme: Japanese Influence on French Art 1854–1910* (Cleveland OH: The Cleveland Museum of Art, New Brunswick NJ: The Rutgers University Art Gallery, and the

Walters Art Gallery with the assistance of Robert G. Sawers Publications, London, 1975).

8. Paul Jeanne, *Les Théâtres d'Ombres à Montmartre de 1887 à 1923* (Paris: Les Editions des presses modernes au Palais-Royal, 1937), 18.

9. For an account of the history of shadow theater in both East and West, see Hetty Paërl, Jack Botermans and Pieter Van Delft, *Ombres et silhouettes*, translated from the Dutch by Jeanne Renault (Paris: Chêne Hachette, 1979).

10. Two such exceptions are the eighteenth-century Théâtre de Séraphim, which combined marionettes with shadow play and the nineteenth-century plays of Louis Lemercier de Neuville.

11. Eudel explains in detail how to construct a home-made theater for shadow plays and includes the texts of some plays that he deems easy to perform.

12. As Phillip Dennis Cate pointed out in "The Spirit of Montmartre," the time and circumstances were right for the rediscovery of this art form. With the invention of photo-mechanical relief-printing processes, high contrast black and white drawings were easily and inexpensively reproduced. Many artists in Rivière's group were involved in experimenting with the aesthetic effects of silhouettes, in art works and in book illustration. Furthermore, the *ukiyo-e* or Japanese color wood-block prints that Rivière admired and collected involved the use of silhouettes for a variety of compositional and aesthetic functions. Eudel himself lived directly across from the Chat Noir in Montmartre, and Rivière would certainly have been aware of his book. All these factors contributed to Rivière's experimentation with shadow play. See Phillip Dennis Cate and Mary Shaw, eds., *The Spirit of Montmartre: Cabarets, Humor, and the Avant-Garde, 1875–1905* (New Brunswick NJ: Jane Voorhees Zimmerli Art Museum, Rutgers, The State University of New Jersey, 1996), 55.

13. Jeanne, *Théâtres d'Ombres*, 50.

14. Jeanne, *Théâtres d'Ombres*, 56

15. "... Enfin pour reproduire les éclairs on allumait du papier salpêtré qu'on jetait ensuite en l'air." Jeanne, *Théâtres d'Ombres*, 58.

16. The chief difference between the satirical and lyrical categories (beside the obvious distinction between satire and the lyrical) is that plays in the former category did not have a fixed written script. The satirical commentary was entirely improvised by Salis for each performance. Salis' mordant wit and the acerbic barbs which he directed at members of the audience or at well known figures from Paris's bourgeoisie, were eagerly anticipated and applauded by the audience. The connections Salis drew between the content of the play and the social and political events occurring at the time in Paris, contributed to the success of these productions as much as Rivière's artistic and technical contributions. Jeanne theorizes that the reason why no other cabaret could equal, let alone surpass, the success of the Chat Noir's Shadow Theater is that there was no other *bonimenteur* (extempore commentator) of Salis' caliber (with the exception, perhaps, of the *chansonnier* Dominique Bonnaud, who sometimes stood in for Salis). In other cabarets, such as La Lune Rousse or the Cabaret des Quat'z'arts, which also presented shadow plays and continued to do so for many years after the Chat Noir closed down, and until the start of World War I, lines to be spoken were written beforehand and recited by actors.

17. *Fantaisie antédiluvienne*, *parabole biblique*, and *mystère* are the French terms.

18. "... imposing, wonderful, and considerable." Lemaître, *Impressions* (Deuxième série), 333.

19. On September 12, 1849, Flaubert completed the first version of his own *Tentation*, begun on May 24, 1848, and invited two friends, Louis Bouilhet and Maxime Du Camp to listen to a reading of the novel. The reading took four days and the verdict of the two friends, related by Du Camp was: "Nous pensons qu'il faut jeter cela au feu et n'en jamais reparler" (We think that it should be thrown in the fire, and never be spoken of again). (Maxime Du Camp, *Souvenirs littéraires* (Tome I) (Paris: Hachette, 1883), 427–30, quoted by Claudine Gothot-Mersch in the introduction to Flaubert's *Tentation de Saint Antoine* (Paris: Gallimard, 1983), 11. Dejected by such an uncompromising condemnation, Flaubert immersed himself in other projects. *Madame Bovary* was published in 1856. During the same year, Flaubert also published fragments of an abbreviated *Tentation* in the journal *L'Artiste*. Convinced that certain portions of the work would land him in court, as *Madame Bovary* had, Flaubert abandoned the project of publishing the complete work. It was only after having completed his other major novels *Salammbô* (1860) and *L'Education sentimentale* (1869), that Flaubert returned to the *Tentation*. He spent several years completely reworking the previous drafts, and a final version of the work was at last published in March 1874. In a letter written on June 5, 1872, to Mlle Leroyer de Chantepie while he was still working on the novel, Flaubert stated, "C'est l'oeuvre de toute ma vie" (It is my whole life's work), Gothot-Mersch, 13.

20. For an extended discussion of the musical components of both the *Tentation* and *Sainte Geneviève*, see Steven Moore Whiting's essay entitled "Music on Montmartre" in Cate and Shaw, eds., *The Spirit of Montmartre*, 184–88.

21. See Fig. 3.14 in Barbara Larson's essay in this volume.

22. Gustave Flaubert, *La Tentation de Saint Antoine* (Paris: Gallimard, 1983), 84–85. ("If you laid your finger on my shoulder, it would affect you like fire running through your veins. The possession of the least place on my body will give you sharper joy than the conquest of an empire. Offer your lips! My kisses taste like fruit ready to melt into your heart! Ah! How you'll lose yourself in my hair, breathing the scent of my sweet-smelling breasts, marveling at my limbs, and scorched by the pupils of my eyes, between my arms, in a whirlwind ... *Antoine crosses himself.*") Gustave Flaubert, *The Temptation of Saint Antony*, trans. Kitty Mrovosky (Ithaca NY: Cornell University Press, 1980), 89.

23. For information about the deities of India, Flaubert apparently referred to the illustrated work entitled *Symbolik und Mythologie der allen Volker besonders der Griechen*, published between 1810 and 1812 by the German Orientalist, Friedrich Creuzer. A modified, reworked version of Creuzer's book was published in French by Guigniaut between 1825 and 1851, under the title *Religions de l'antiquité*. Henri Rivière appears to have consulted these works while preparing the shadows for the Chat Noir *Tentation*, because his depiction of the Hindu God Vishnu asleep on the ocean of milk, cradled in the folds of a multiheaded cobra, closely resembles a plate from Creuzer's book.

24. "... angels from the Middle Ages, very long, with the hem of their robes fanned out in a circle, forming complicated folds." Lemaître, *Impressions* (Deuxième série), 342.

25. "... rediscovers his chosen ground, the evocation of nature."

26. "... the greed and lechery that tempt Saint Anthony ... would have made a nun laugh. Despite an orgy of colors and an unbelievable number of characters, it was hardly 'tempting.' As

for the final paradise scene, a vendor of pious images in the Saint-Sulpice district would have made a good profit out of it." Fossier et al., *Henri Rivière*, 7.

27. "The whole thing offers an impression of extreme splendor, greater than that of the most magnificent ballets at the Eden-Théâtre. It has the luminosity of a stained-glass window blazing with light. And the comparison is absolutely apt; for the tableaux are actually made like stained-glass windows, the only difference being that the outlines are defined not by ribs made of lead, but by zinc cut outs, and that glass is replaced by colored paper through which light passes from an oxy-hydric lamp." Lemaître, *Impressions* (Deuxième série), 341–42. (The same passage is quoted by Harold B. Segel in his discussion of the Chat Noir shadow show in *Turn-Of-The-Century Cabaret: Paris, Barcelona, Berlin, Munich, Vienna, Cracow, Moscow, St. Petersburg, Zurich* (New York: Columbia University Press, 1987), 72.

28. *Sainte Geneviève de Paris* (Paris: Au Ménestrel, 1893).

29. See Edouard Sarradin's article "Henri Rivière et son Oeuvre" in *Art et Décoration: Revue mensuelle d'art moderne*, Tome III, janvier-juin 1898. (Paris: Emile Lévy, 1898).

30. *Golden Legend*, Vol. 3. (http://www.fordham.edu/halsall/basis/goldenlegend/GoldenLegend-Volume3.htm#Genevieve)

31. "'It is in order to sing the praises of the Almighty,' Salis would reply to the scruples of the parish clergy." Jeanne, *Théâtres d'Ombres*, 54.

32. See note 20 above.

33. "A road, near the town of Nanterre. Dissipating the morning fog, little by little, the sun appears on the horizon, behind the nearby hills. Peasants, scythes at their shoulders, drive heavy empty oxcarts on their way to the harvest, while singing a rustic hymn. Women, carrying sickles or baskets of provisions follow them. Bright-eyed and full of laughter, they greet the return of day with their morning song."

34. A reproduction of this tableau adorns the cover for the play's musical score (*Sainte Geneviève de Paris: partition, chant et piano* (Paris: Au Ménestrel, 1893).

35. "On the hilltops, the sinking sun outlines the clouds in gold, the crescent of the silver moon brightens, even as the first stars begin to twinkle."

36. "... clouds the color of blood eclipse the moon: They take on the vague shapes of barbaric warriors armed with fiery lances."

37. "As in a sunlit stained-glass window, Paradise appears."

38. Whiting, "Music on Montmartre," 187.

39. Cate, "The Spirit of Montmartre."

40. "Shadows cannot tolerate mediocrity. Be they decorative and lyrical, humorous, or meant to accompany a beautiful work in verse ... they must attain perfection." (Jeanne, *Théâtres d'Ombres*, 7).

41. Elena Cueto-Asín, "The Chat Noir's Théâtre d'Ombres: Shadow Plays and the Recuperation of Public Space" in Gabriel P. Weisberg, ed., *Montmartre and the Making of Mass Culture* (New Brunswick NJ & London: Rutgers University Press, 2001), 231–32.

PART TWO

THE "SCIENTIFIC" EXAMINATION OF SAINTS' VISIONS

3

Odilon Redon's *Temptation of Saint Anthony* Lithographs

Barbara Larson

Gustave Flaubert's hallucinatory *La Tentation de Saint Antoine* became a virtual cult object in certain progressive literary and artistic circles in the last quarter of the nineteenth century. His powerful descriptive imagery, erotic references and exploration of the dark side of the psyche reverberated with Decadents and Symbolists alike. The author's fantastic scenes, inspired in part by the fabulous, grotesque hybrids found in Saint Anthony paintings and prints of the fourteenth to the seventeenth centuries, appealed to a taste for the macabre and visionary at the fin de siècle.

The artist Odilon Redon created three sets of lithographic prints between 1888 and 1896 based on the text by Flaubert. No other theme absorbed him to this extent; there are approximately forty prints in all, which follow the monstrous nightmares that plagued Flaubert's saint. Anthony experiences a series of hallucinations in a single night that include personifications of lust, greed and gluttony, among other sins. He is taunted by believers of diverse faiths as well as pagan cults. However, no temptation proves a greater threat to Anthony's Catholic ideals than the idea that man's origins are in nature, not creation. Redon's attraction to the fantastic aspects of Flaubert's work arose at a time when evolutionary theory was gaining credibility and when contemporary theories of the mind (illuminating the existence of hidden motivations in the unconscious) and human pathologies had led to an imaginative fusion of myth and divisive behavior in literature and art. For both Flaubert and Redon the legend of Saint

Anthony provided a vehicle through which to explore modern concerns about illness, madness and man's natural past.

The writer Emile Hennequin first introduced Redon to Flaubert's novel in 1882 after seeing trial proofs for Redon's fantastic lithographic series *Origins* (1883), based on the theme of evolution.[1] In Flaubert, Redon found a kindred spirit interested in the natural past of biological monstrosities, the primordial life of cells and the exploration of mental pathologies. Both artist and writer were also interested in the relationship between the revelations of science and spiritual life with the possibility of a reconciliation between the two. Redon would call *La Tentation de Saint Antoine* "une merveille littéraire et une mine pour moi."[2] His first set of ten lithographs plus a frontispiece and the third set of twenty-three prints plus a frontispiece were entitled *La Tentation de Saint Antoine*; the second, done in 1889, was given the title *A Gustave Flaubert*. That Redon would specify the second series to be an homage to Flaubert, while following the text of the literary work, reflects the artist's affinity and identification with the writer and his interpretation of the Saint Anthony legend.

Saint Anthony was born in Egypt in 250 A.D. and is said to have lived for nearly a hundred years despite an eremitical existence in which he was supposedly assaulted by demons representing all the vices known to man. His story was written down as a biography by Saint Athanasius, who had known Saint Anthony well.[3] In centuries to come, Saint Anthony would be thought of as a pure and elevated soul; he was assured a central place in the pantheon of Catholic saints by the fact that he is credited with being the founder of the monastic tradition. Anthony was identified as a "plague saint" by the medieval period, and more particularly was associated with diseases that affected the skin like ergotism (Saint Anthony's fire) and syphilis.

Anthony's ability to deliver one from the pains of the flesh (that may indeed seem like the attack of so many demons) has roots in the French national past. Whether true to historical fact or mere legend, Saint Anthony's body is said to have been removed from Egypt and reburied in France in the eleventh century in the abbey Saint-Antoine-en-Viennois, where a miracle cure involving a skin disorder supposedly took place. The abbey became a major pilgrimage site rivaling that of Santiago de Compostela. It was here that the monastic community of Antonines, which dedicated itself to the art of healing skin disorders, was founded. The Antonine order spread throughout France to Germany and the Netherlands. It is in the north that the most memorable and horrific Saint Anthony imagery was created, from fantastic works by Bosch to Jan Mandyn and Schoengauer. These artists had been influenced by the thirteenth-century *Golden Legend* of Jacobus de Voragine, who emphasized the terrible nature of Anthony's visions. The tribulations and torments of Saint Anthony from lust to demonic attacks had an enormous appeal from the fourteenth to the sixteenth centuries at a time when syphilis and fears of witchcraft were on the rise.

Flaubert first began to think about a work based on the Saint Anthony legend after seeing Mandyn's *Temptation of Saint Anthony* (then attributed to Breughel) in Genoa in 1845. In the Mandyn, the devout saint turns his back on the Bosch-like hybrids that personify mortal sin. Shortly after his trip to Italy, Flaubert bought a print on the theme by the seventeenth-century French artist Jacques Callot, who specialized in works of contemporary social ills as well as monstrous horrors (Fig. 3.1).[4] The fact that Callot's print with its staged vignettes was based on baroque theatrical sets of hell may have held particular appeal for Flaubert since his text was originally conceived as a play. While Mandyn and Callot's saint follows the traditional interpretation of Anthony as a model of virtue and steadfastness in the face of overwhelming adversity, Flaubert's saint, and that of Redon, would be vulnerable and self-doubting, a kind of contemporary everyman, prey to guilt, tricks of the mind and weakness of the flesh.

By 1849, when Flaubert was finishing the unpublished first version of *La Tentation de Saint Antoine*, the theme of Saint Anthony's temptations was a popular one in art. In part, this was due to a religious revival at midcentury and a renewed interest in the lives of saints, but it also had to do with a Second Empire taste for themes of seduction and religious crises. Among the artists who depicted the erotic side of the saint's temptations were Tassaert, Morot and Delaroche.[5] In popular culture, Saint Anthony had been a favorite subject for puppet shows for decades; here, the tales of temptation were designed to amuse and satirize hypocritical monks and the religious elite.[6]

Revised in the 1850s, then rewritten once again during the Franco-Prussian War and its immediate aftermath, Flaubert's work was finally published in 1874. The date of its appearance was timely. The loss of the Franco-Prussian War was blamed by many on a self-indulgent, decadent Second Empire; in the early 1870s, a new moral order and a revived Catholicism attempted to compensate for the immediate past. At the same time, an anticlerical Republican faction, which would gain authority throughout the decade, promoted progressive science as the way out for a defeated France. When *La Tentation de Saint Antoine* was first published, it was unclear whether religious instruction or science would act as a future infrastructure in guiding a recovering nation. In Flaubert's text, the saint tried to hold on to dogmatic Catholic faith, but was eventually overwhelmed by nature's own truths. Only loosely based on Saint Athanasius' account of Anthony's life, Flaubert's work explored the mystery of existence and

Fig. 3.1. Jacques Callot, *The Temptation of St. Anthony* (second version), 1635. Etching. Musée historique lorrain, Nancy. Giraudon/Art Resource, NY.

questioned life's ultimate purpose through a modern interest in pantheism, medicine, comparative religions and the mysteries of the mind.

The appeal of *La Tentation de Saint Antoine* was such in the literary world that Verlaine had considered doing an opera libretto based on it as early as 1878. Jean Moreás would include it in his *Symbolist Manifesto* of 1886, comparing it to Shakespeare's *Hamlet*, the second part of Goethe's *Faust* and Dante's *Vita Nuova*. Flaubert's work is directly invoked in a scene in Huysmans' *A Rebours* of 1884, in which a hybrid chimera and sphinx engage in a conversation that derives from the Flaubert. *A Rebours* also contained numerous references to Redon's morbid charcoal drawings and the artist's close friendship with Huysmans may well have encouraged his interest in Flaubert's work. Huysmans' devotion to *La Tentation de Saint Antoine* led him to arrange a deluxe edition of the Flaubert in 1887, with lithographic illustrations by Redon.[7] Although this project fell through, it prompted Redon's work on his first set of Saint Anthony lithographs.

The theme of Saint Anthony's temptations, especially the more erotic of them, interested many late nineteenth-century artists—Saint Anthony

Fig. 3.2. C. Daux, *La Tentation de Saint-Antoine*, **1884** salon. Oil on canvas. Location unknown.

paintings populated the French salon by the 1880s (Fig. 3.2). The saint's story and its more satirical side also remained alive at the popular level. The first major shadow play at the Chat Noir cabaret, performed in December of 1887, was based on the legend.[8] Like Flaubert and Redon, the set designer Henri Rivière modernized aspects of the tale, not only through references to science (in this case, industry and astronomy), but by setting many of the scenes in the here and now. In a number of them, contemporary Paris was used as a backdrop. Other scenes were more closely based on Flaubert. In this shadow play, Rivière used silhouettes placed at set distances from the screen to create varying effects of intensity and depth. Colors were used for the first time in the history of the shadow play, but the spatial effects, silhouettes and nuances of tone would have appealed to Redon, who no doubt knew this hugely popular production.

Saint Anthony and the Femme Fatale

While the Chat Noir shadow play was an immediate precedent in date for Redon's own lithographic scenes, whose sequence of images faithfully followed Flaubert's text, the artist's decision to undertake a major project based on the Saint Anthony legend may well have been encouraged by the popularity of the theme among avant-garde artists in Belgian circles, which he frequented. Khnopff (*After Flaubert*, 1883), Ensor (*The Tribulations of St. Anthony*, 1887) and Rops (*The Temptation of St. Anthony*, 1878) had all taken up the subject of the temptations of Saint Anthony. Indeed, it was with the assistance of his Belgian friend Verhaeren that Redon's first *Temptation of Saint Anthony* album was published in Brussels by Edmond Deman.[9] Rops' *Temptation of Saint Anthony* was considered the artist's masterpiece and was owned by Edmond Picard, one of Redon's early Belgian patrons (Fig. 3.3). This work, later referred to by Freud as "a typical case of repression," envisions temptation in the body of a voluptuous female nailed to a cross. The erotic female is a sacrilegious object that is at once Christian martyr and the devil, lust and death.

Saint Anthony's erotic temptations, which are featured prominently in the Flaubert text, had become absorbed in nineteenth-century decadence as a masochistic, morbid theme. While Redon addressed many themes of temptation in Flaubert's novel, approximately one-third of all of the artist's Saint Anthony lithographs respond to the popular Romantic and Symbolist theme of the monk's lust. By the late nineteenth century, the subject of the fatal woman became tied to the growing dread associated with rising statistics of venereal disease linked with "women of pleasure." The voluptuous beauty who embodies death is one of the most pervasive of all Symbolist themes.

In his first *Temptation of Saint Anthony* album, Redon depicted fatal women in four out of ten of the lithographs. In Plate 1, the coquettish female with a backward glance is a prostitute and comes from a hallucination suffered by Saint Anthony at the end of Chapter 1 of Flaubert's text, in which the saint sees a sequence of visions beginning with a prostitute and followed by a corner of a temple, a soldier's face and a chariot with two rearing white horses (Fig. 3.4). The woman personifies one of the seven deadly sins referred to by this hallucination. Temptation of the flesh is revisited in Plate 3, where Redon illustrates the appearance of the queen of Sheba as an enigmatic bust-length figure with an impassive expression. Her dark, magical powers are suggested not by her appearance, but by the presence of the macabre legendary Persian Simorg-anka bird that accompanies her. In Flaubert's account, the Queen of Sheba offers Anthony worldly stature, marvelous goods and the delights of the flesh. That she hops away when rebuffed by the saint suggests she is the devil incarnate. In the Redon, it is the bird with its humanoid grimace that appears diabolical.

Fig. 3.3. F. Rops, *The Temptation of St. Anthony*, 1878. Oil on canvas. Bibliothèque Royale Albert Ier, Brussels.

Fig. 3.4. Odilon Redon, French, 1840–1916. "First a pool of water, then a prostitute, the corner of a temple, a figure of a soldier, a chariot with two rearing white horses," Plate 1 from *The Temptation of Saint Anthony,* 1888. Lithograph, 29 × 20.6 cm. Charles Stickney Collection, 1920.1632. Reproduction, The Art Institute of Chicago.

3. Redon's *Temptation* Lithographs—*Barbara Larson*

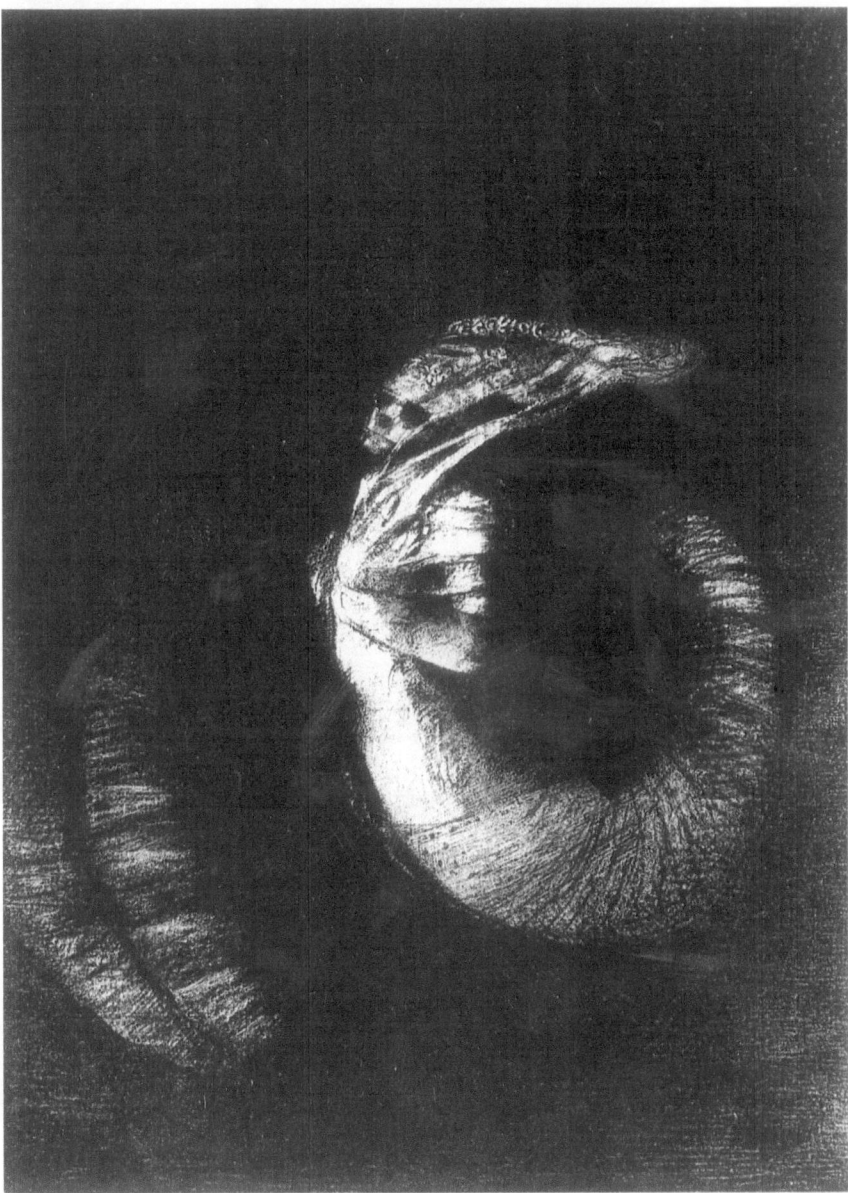

Fig. 3.5. Odilon Redon, French, 1840–1916. "It is a skull wreathed in roses. It dominates a woman's torso of pearly whiteness," Plate 6 from *The Temptation of Saint Anthony*, 1888. Transfer lithograph on mounted ivory China paper, 29.7 × 21.7 cm. The Stickney Collection, 1920.1639. Reproduction, The Art Institute of Chicago.

Fig. 3.6. Odilon Redon, French, 1840–1916. "And all sorts of frightening beasts arise," Plate 8 from *The Temptation of Saint Anthony*, 1888. Lithograph, 31.2 × 22.8 cm. Charles Stickney Collection, 1920.1641. Reproduction, The Art Institute of Chicago.

In the following plate, Redon illustrates the story of Helen, who, in Flaubert's work, represents a notable prostitute of classical times. She makes an appearance as a somnambulist, hypnotized by the magician Simon, in Chapter Four. Redon depicts her drifting in mid-air, dressed from head to toe in classical garb, as remote and inaccessible as a Greek goddess. Plate 6, which illustrates a passage from the last chapter of the Flaubert, is the most horrific incarnation of the *femme fatale*: "It is a skull wreathed in roses. It dominates a woman's torso of pearly white" (Fig. 3.5). She is the death rattle itself, who makes an appearance after Saint Anthony has been accosted by lust and death, seen as a young and an old woman. Together, lust and death dance and sing a song of life and death in which one is found in the other. After this vision disappears, Anthony sees the death's head and the passage continues, "En dessous, un linceul étoilé de points d'or fait comme une queue; et tout le corps ondule, à la manière d'un ver gigantesque qui se tiendrait debout."[10] Her skeletal appearance and leaping form link this figure to the grotesque figures of the medieval dance macabre, several of which appear in Flaubert's Callot print (see Fig. 3.1).

Fin-de-siècle imagery where death is embodied in lust has roots in fears of contamination and with syphilis. Syphilitic cures, as we have seen, were associated with Saint Anthony. At the time Flaubert first considered writing a book based on the legend of Saint Anthony, he had a skin eruption that he feared to be syphilis.[11] In 1849, a doctor confirmed Flaubert's self-diagnosis.[12] Redon may take the biological dimensions of this pervasive nineteenth-century condition a step further in his "And all sorts of frightening beasts arise," also from the Saint Anthony series of 1888 (Fig. 3.6).

A number of Redon's late nineteenth-century works were done in response to Pasteur's discoveries of the true origin of contagious disease, deadly microorganisms that cause death. In reference to this print, Huysmans would write in his essay "Le monstre" that the "districts des imperceptibles" in Redon's work were "plus terrifiants que les fauves exagérés des vieux maîtres."[13] He describes the image in terms of deadly bacilli and protoplasm in a gelatinous environment.

Venereal disease and the prostitution it was associated with were major themes in literature in the last decades of the century. Disease and prostitution figure in Barbey d'Aurevilly's "Vengeance d'une femme" in *Les Diaboliques*, a story of self-destruction and syphilitic death. The more venal aspects of the prostitute became increasingly pronounced in literature and art as the century progressed. Huysmans had often treated the theme of the sexual temptress, including in his first book, *Marthe*, which dealt with state-controlled prostitution. But it was Des Esseintes of *A Rebours* whose nightmarish visions of lust and death matched only that of Flaubert's Saint Anthony. Des Esseintes imagines he sees a woman who is shaking with fever and whose arms become fleshless. He attempts to run, but is pursued by her again. She is the embodiment of syphilis, "la grande variole."[14] Des

Esseintes' symptoms, including migraines, vertigo and nightsweats, are those of a syphilitic. Des Esseintes not only brings up the dread of syphilis, but also its bacteriological origins. His gloomy meditations on life would have struck a chord with his audience now so aware of the lethal potential of microorganisms, "Tout n'est que syphilis.... Et il eut la brusque vision d'une humanité sans cesse travaillée par le virus des anciens âges.... Elle avait couru, sans jamais s'épuiser à travers les siècles; aujourd'hui encore, elle séduisait, se dérobant en de sournoises souffrances."[15]

In the year Redon was beginning his first *Temptation of Saint Anthony* album, a program of reforms focusing on regulating prostitution through the state had begun in an attempt to control the "péril vénerien."[16] At the same time, Saint Anthony's association with syphilitics came up in the medical literature of the period. In a chapter called "Les Syphilitiques dans l'art" in his 1887 *Nouvelle iconographie de la Salpêtrière*, the prominent pathologist Charcot attempted to identify syphilitic figures in medieval and other art. He discussed the Saint Anthony legend and illustrated a figure at lower left in Grünewald's *Temptation of Saint Anthony* panel from the famous Issenheim Altarpiece, created for the Antonine community at Colmar (Fig. 3.7).[17] Charcot described the syphilitic symptoms of the figure, including a partially destroyed nose and ear. Huysmans, who wrote an essay on the Issenheim altarpiece some years later, would note Charcot's diagnosis and responded to the figure in the following way:

> Est-ce une larve, est-ce un homme? En tout cas, jamais peintre
> n'a osé, dans le rendu de la putréfaction, aller aussi loin.
> Il n'existe pas dans les livres de médecine de planches sur les
> maladies de la peau plus infâmes. Imaginez un corps boursouflé,
> modelé dans du savon de Marseille blanc et gras marbré de bleu,
> et sur lequel mamelonnent des furoncles et percent des clous.
> C'est l'hosanna de la gangrène, le chant triomphant des
> caries![18]

Huysmans may have informed Redon further about the Saint Anthony legend and its medieval connection with syphilis.

Redon continued to explore Flaubert's fascination with lust and its consequences in subsequent albums. Two of the six plates in Redon's *A Gustave Flaubert* also deal with the theme of lust. In the first plate, a figure of a martyred female whose body remains a locus of desire ranks with Rops

Opposite: Fig. 3.7. Matthias Grünewald, The Temptation of St. Anthony, Issenheim Altarpiece, wing on the high altar of the Anthona Church at Issenheim, 1510–1515, Musée Colmar. Giraudon/Art Resource, NY.

Fig. 3.8. Odilon Redon, French, 1840–1916. "Saint Anthony: 'Beneath her long hair, which covered her face, I thought I recognized Ammonaria,'" Plate 1 of *A Gustave Flaubert*, 1889, lithograph, Charles Stickney Collection, 1920.1648. Reproduction, The Art Institute of Chicago.

in its disturbing psychology. The image "Beneath her long hair ... I thought I recognized Ammonaria" conflates a scene of torture with the memory of a beloved female from Saint Anthony's past, one of Flaubert's inventions (Fig. 3.8). It is an image of obsessive sexual infatuation and sadomasochism, which had great appeal at the fin de siècle. Here a male with a whip ambiguously turns away from the woman and seems to be self-flagellating. The reference is to Anthony's self-reproach over lustful thoughts. This plate is contemporaneous with the first series and was included in the Paris salon in 1888. The second reference to lust in the 1889 album is the celebrated "Death: My irony surpasses all others," considered by Mallarmé, Gauguin and other contemporaries of Redon to be one of his best works. It is quite similar to "It is a skull" of 1888 and, in an unusual departure, does not depict the scene from which the quote derives, but rather one slightly later, that of "It's a death's head." Death is the narrator in the Flaubert text, as an old woman dressed in a shroud. It is she who says "My irony surpasses all others!" Death refers to sadistic pleasure found in suffering, and the narrator continues, "Il y a des convulsions de plaisir aux funérailles des rois, à l'extermination d'un peuple—et on fait la guerre avec de la musique, des panaches, des drapeaux, des harnais d'or, un déploiement de cérémonie pour me rendre plus d'hommages."[19] The choice of this text to accompany an image that illustrates another passage may have to do with Redon's self-consciousness over creating a work that is so close to a plate from his first Saint Anthony album. That the caption brings up not death, but the image of lust once again, underscores the powerful psychological orientation of the work. In the album *A Gustave Flaubert*, the artist may be responding not just to the text of *La Tentation de Saint Antoine*, but to the life of Flaubert himself. After the writer's death in 1880, the details of his personal life fed his myth. His taste for prostitutes and failings in love were well known. He never married and lived much of his life in solitude, which raised comparisons with the eremitical monk and the erotic desires that had so consumed him from his youth to his old age.

Sexual temptation is once again a major theme in the 1896 Saint Anthony lithographs, but in some cases the references are subtle or even seem nearly effaced. The mood of this album is more restrained. For example, the Queen of Sheba makes another appearance, but this time her face is in near profile and her eyes are closed. She is a remote introverted figure despite the emotional intensity of the words repeated in Redon's caption: "My Kisses Taste Like Fruit ready to melt into your heart! ... You Scorn Me! Farewell!" She is hardly the sensual creature who has also just said, "Ah! Comme tu vas te perdre sous mes cheveux, humer ma poitrine, t'ébahir de mes membres, et brûlé par mes prunelles, entre mes bras, dans un tour-

billon."[20] Helen is depicted, but turns aside. Although her bust, with face in profile, bears a resemblance to Redon's prostitute in plate 1 of 1888, she does not cast a glance toward the viewer; her eyes are little more than dark sockets. There is no reference to Flaubert's text in the caption, she is simply "Helen."

In a complex image of the ruined palace of Nebuchadnezzar, the dark face of a woman who seems to be veiled is disembodied and recedes into shadows between two pillars. In this plate, a snake appears as a separate undulating form that wraps itself around one column. Inexplicably, a head or tail slithers across the foreground column. In another plate, a female Christian martyr takes a sponge soaked in the blood of a lovely young male who had been martyred in a horrific fashion and covers it with kisses. Lust and death are only subtly suggested here; readers of Flaubert would know that following this melancholy scene, an orgy of sex and drink take place in a graveyard of martyred Christians. A new goddess appears in Redon's 1896 album: the Syrian fertility goddess Cybèle, described by Flaubert as a mountain deity with the sun as a halo. Despite Flaubert's discussion of her sadistic nature and her masochistic appeal to her followers, Redon depicts her as a flat-chested introspective figure whose head is, once again, turned in profile. Isis, the voluptuous nature goddess whose cult was followed by many throughout the Mediterranean world during Anthony's time is represented by Redon as a more imposing Egyptian deity whose incestuous relationship with her brother Osiris has resulted in the weak failing child she holds in her arms. Although her substantial figure faces forward, her head is entirely obstructed from view by a back veil. Death as a shrouded old woman appears in 1896, with no erotic overtones. As a skeleton, death also appears dancing with the curvaceous figure of lust; as two separate figures their fusion is suggested by a sinuous arabesque (Fig. 3.9). Again, the narrator Death is included in the caption. She speaks first to Saint Anthony: "But I alone make you serious" and then to Lust, "Why don't we embrace?" The recipient of both messages is ambiguous, for the figures face the viewer. While the medieval dance macabre is reenacted once again, the references to fatal women in the majority of the 1896 images are enigmatic and remote. Subdued, introspective females that personify powerful erotic legends are part of Redon's exploration of psychology.

Opposite: Fig. 3.9. Odilon Redon, French, 1840–1916, Plate 20 of 24: "Death: It is I who make you serious; let us embrace each other." *The Temptation of Saint Anthony,* 1896. Lithograph in black on cream chine affixed to ivory wove paper, 30.2 × 21.2 cm. The Stickney Collection, 1920.1785. Reproduction, The Art Institute of Chicago.

SAINT ANTHONY AND MADNESS

Flaubert's text is filled with hallucinations. To prepare to write the work, he read medical texts on mental illness including Esquirol's *Des Malades mentales*, works by Pierre Cabanis, who related the intellect to the nervous system and recounted states of delusion, and Dr. Hector Landouzy's *Traité complet de l'hystérie*.[21] Saint Anthony often seemed unsure if what he experienced was real or the result of mental debilitation. In Chapter 2, for example, he is described as cataleptic. The figures that appear to him often seem to be in trances themselves, like the Christian martyr in Chapter 4 who is "sans rien voir, comme un somnambule."[22] Helen's eyes "Paraissent insensibles à la lumière" and "elle tourne ses prunelles comme sortant d'un songe."[23] Flaubert had thought to subtitle his 1874 revision, "le summum de la folie." The morbid psychology of *La Tentation de Saint Antoine* would have had great appeal in the 1880s, when psychiatry was validating the importance of dreams, hallucinations and altered states. Anatole France, whose *Thaïs* of 1890 was influenced by Flaubert, had written a year earlier that Saint Anthony awaited scientific analysis of behavior in terms of emerging psychology.[24]

Pathologies of the mind revived interest in mesmerism (now called hypnosis), and the relationship between vision and reality were the obsession of numerous scientists and laymen under the Third Republic. Charcot wrote a book called *Les Démoniaques dans l'art* in 1887 in which he interpreted medieval imagery of suffering martyrs and the possessed in terms of hysterical conditions.[25] His diagnosis of delusional states mainly among women, many of whom saw themselves as possessed by demons or to be themselves saints, was made largely through his work at the mental hospital the Salpêtrière. That certain of Redon's images could be interpreted in this way is suggested by plans for the inclusion of his "Ammonaria" print in an 1889 exhibition called "Folles de la Salpêtrière."[26] By the 1880s and the 1890s, the painful ecstasies of many saints, such as Teresa, were being reinterpreted in terms of hysteria.[27]

There is a personal side to the aberrant states recounted by Flaubert that may well have intrigued Redon. The writer was an epileptic who, in his youth, experienced seizures that were accompanied by hallucinations. He described his attacks as a kind of hemorrhage of the nervous system, where thousands of images seem to explode all at once.[28] Flaubert was plagued by this condition in the 1840s; it seemed to abate around 1849 when he was finishing the first version of *La Tentation de Saint Antoine*, only to begin again around 1870 when he was writing the final version. Among his readings on psychology, he was familiar with medical books on nervous diseases kept in the library of his father, a prominent medical doctor who attempted to cure him. The reason he lived much of his life in seclusion at the country estate of Croisset may have had to do with the fact that epileptics were then regularly prescribed rest in the country. Kitty Mrosovsky in her informative introduction to her English translation of *The Temptation of Saint Anthony* interprets the appearance of the mercurial monstrous chimera in Flaubert's last chapter as a symbol of the fluid stream of images and thoughts Flaubert experienced when ill.[29]

Redon too had been an epileptic when young and also lived a solitary life on a country estate outside of Bordeaux. Whether his episodes continued beyond childhood is unknown, for according to church records he was an example of a miracle cure in 1846.[30] Epilepsy was stigmatized as a degenerative disorder and associated with hysteria; if Redon knew of Flaubert's condition, which was likely in the years after his death, he may have felt a special affinity for the writer and his fascination with a monk who lived apart from the world, plagued by his demons. Many of Redon's Saint Anthony figures stare, adrift as if in a dream or are entirely lost in an interior world. The example closest to "the fugue of images" Flaubert claimed to have experienced during his seizures is Plate 1 of the 1888 *The Temptation of Saint Anthony* lithographs (Fig. 3.4). In more general terms, Redon makes use of the contemporary interest in other states of mind in his iconography. In the first two lithographic albums one finds an allusion to Hypnos, god of sleep, in the diabolical figures that represent the devil where one wing is open, the other closed. This symbol of the dark side of the mind would have been readily recognizable in the Symbolist circles Redon frequented. It is found, for example, in the work of Khnopff.

MONSTERS AND MODERN SCIENCE

Half of Redon's Saint Anthony prints were based upon the composite monsters envisioned by Flaubert. Oriental hybrids like the sphinx and chimera come to life, along with fabulous creatures not unrelated to those of medieval bestiaries. Of all the fantastic creatures Redon represented in *The Temptation of Saint Anthony* albums, the chimera appears most often. It is a mercurial creature in the final chapter of the Flaubert: Its composite characteristics of bird and reptile suggest that its iconographical source is in the Callot with its fabulous flying beast (Fig. 3.1). In Redon's Saint Anthony lithographs, it is a heraldic linear symbol in the frontispiece of the 1888 album; a fabulous winged horse that leaps toward heavenly realms like Apollo's horses in the 1888 plate "the green-eyed chimera turns, barks";

Fig. 3.10. Odilon Redon, French, 1840–1916. "The Sphinx: Mon regard que rien ne peut dévier, demeure tendu à travers les choses sur un horizon inaccessible. La chimère: Moi, je suis légère et joyeuse." Plate 5 of *A Gustave Flaubert*, 1889, lithograph, 28.2 × 20.2 cm. Charles Stickney Collection, 1920.1654. Reproduction, The Art Institute of Chicago.

a diabolical serpent in "The Sphinx: My gaze, which nothing can deflect remains fixed across all things on an unreachable horizon. The chimera: I am full of lightness and joy" of 1889 (Fig. 3.10); a shadowy, dim presence in "I have sometimes caught sight in the sky of what seemed to be the forms of spirits," of 1896; and a veritable seahorse in "The Beasts of the Sea," also from the last album. Two years before the first Saint Anthony album, Redon created the lithograph, "The chimera looked at everything with terror," for the album *Night*. By this time, Flaubert's chimera as a symbolic image had become a kind of touchstone for literary symbolists. Jules Destrée expressed regret that he could not use one of Redon's 1888 Saint Anthony prints as the frontispiece for his book of poems, *Chimères*.[31]

While the chimera suggests thought and the imagination, other beasts are related to the origins of life. Monsters as evolutionary creatures led Saint Anthony to a study of the details of nature. Flaubert moved the passages on monsters from a former more obscure section of the book to the final climactic chapter in the 1874 *La Tentation de Saint Antoine*, demonstrating the increased importance of biological as well as spiritual origins for Flaubert. Monsters are a vehicle through which Anthony passes quickly back through the centuries as forms mutate or devolve.

Flaubert's interest in monstrosities came from several sources. He had been fascinated by hybrid creatures he saw in medieval cathedrals and thought that they might have represented a carryover from prehistoric times. The grotesque multiforms he saw in the work of Jan Mandyn and Callot, among other representations of the Saint Anthony theme provided another source, as did his reading of Montaigne, who had written about the natural origins of monsters.[32] Flaubert's close friend Georges Pouchet was also interested in the natural origins of medieval monsters, having written the book *Histoire des sciences naturelles au moyen âge* in 1853. Yet another source had to do with the medical training of his father. Dr. Flaubert had studied under Dupuytren, famous for his studies of physical malformations such as defective fetuses and degenerative skeletal structures. These biological monstrosities were preserved at the Dupuytren Museum in Paris, which still exists today. A final source had to do with nineteenth-century theories of evolution. Both artist and writer would have been able to gather considerable information regarding the history of life at the Museum of Natural History in Paris, which they both frequented. The biological origins of the monster and its relationship to evolution through time was incorporated into nineteenth-century ideas on biological transformation. The science of teratology, or monstrosities, was established by Etienne Geoffroy Saint-Hilaire, who worked at the Museum of Natural History in the 1830s. In his famous treatises *Considérations générales sur les monstres* and

Des Monstruosités humaines Geoffroy Saint-Hilaire asserted that embryonic deviations from the norm reveal true biological secrets and can offer insight into catalysts behind evolution.[33]

One of Redon's favorites of Flaubert's biological inventions was the Chaldean god Oannes, part man and part fish, who made his appearance in the writer's pantheon of false gods in Chapter 5 (Fig. 3.11). In a passage that prefigures the de-evolutionary episode of natural origins that will eventually undermine the saint's rigid beliefs at the end of the novel, Oannes claims to have "vu dans les étangs qui restent du déluge."[34] The artist's first response to Flaubert's book occurred in 1883 in the form of two charcoals that depict Oannes. One, called "Tadpole," shows Redon's interest in creatures whose bodies undergo metamorphosis in the real world. Created at the same time he published his lithographic album *Origins*, Redon had evolutionary theory very much in mind, and a fish-humanoid creature introduces that series. The fish may also allude to the Christian symbol and suggest interchangeable aspects of world religions, with common roots in nature mysticism. Oannes is both god and nature intertwined and only through his awakening can nature proliferate in its multiple forms. Redon's interest in composite creatures that inhabit the boundaries between different species owes a great deal to his intellectual mentor, the botanist Armand Clavaud, who specialized in research on tiny aquatic organisms that exhibited both plant and animal characteristics. Although Redon's depiction of Oannes may recall something of the bizarre composite creatures of Bosch, Grünewald or Schongauer, it was also informed by modern science.

While Redon was undertaking his scientific studies, his growing awareness of the philosophical potential of science applied to mankind's past and future was also indebted to the legacy of romantic Naturalism, including the work of great luminaries such as Balzac, Michelet and Hugo, who drew from discourses in zoology in the late eighteenth and early nineteenth centuries and openly acknowledged the considerable importance of Cuvier, Geoffroy Saint-Hilare and Buffon in their investigations. Hugo used contemporary ideas on science in his *La Légende des siècles* with its meditations on the ascent of the human spirit from its origins in a prehistoric milieu. Balzac, most notably in his 1845 preface to the *Comédie Humaine*, credits both Buffon and Geoffroy Saint-Hilaire for his analogies. Michelet sub-

Opposite: Fig. 3.11. Odilon Redon, French, 1840–1916. Plate 5 of 10, "Then there appears a singular being, having the head of a man on the body of a fish," *The Temptation of Saint Anthony*, 1888. Lithograph in black on ivory chine affixed to ivory wove paper, 27.6 × 17.1 cm. Elizabeth Hammond Stickney Collection, 1920.1637. Reproduction, The Art Institute of Chicago.

70 TWO: THE "SCIENTIFIC" EXAMINATION

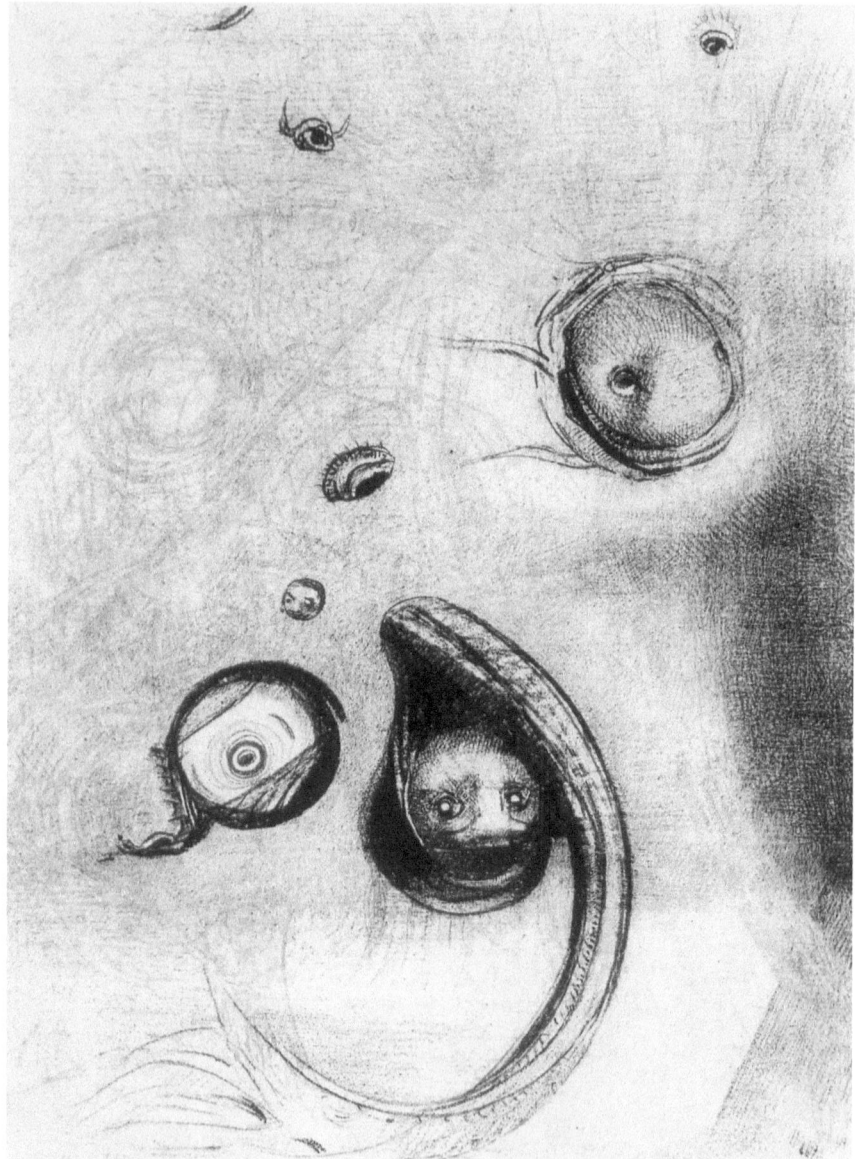

Fig. 3.12. Odilon Redon, French, 1840–1916, Plate 13 of 24: "And that eyes without heads were floating like mollusks," *The Temptation of Saint Anthony,* 1896. Lithograph in black on light grey chine affixed to ivory wove paper; image: 31.1 × 22.6 cm, sheet: 52.6 × 34.9 cm. Elizabeth Hammond Stickney Collection, 1920. 1769. Reproduction, The Art Institute of Chicago. (Photograph by Greg Williams.)

merged Naturalism in many of his works and wrote four books on the natural sciences. Long before Redon and Flaubert began to make trips to the Museum of Natural History, Michelet and other writers of the Romantic generation had gone there to find inspiration. For Michelet, the monster was an experimental step in nature, full of tragic implications. He was most interested in middle zones, creatures that exist between the land and the sea or species that he believed belonged to two kingdoms. The whale was an example of what Michelet saw as a tragic monstrosity, a survivor of nature's shot at the sublime. For Michelet, the jellyfish was an emancipated polyp, half vegetable and half animal. The polyp, having recently been attributed to the animal kingdom, was a favorite image of his, as it would be for Redon. Michelet described it in terms of assuming all shapes and colors and even playing the part of a plant or fruit. Redon's jellyfish of Plate 21 of the 1896 Saint Anthony lithographic series illustrates Flaubert's passage, "Au loin des jets d'eau s'élèvent, lancés par des baleines; et du fond de l'horizon rondes comme des outres, plates comme des lames, dentelées comme des scies, s'avancent en se traînant sur le sable."[35]

The monsters are the only vision that the saint seems not to regret; they lead him to scrutinize nature. Anthony wishes to merge with nature, to see the very stirrings of life. He is eventually overcome with amoebic bliss and lies on his belly, studying the minutiae of nature. Animals and plants merge, then the ocean transforms and seaweed becomes grass, and forests of coral give way to trees. Interested in pantheism from his earliest years, Flaubert directs Saint Anthony ultimately toward the loss of narrow Catholic faith, but this is countered by a near spiritual vision of nature. After his revision of the 1870s, Flaubert noted to a friend that Anthony had lost his narrow belief system because of the scientific cell. In Redon's image "And that eyes without heads were floating like mollusks" is a single cell with a nucleus, as if seen through a microscope on a glass slide (Fig. 3.12). Cells also drift through a number of other Saint Anthony plates including "Beasts of the Sea," "Various Populations inhabit the countries of the ocean," and "Then there appears a singular being, having the head of a man on the body of a fish" (Fig. 3.11). Jean Doin, who consulted the artist in an article on his work in 1914, noted Redon's fascination with the cell: "Mais, c'est surtout la cellule, unité élémentaire de la vie, qui séduisit alors M. Redon."[36]

In Flaubert's text, Anthony watches life eventually become inanimate matter, then observes: "Des diamants brillent comme des yeux, des minéraux palpitent.... Enfin, il aperçoit de petites masses globuleuses, grosses comme des têtes d'épingles et garnies de cils tout autour, une vibration les agite."[37] In the passage regarding "the birth of life," Flaubert is referring to the still widely held belief of, among others, Georges Pouchet's famous father, Félix-Archimède Pouchet (whose work on spontaneous generation Flaubert had read), that life could originate from inorganic matter.

At the end of the novel the night with its many visions has passed and Saint Anthony looks up to see Christ's face in the sun. The last change to Flaubert's novel was made as late as 1873, when he replaced what had been the final episode of the three theological virtues with the image of the Christ-sun. The reference is to a final pantheistic reconciliation of the natural and the spiritual world and an abandonment of rigid dogma. Anthony peacefully accepts this vision, which some episodes ago may have seemed a sacrilege.

THE LITHOGRAPHIC PROGRAMS

The Temptation of Saint Anthony, 1888

From the late 1880s through the 1890s, when Redon was creating his Saint Anthony albums, there was renewed interest in religion. Many had turned back to Catholicism or had sought spiritual refuge from the Republican culture of science in the growing interest in the occult, mysticism and eastern religions. Redon himself was thought to have undergone some sort of religious crisis around 1895, perhaps prompting his last and most extensive Saint Anthony album.

Redon's lithographic program varies within the individual albums. His first may be interpreted in terms of paired images. The first two plates concern the seven deadly sins. Plate 1 is his "First a pool of water ..." (Fig. 3.4) and Plate 2 features a grotesque devil who "holds the seven deadly sins" in the form of a degenerate infant. The second two both have temptresses, the Queen of Sheba and Helen. The third pair seem to be about the birth and death of life with serpent or fish and human conflations but have vastly different moods: One represents Oannes as an amusing creature, and the other is the horrific "It is a skull" (Figs. 3.11, 3.5). The fourth pair of plates have horrible beasts that represent the invisible dark dimensions of matter and the mind: "And all sorts of frightening beasts arise" and "The green-eyed chimera, turns, barks" (Fig. 3.6). The final pair both have round ciliated forms and suggest origins of matter and spirit and their interconnectedness: One is a disembodied eye that looks up toward heavenly realms, and the other is the sun with its face of Christ. Nature and spirit find one another.

A Gustave Flaubert, 1889

Redon's second Saint Anthony album was published on the heels of the first, and when it was advertised in the Belgian periodical *L'Art moderne* in June 1888 the reviewer announced an album of six plates that would "complete" the first.[38] In this set, Redon seems to explore Flaubert's own obsessions, not only venturing as far as he ever will into libidinal territory, but by exploring a monstrous hybrid from *La Tentation de Saint Antoine* that had held a particular appeal for Flaubert: the snake-human Knouphis.

Knouphis was worshiped by the gnostic faction the Ophites, who practiced heretical Christian beliefs during Anthony's lifetime. The Ophites identified the serpent with the savior through the staff held up by Moses, which had been transformed from a serpent. The description of a serpent with a human head in Flaubert's novel derives from a plate in Jacques Matter's 1828 *Histoire critique du Gnosticisme*, which reproduces human-headed serpents, symbols of the Ophite sect.[39] They believed that matter was evil but infused with divine sparks. In the course of salvation, the soul with its connection to divinity could be released from the material body. For both artist and writer, Knouphis could be used as a vehicle to further explore the relationship of the spiritual to the material world and matter to thought; it also represented roots of religious history in nature worship. Redon refers directly to Knouphis in Plate 2 where the serpent rests his human head on an altar (Figure 3.13). Light radiates from the creature's calm visage like the divine sparks the gnostics believed existed in all matter. Knouphis is also the subject of Redon's dark, mysterious "Flowers fall and the head of a python appears" from the 1896 album. This image suggests not light and salvation but the dark side of matter, and an atmosphere of evil prevails. Redon may have known that Flaubert had intended to write a history of Gnosticism, but regardless, as an astute reader of *La Tentation de Saint Antoine*, he would have noted Flaubert's personal fascination with this form of belief, which contains pagan and eastern components.

While the six plates of the 1889 album illustrate various passages of Flaubert's text, all the images include serpentine tails or imply a serpentine creature in the sinuousness of their bodies. The figure of Ammonaria is almost boneless in its curves; long hair hides much that is human in this body (Fig. 3.8). "Death: My Irony Surpasses all others" fuses snake and human as does the worm-like creature of "There must be somewhere primordial creatures where bodies are nothing but images." The chimera and the sciapode of the last two plates all have humanoid faces and snake-like tails.

The snake can be tied to dark eroticism as well as to the history of religion, one of Flaubert's fields of study.[40] The serpent of Eden would have reverberations as a meaningful symbol in late nineteenth-century Catholic France with its moralizing currents. Eroticism and evil in the body of the *femme fatale* who emerges from a coiled snake in "Death, my irony surpasses all others" of Plate 3 may suggest Eve after the fall. Flaubert explored the snake as a religious symbol from its association with nature mysticism to its affiliation with the great religions such as Hinduism. The snake has had magical connotations as uruboros or symbol of the never-ending circle of life and was ascribed healing powers during pagan times. The snake can be seen as a transmythological symbol uniting world religions and sometimes evoking concerns about dark aspects of the material realm.

While Redon seems to explore Flaubert's personal obsessions in the 1889 lithographs, the recurring symbol of the snake may refer to another aspect of the timeliness of Flaubert's text in fin-de-siècle France: the growing interest in comparative religions and the occult. That Anthony is a Catholic saint plagued by the possibility that other religious systems embody similar truths and symbols would have reverberated at a time when occult systems, incorporating common aspects of world religions, were finding popularity and challenging Catholic beliefs. After the mid–1880s there was a great deal of interest in theosophy, for example, which combined aspects of Hinduism, Buddhism and Christianity, among other beliefs, with references to modern science, including Darwinism and evolutionary theory. Theosophy revived the symbol of uruboros as a self-perpetuating snake that consumes its own tail. Redon owned a copy of Schuré's *Les Grands initiés* (1889), one of the great theosophical documents of the period. It was personally dedicated to the artist with the words, "in very sympathetic homage." Redon frequented theosophical circles and began, by 1890, to sell prints through Edmond Bailly's Librairie de l'art indépendant, a gathering place for those interested in the occult and theosophy.

The Temptation of Saint Anthony, 1896

Fin-de-siècle interest in eastern religions and their connection with nature mysticism informs Redon's interest in the false gods that confronted Anthony. Both Isis and the Buddha made their first appearance in Redon's 1896 *The Temptation of Saint Anthony* plates. He must have been thinking seriously about illustrating Flaubert's novel once again by 1895 when he created a print of the Buddha with its pantheistic reference to the cosmos and its title taken from Flaubert, "I was taken to schools. I knew more than the scholars." Redon's 1896 Buddha from his Saint Anthony plates com-

Fig. 3.13. Odilon Redon, French, 1840–1916, Plate 2 of 6: "A Long Chrysallis, the Color of Blood," *A Gustave Flaubert*, 1889, lithograph in black on ivory chine, 21.9 × 18.4 cm. The Stickney Collection, 1920.1649. Reproduction, The Art Institute of Chicago.

bines the figure with a python. Unity with nature is suggested by the caption, "Understanding was mine! I became the Buddha."

The plates of 1896 draw from the works of 1888 and 1889, but the album is mellower in mood in keeping with the increased spiritualism of the decade of the 1890s. The chimera is alluded to but is no longer a specific

Fig. 3.14. Rivière, "Le ciel," "La Tentation de St. Antoine," 1887. Norma B. Bartman Purchase Fund. Jane Voorhees Zimmerli Art Museum. Rutgers, The State University of New Jersey.

presence. Grimacing diabolical faces are no longer to be found in 1896; even the devil seems less deadly. In his single appearance in the twenty-four works he is a seductive figure in "Anthony: What is the meaning of all this? The devil: there is no meaning." Redon's image alludes to a passage in *La Tentation de Saint Antoine* in which the devil takes Saint Anthony on a flight through the heavens not unlike that of Faust, which Redon depicts in the frontispiece to *A Gustave Flaubert*. The space flight is prefigured in Flaubert's own *Smarrh*, as in *Bélial*, by his close friend Poittevin, and in Byron's *Cain*, but in *La Tentation de Saint Antoine* it represents the temptation of positivism, where the heavens are revealed as governed by cosmic laws rather than by the hand of god. This modern concept of the spiritually meaningless but fascinating space voyage had also been the subject of one of the scenes at the Chat Noir Saint Anthony play (Fig. 3.14). In the 1896 lithograph we see only the head of Saint Anthony and the devil who emerges, along with a bat-wing, from Anthony's mind as evil thought. The tiny whispering figure of the devil may allude to the power of hypnotism over the weak and the ill, an acceptable form of medical therapy in the 1890s. The life of the mind is an important aspect of the 1896 album. The many faces in profile or those with closed eyes in 1896 suggest an atmosphere of interiority or meditation upon the failings of the flesh.

Childhood memory is also explored in 1896. When he rewrote *La Tentation de Saint Antoine* in the early 1870s, Flaubert had decided to use youthful memories of Anthony's and their later life in hallucinations as an organizing principle, including specific locales. In the 1896 album, settings with or without the presence of humans take on importance as in the empty desert, "And he made out an arid plain with nipple-like hillocks," the tree with its enormous hole of "I have sunk into solitude. I once lived in the tree behind me," the encrusted baroque interior of Nebuchadnezzar's palace of "All around are columns of basalt ... light falls from the vaults," or the haunting prison of Christian martyrs, "In the shadows, people crying and praying are surrounded by others who exhort them." Redon used many of his own memories with imagery taken from Flaubert's text. For example, the tree of "I have sunk into solitude ..." is based on sketches of a tree from the country estate of Peyrelebade and the hills "And he made out an arid plain ..." are similar to those he etched under the tutelage of the printmaker Bresdin when young.

Six lithographs of 1896 (Plates 4 to 9) follow passages from Chapter 4 of *La Tentation de Saint Antoine* in rapid succession as if Redon is experimenting with another way to represent the "fugue of images" experienced by Saint Anthony in his hallucination of the seven deadly sins of Plate 1 in 1888. In Plate 1 of the 1896 album, however, we begin not with a vision, but with a profile view of Saint Anthony himself (Fig. 3.15). Redon refers here to a standard medieval practice of representing Anthony after an initial series of demonic attacks at a moment when he cries out for divine intervention, the apparitions still visible. In the Grünewald *Temptation of Saint Anthony* panel, the saint holds a piece of paper with the words, "Where were you good Jesus, where were you? And why did you not come to dress my wounds?" Similarly, the Redon illustration is accompanied by the words, "Help me, O my God!" Unlike the distraught monk of the Grünewald, however, Redon's Anthony, with his calm face radiating light, is very much a fin-de-siècle *voyant*. As a Rimbaudian seer the experiences that will disrupt Anthony's senses will give him the means to understand universal principals.

By exploring the visions of a saint, Flaubert and Redon play upon periods of Catholic and medieval revival, but unlike medieval representations

that focus on the monsters of the seven deadly sins, Redon and Flaubert venture beyond this, exploring questions about the origins of life, the mysterious depths of the mind and the relationship between spirit and matter that was part of the quest for meaning in late nineteenth-century France.

Notes

1. Letter from Redon to André Mellerio, 21 July 1898, in *Lettres d'Odilon Redon 1878-1916*, ed. Marius Leblond (Paris: Floury, 1923): 32.

2. "A literary marvel and a mine for me." Quoted in Roseline Bacou, *Odilon Redon*, 2 vols. (Geneva: Pierre Cailler, 1956), I: 77-78.

3. Saint Athanasius, *Life of Saint Anthony*. Ancient Christian Writers, Vol. 10, trans. Robert T. Meyer (Westminster MD: Newman Press, 1950).

4. Jean Seznec, *Nouvelles Etudes sur la Tentation de Saint-Antoine*, ed. F. Saxl, Studies of the Warburg Institute (London: University of London, 1949): 61.

5. See Theodore Reff, "Cezanne, Flaubert, Saint Anthony and the Queen of Sheba," *The Art Bulletin* 44 (Spring 1962): 113-25 on the Saint Anthony theme at mid-century.

6. The first version of *La Tentation de Saint Antoine* was indebted to a puppet show Flaubert saw at the annual fair in Rouen when he was young. Later in life, he took George Sand to see the production. The words were printed and published in 1843, with lithographic illustrations by Daubigny. See "La Tentation de Saint-Antoine, pot-pourri par Sédain, dessins par M. Trimolet, gravures par M. Daubigny," *Chants et chansons populaires de la France* (Paris: H. L. Delloye).

7. *Lettres ... à Odilon Redon*, ed. A. Redon and R. Bacou (Paris, 1961): 111-12.

8. On the *Temptation of Saint Anthony* shadow play at the Chat Noir, see Madhuri Mukherjee's contribution to this volume. See also Steven Moore Whiting, "Music on Montmartre," *The Spirit of Montmartre: Cabarets, Humor and the Avant-garde, 1875-1905*, ed. Phillip Dennis Cate and Mary Shaw (Rutgers: The State University of New Jersey): 14-88.

9. See Fred Leeman, "Odilon Redon: The Image and the Text," *Odilon Redon: Prince of Dreams*, ed. Douglas Druick and Peter Zeegers (Chicago: The Art Institute of Chicago, 1996): 191-92 for details on the publication agreement between Redon and Deman. The fifty-eight volumes were distributed in Paris through the bookshop associated with the journal *La Revue Indépendante*.

10. Gustave Flaubert, *La Tentation de Saint Antoine, Oeuvres Complètes de Gustave Flaubert*, 10 vols. (Paris: Louis Conard, 1902), 5:186.

11. Roger Williams, *The Horror of Life* (Chicago: University of Chicago Press, 1980): 130.

12. Williams, 154.

13. "... the imperceptible worlds enlarged and made visible were more terrifying than the fantastic beasts of old masters." J.-K. Huysmans, "Le monstre,"

Opposite: Fig. 3.15. Odilon Redon, French, 1840-1916. Plate 2 of 24: "Saint Anthony: Help me, O my God!" The Temptation of Saint Anthony, 1896. Lithograph in black on light grey chine affixed to ivory wove paper, 21.7 × 13.2 cm. The Stickney Collection, 1920.1740. Reproduction, The Art Institute of Chicago.

Certains (Paris: UGE, 1975): 334. Unless otherwise indicated, all translations from the French in this chapter are by Barbara Larson.

14. J.-K. Huysmans, *A Rebours, Oeuvres Complètes de J.-K. Huysmans*, 18 vols. (Paris: Les Editions G. Crès, 1929), 7: 79.

15. "All is syphilis.... And he had the abrupt vision of a humanity unendingly tormented by this virus from ancient times.... She [syphilis, feminine in French] had run her course through the ages without tiring; even today, she seduced, stealing away through underhanded suffering." Huysmans, *A Rebours*, 141.

16. See Alain Corbin, *Les filles de noce: misère sexuelle et prostitution* (Paris, 1982) for a discussion on "syphilophobia" and politics.

17. Jean-Martin Charcot, *Nouvelle iconographie de la Salpêtrière* (Paris, 1889): 236–38.

18. "Is this creature a larva or a man? In any case, no painter has ever gone so far in the representation of putrefaction. In no medical textbook is there a more frightening illustration of skin disease. The bloated body of the figure seems to be modeled in greasy blue-veined white soap, and full of boils and warts. It is the hosanna of gangrene, the triumphal chant of decay!" J.-K. Huysmans, *Trois Primitifs, Oeuvres Complètes de J.-K. Huysmans*, 18 vols. (Paris: Les Editions G. Crès, 1930), 11: 291–92.

19. "There are convulsions of pleasure at kings' funerals, at the extermination of a people, and one makes war with music, plumes, flags, gold harnesses, a whole ceremonious display to give me greater homage." Flaubert, *La Tentation de Saint Antoine, Oeuvres*, 185.

20. "Oh! How you will lose yourself in my hair, smelling my breasts, marveling at my limbs, and scorched by the pupils of my eyes, in my arms, in a whirlwind...." Flaubert, *La Tentation*, 37.

21. Seznec, 59, n. 5; Jan Goldstein, "The Uses of Male Hysteria: Medical and Literary Discourse in Nineteenth-Century France," *Representations* 34 (Spring 1991): 135.

22. "Sees nothing, like a somnambulist," Flaubert, *La Tentation*, 81.

23. "Seem unresponsive to light and she rolls her eyes as if coming out of a dream," Flaubert, *La Tentation*, 89.

24. Reff, 116.

25. Jean-Martin Charcot, *Les Démoniaques dans l'art* (Paris: Adrien Delahaye, 1887).

26. The image was selected by the artist Armand Gautier, who specialized in painting the insane. André Mellerio Archive, The Art Institute of Chicago, Chicago.

27. In the article "La foi qui guérit," Charcot diagnosed both Teresa and Francis of Assisi as hysterics able to cure others of hysterical conditions. Jean-Martin Charcot and Paul Richer, *Les Démoniaques dans l'art suivi de "La foi qui guérit"* (Paris: Macula, 1984): 111–23. Flaubert himself read a biography of Saint Teresa's life in preparation for the final writing of *La Tentation de Saint Antoine* and would later say that he had experienced during periods of illness all that Saint Teresa had. On saints and hysteria in the late nineteenth century, see Cristina Mazzoni, *Saint Hysteria: Neurosis, Mysticism and Gender in European Culture* (Ithaca: Cornell University Press, 1996).

28. Williams, 129. On Flaubert and psychology see John C. Lapp, "Art and Hallucination in Flaubert," *French Studies* 10 (1956): 311–22.

29. Kitty Mrosovsky, "Introduction," Gustave Flaubert, *The Temptation of Saint Anthony* (Ithaca: Cornell University Press): 220.

30. Robert Coustet, "Odilon Redon miraculé," in *Revue de l'art* (1993): 83–85.

31. See a letter from Destrée to Redon in *Lettres ... à Odilon Redon*, 178.

32. Seznec, 75.

33. In a letter to George Sand as early as the 1850s, Flaubert had written, "Aesthetics awaits its Geoffroy Saint-Hilaire, that great man who demonstrated the viability of monsters ...," quoted in Seznec, 80.

34. "[... seen] into ponds remaining from the flood." Flaubert, La Tentation, 129.

35. "In the distance rise jets of water, spouted by whales, and from the far reaches of the horizon, come the beasts of the sea, like round wineskins, jagged like saws and flat like blades, dragging themselves across the sand." Flaubert, La Tentation, 199.

36. "But it was especially the cell, elementary unit of life, that absorbed Redon's interest." Jean Doin, "Odilon Redon," Mercure de France 60 (July–August 1914): 10. By mid-century the cell had been found to be the fundamental unit of organic structure and thus the conceptual bond that brought together the study of plants and animals. This unified biology into one science. By the mid–1870s, the role of the nucleus, which can be seen in Redon's image, became of central importance in the study of the cell. Due to contemporaneous developments in the microscope, scattered and diverse information about the cell nucleus could be organized.

37. "Finally, he perceives small globular masses, as big as pinheads and covered by eyelashes, shaken by a vibration." Flaubert, La Tentation, 200.

38. "Petite Chronologie," L'Art moderne, June 17, 1888: 199. This album was printed by Bequet in an edition of sixty copies and sold through Laurent Dumont. Forty-five were sold within the first year; the remaining fifteen were bought by Deman and sold in Belgium.

39. Seznec discusses the origin of Flaubert's snakes with human heads and illustrates a plate.

40. Flaubert had read and taken notes on Creuzer's Les Religions de l'Antiquité, among other texts.

4

The Golden Legend in the Fin de Siècle: Zola's *Le Rêve* and Its Reception

Elizabeth Emery

Comment arriver à exprimer aujourd'hui le suc dolent et le blanc parfum des très anciennes traductions de la *Légende dorée* de Voragine? Comment lier en une candide gerbe ces fleurs plaintives que les moines cultivèrent dans les pourpris des cloîtres, alors que l'hagiographie était la soeur de l'art barbare et charmant des enlumineurs et des verriers, de l'ardente et de la chaste peinture des Primitifs? On ne pouvait cependant songer à se livrer à de studieux pastiches, s'efforcer de singer froidement de telles oeuvres. Restait alors la question de savoir si, avec les ressources de l'art contemporain, l'on parviendrait à dresser l'humble et la haute figure d'une sainte; et c'était pour le moins douteux, car le manque de simplesse réelle, le fard trop ingénieux du style, les ruses d'un dessin attentif et la frime d'une couleur madrée transformeraient probablement l'élue en une cabotine. Ce ne serait plus une sainte, mais une actrice qui en jouerait plus ou moins adroitement le rôle; et alors, le charme serait détruit, les miracles paraîtraient machinés, les épisodes seraient absurdes! ... puis ... puis ... encore faudrait-il avoir une foi qui fût vraiment vive et croire à la sainteté de son héroïne, si l'on voulait tenter de l'exhumer et de la faire revivre dans une oeuvre.[1]

—J.-K. Huysmans, *En Route*

In this passage of Huysmans' 1894 novel *En Route*, his protagonist Durtal has recently converted to Catholicism and revels in the medieval religious texts that he has discovered as a result of his newfound faith. Above all, he admires hagiography, particularly the early French translations of Voragine's lives of saints, which he equates to the medieval arts of manuscript illuminators, stained-glass artisans and *Primitif* painters such as Rogier van der Weyden.[2] Believing that portraying faith through beautiful style is of the utmost importance in writing a good saint's life, Durtal questions his contemporaries' ability to write hagiographies. He dismisses the *bondieuseries* of most Catholic artists and writers who, he feels, lack both style and religious sentiment (see Figs. 0.1 and 4.4). While he admires the style of Flaubert's "Saint Julien l'Hospitalier," he finds it lacking in belief: The story is nothing but a legend and thus lacks "le cri de l'amour qui défaille, le don de l'exil surhumain, l'âme mystique!"[3] Ernest Hello's *Physionomies de saints*, on the other hand, contains the necessary faith, but is marred by its style. The emphasis Durtal places on distinguishing popular portrayals of saints—such as those on sale in Paris or on display at the Chat Noir shadow theater—from medieval saints motivated by their "flame," their belief in God, reflects contemporary debates about the representation of saints in fin-de-siècle art and literature. How, in an increasingly secular, scientific and commercial age, could, as Durtal asked, one reproduce the "suc dolent et le blanc parfum" of the *Golden Legend*?

An unusual novel, Emile Zola's 1888 bestseller *Le Rêve*, lies at the center of fin-de-siècle discussions about medieval and modern saints' lives.[4] In this book, an orphaned protagonist, the aptly named Angélique Marie, reveres the *Golden Legend* and models her behavior on the lives of the saints she finds in it. Zola surprised the public with *Le Rêve*, the sixteenth volume of the *Rougon-Macquart* series, because it seemed a far cry from his usual brand of Naturalism. In fact, unlike *La Terre*, the "degenerate" novel that had preceded it, *Le Rêve* was immediately praised by many readers, who pronounced it an "appendix to the *Golden Legend*," a "quasi-Biblical idyll" and a "poem of grace."[5] They appreciated the way in which his style captured the mystical development of the heroine: "la Légende et la Cathédrale, s'aidant l'une l'autre dans leur oeuvre de purification, modifiant peu à peu l'âme d'Angélique, la dépouillant enfin de la robe héréditaire pour la faire semblable à la Légende, à ses saintes de chair et d'os ...."[6] Others, however, ridiculed the "imbecility" of the novel. Huysmans, for example, labeled it "une ridicule bondieuserie dans laquelle ce pataud a simplement oublié la messe et les sacrements—Une jeune fille, pure, céleste, rêvant d'un Prince Charmant mais voulant de l'ARGENT!!!"[7] Huysmans rejected the book on the same terms that he had the works of Catholic writers and artists who subordinated religious faith to simplistic or sentimental storytale fables.

This essay examines the battles that took place in the fin de siècle among those who appropriated saints' lives as legends, appreciating them for their entertainment value, those who used them as examples of psychological abnormalities and those who hoped to reclaim them for their edifying religious or historical value. As the exemplary aspects of saints' lives devolved into mere biography or legend in the French mainstream, Catholics worked valiantly to re-invest them with their medieval signification: as outstanding examples of the powers of faith and of God's presence in the world. The immense popularity of Zola's *Le Rêve* and its operatic adaptation, both of which gave a prominent position to *The Golden Legend*, provides a valuable reference for evaluating fin-de-siècle attitudes toward the representation of medieval saints' lives.

LE RÊVE AND THE GOLDEN LEGEND

Hagiographical stories permeate *Le Rêve* from its first scene, which takes place on the day after Christmas in 1860; we find the nine-year-old Angélique seeking refuge from the snow (she has run away from her foster parents) under the cathedral's portal of Saint Agnes. Her back is against the trumeau next to the statue of Saint Agnes, who is sculpted with her martyr's palm branch and sheep at her feet. In the tympanum just above, Angélique follows the legend of the thirteen-year-old saint, fiancée of Jesus, who refused marriage, was sentenced to burn to death, but who was miraculously saved as the flames spared her and turned themselves upon her executioners. The sculptures also chronicle the miracles accomplished by her bones, as well as her union with Christ in Heaven.[8]

Agnes protects Angélique from the snow, as do Dorothy ("nourished, in prison by miraculous bread"), Barbe ("who lived in a tower"), Genevieve ("whose virginity saved Paris"), Agatha, Christina, Cecilia and three more rows of virgins who are represented as being martyred at the bottom of the sculpture and triumphantly welcomed to heaven at the top. Henceforth, Angélique respects these saints and considers them her friends because they protected her. Zola returns often to descriptions of these statues, dwelling on the richness of the sculpture and the precious gems with which they are embellished.[9]

Angélique is found and adopted by a couple of chasuble makers, the Huberts, who live in the shadow of the cathedral. She grows up in this simple pious world, working, attending mass at the cathedral, helping the

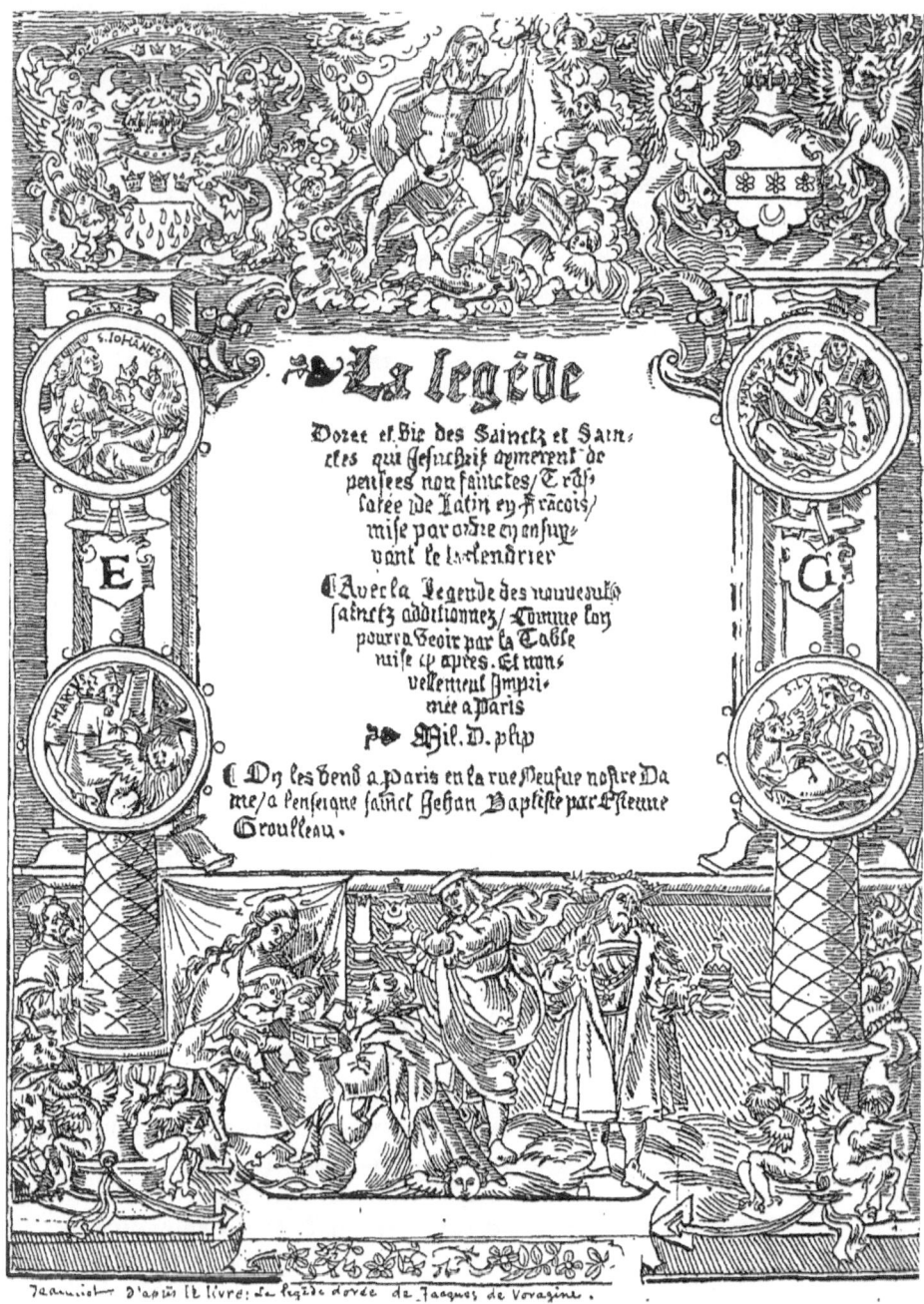

Fig. 4.1. Jeanniot, *La Légende dorée*, after the frontispiece of a translation of Jacques de Voragine's text published in 1549 by Estienne Groulleau. Illustration for Emile Zola's *Le Rêve*, first printed in *La Revue Illustrée* 5 (1887–1888: 267).

poor and emulating her friends the saints. The *Golden Legend* appears throughout the book, in the form of a 1549 illustrated French translation, written in Gothic script and full of "old woodcuts marked by their naive faith." Zola devotes an entire chapter of his novel to the description of this volume and its contents, from its initial images of the four evangelists to those of the Annunciation, Saint Nicholas and the three little children, Saint Agnes, her neck pierced by a sword, Saint Christine, her flesh torn with hooks and Saint Genevieve and her sheep. In fact, Zola was describing in great detail a real sixteenth-century French translation of the *Golden Legend*, which he had consulted at the Bibliothèque Nationale, and which he follows carefully[10] (Fig. 4.1).

Zola's detailed descriptions of this volume brought attention to Jacobus de Voragine's thirteenth-century text, which had been wildly popular in the Middle Ages; some 1,000 manuscripts of it survive and it is thought to have been the most widely read medieval text after the Bible.[11] The work fell into disfavor in the Renaissance and had been all but forgotten until the middle of the nineteenth century (Gustave Brunet's 1843 French translation of the Latin text was allegedly the first in 300 years).[12] Zola, in closely following the 1549 manuscript (and quoting, periodically, from the sixteenth-century French text) brought new attention to the *Golden Legend*, especially because he published *Le Rêve* in illustrated installments for the popular *La Revue illustrée* (from April to October 1888). Although most of Jeanniot's accompanying illustrations were modern, he also copied a number of the sixteenth-century woodcuts of saints referred to in Zola's text, including the frontispiece to the 1549 edition Zola had consulted[13] (Fig. 4.1).

As paradoxical as it may seem, it was the agnostic Naturalist writer who, in devoting his novel to *The Golden Legend*, served as a catalyst for bringing the contents of this medieval book of piety widespread popular attention; *Le Rêve* elicited over thirty reviews in 1888–1889, while several hundred critical studies were dedicated to the opera based on the book.[14] Zola's influence in this regard has not yet been recognized. In fact, scholars persist in seeing art historian Emile Mâle's 1898 doctoral thesis as a "milestone" for the popularity of saints in the fin de siècle (the five years after its publication witnessed an enormous growth in interest about the *Golden Legend*).[15] Mâle's text was surely influential, though only one of many contributions to interest in the saints that had begun earlier and that was encouraged by two best-selling novels of the 1880s: Anatole France's 1881 *Le Crime de Sylvèstre Bonnard, membre de l'Institut* and Zola's 1888 *Le Rêve*.[16]

In France's work, an erudite bibliophile discovers that a fourteenth-century manuscript of the *Légende dorée* is for sale and goes through great lengths to obtain it. Bonnard is a specialist of Christian Gaul and has collated many manuscripts of the *Golden Legend*, which he knows well; he describes Voragine's work as "a vast and gracious work" (158). The eponymous hero thus covets this manuscript (it did not exist; France created a composite from extant manuscripts to create an apocryphal and ideal edition), which miraculously comes to him as a gift. The novel then traces the psychology of this scholar who must sell his library to provide a dowry for his ward, Jeanne Alexandre. Incapable of giving up the most beloved of his treasures, including the *Golden Legend*, he withholds them from the sale (hence the crime). In contrast to Zola, who focused on content, on the individual stories of the *Golden Legend* and their influence on Angélique, France portrayed the manuscript as an object worthy of collection: Bonnard cherishes the work above all for its pedigree and for his scholarly attachment to it; it is a museum piece. Zola underlined the particulars of medieval hagiography by drawing attention to the text itself; he treated medieval literature while France drew attention to art history, to the rarity of *Golden Legend* manuscripts. Both brought new attention to the *Golden Legend*.

ZOLA'S REPRESENTATION OF MEDIEVAL HAGIOGRAPHY

Though his penchant for the Middle Ages is little discussed, Zola was an avid collector of medieval art and artifacts; he filled his home in Médan with armor, tapestries, missals and stained glass. Flaubert compared his bedroom to that of Saint Julian.[17] It is thus not surprising that he would have taken over 100 pages of notes from *The Golden Legend*, nor that he would give it a critical place in the structure of his novel.[18] The details he chose to incorporate reveal a great deal about late nineteenth-century impressions of saints' lives.

First, he echoes stereotypes about the Middle Ages as "simple," "candid" and "pure," ideals expressed in works such as those of Chateaubriand and Hugo and adopted by scholars until the twentieth century to refer to medieval art and literature.[19] These are the terms used by Brunet in his 1843 preface to his translation of the *Golden Legend* (copied by Zola in his notes): "the most sincere and naive expression" of a lost faith.[20] Angélique's understanding of saints' role in the world is similarly simple, naive and sincere:

> Dieu est débonnaire, et ce sont d'abord les saints et les saintes.
> Ils naissent prédestinés, des voix les annoncent, leurs mères ont
> des songes éclatants. Tous sont beaux, forts, victorieux. De grandes
> lueurs les environnent, leur visage resplendit.... Leur histoire à

> tous est la même, ils grandissent pour le Christ, croient en lui, refusent de sacrifier aux faux dieux, sont torturés et meurent pleins de gloire.... Des conversions en masse se produisent, quarante mille hommes sont baptisés d'un coup.... La prospérité, la santé sont en mépris, la joie commence aux privations qui tuent le corps. Et c'est ainsi que, triomphants, ils vivent dans des jardins où les fleurs sont des astres, où les feuilles des arbres chantent.[21]

Zola represented Angélique's belief as a reflection of what he understood as the medieval spirit. Indeed, it was common practice in the late nineteenth century to accept the *Golden Legend* as a mirror of all medieval thought, and the cult of the saints was seen as a particularly medieval phenomenon, even if all saints were not medieval. Huysmans called it "the book where the soul of the Middle Ages was most candidly stamped," while Emile Mâle referred to it as "one of the most interesting books of its time for those who seek in medieval literature for the spirit of the age to which it belonged."[22] As Reames has shown, however, this modern notion of the *Golden Legend* as "an exemplary piece of medieval piety or learning, or both, has surprisingly little behind it." She convincingly argues that such beliefs derive largely from a romanticized identification of the *Golden Legend* with all saints' lives, which nineteenth-century writers tended to categorize as democratic works that brought religious ideals to the people.[23]

As Zola further develops Angélique's thoughts about the saints in a passage that continues the one cited above, he also emphasizes her particularly modern appreciation for the entertainment value of the "legends" of the saints by underlining the unusual, the extraordinary:

> Ils exterminent des dragons, ils soulèvent des tempêtes et les apaisent, ils sont ravis en extase à deux coudées du sol.... Des histoires extraordinaires leur arrivent, des aventures merveilleuses, aussi belles que des romans. Et, après des centaines d'années, lorsqu'on ouvre leurs tombeaux, il s'en échappe des odeurs suaves. Puis, en face des saints, voici les diables, les diables innombrables ... dans ce combat des saints et des saintes contre Satan, se déroulent les effroyables supplices des persécutions.... Un continuel miracle d'ailleurs protège les saints, ils fatiguent les bourreaux.... Des secours continuels, des apparitions descendent du ciel ouvert, où Dieu se montre tenant une couronne de pierreries....[24]

Angélique is thus clearly drawn to the seemingly fictional and legendary aspects of saints' lives, as were her nineteenth-century contemporaries. The

Golden Legend fascinates Angélique because of its marvelous stories: they are exotic vestiges of the past, figures as interesting as those of novels. Emile Mâle, too, likened saints' lives to romances, calling the book "a picture of human life, a summary of the world's history, strange adventures, and wonderful miracles."[25] This kind of attraction to the incredible or marvelous aspects of the saints' lives is akin to that evident in Flaubert's "Légende de Saint Julien l'Hospitalier" and *La Tentation de Saint Antoine* or in Henri Rivière's shadow puppet presentations of the lives of Anthony and Genevieve: Marvelous encounters with mythical beasts and demonic figures make for good entertainment that mixes charm with local color.

Zola's novel thus echoed nineteenth-century stereotypes about the simplicity of medieval faith and the fairy-tale qualities of saints' lives, yet he also went further, whether he realized it or not. By depicting Angélique as the reader of an authentic medieval text, he actually cites medieval accounts of the saints and their miracles. Because Zola presents the book through Angélique, who is reverent toward its content, the reader is encouraged to respect her point of view. Zola thus validates her understanding of a world in which God and his saints play an active role: They intercede on behalf of believers. In this sense, Zola presents saints in thirteenth-century terms: God played a daily part in human activities, participating actively in the battles between good and evil. As William Granger Ryan has pointed out, the multiplication of such scenes of good triumphing over evil served to reinforce the belief in God's presence and active intervention in such battles.[26] In stating that the people of the Middle Ages believed these stories, it is important to note that, in the Middle Ages, history was not determined principally by the authenticity of events and facts as it is today. Rather, it consisted of what one was willing to believe, events that belonged to a widely accepted tradition.[27] It was not until the Renaissance that the volume's veracity became a significant issue, thus leading to arguments about it as "full of nonsense," "dangerous," or "superstitious."[28] Angélique's belief in these stories reflects that of her medieval ancestors and Zola's narrative—filtered through her point of view—does not cast doubt on the existence of the saints and the authenticity of their miracles.

Although Angélique is attracted to the fairy-tale aspects of the story, she respects this book and its lessons above all else, modeling her comportment on that of her beloved saints. Her personal visions of saints reinforce the message of the *Golden Legend*: that God does intervene in human affairs. Taught by the medieval text, the nineteenth-century Angélique believes in the saints and understands the rewards she receives as a product of her faith. Angélique feels, as does Huysmans' character, Durtal, that faith is the key element in hagiography. Her reading of the saints' devotion to God is a key element in her own philosophy, which posits that faith conquers all.

Her angelic name (which contains that of Agnes, her favorite saint) suggests that Angélique very much belongs to the medieval world of the saints she so loves. She embroiders chasubles using medieval tools and techniques; she lives in the shadow of the cathedral in a medieval village. Indeed, Angélique even falls in love with a young man who resembles both the Saint George of the cathedral's stained-glass window and Jesus himself.[29] He is the man of her dreams. Later she discovers that he is not a vision, but a real boy, the bishop's son. After many tribulations, including the families' refusal to allow them to marry, Angélique's near death of a broken heart and a miraculous blessing by the bishop, who allows the couple to marry after all, Angélique achieves her story book ending: a princely wedding. In an ultimate plot twist, however, she dies upon leaving the cathedral after the ceremony, thus remaining faithful to her friends the saints. Like Saint Agnes, she refuses to surrender her virginity.

The ending of this novel was perplexing for many readers, who could not decide whether the narrator's commentary on Angélique's death—"all is but a dream"—confirmed the story's legendary aspects or criticized them. This is the question posed by most modern critics of the novel, and without reading his preparatory notes, Zola's relationship to the saints he describes in such detail remains unclear. It is likely that much of the ambiguity comes from the context surrounding the publication of the novel: Zola attempted to please his contemporaries with a fairy tale while criticizing the escapism of those who, like Angélique, lived in the dream worlds motivated by fiction and religion.[30] What interests us here, however, is less Zola's intent, than the effect his book produced. The attention he devoted to the stories and the images contained in *The Golden Legend* brought them to the public eye and familiarized readers with the ways in which the Middle Ages had represented the saints. The years following Zola's novel saw a flourishing of interest not just in the saints, but in the *Golden Legend* as a masterpiece of medieval literature: Illustrated editions, versions for children and new translations quickly appeared on the market.[31]

The reception of this unusual novel provides a marvelous vantage point from which to study late nineteenth-century relationships to the lives of saints. Zola's text, in its very ambiguity, epitomized the different appropriations of saints' lives that took place in the 1880s and 1890s. It mirrored the Symbolist movement's fascination for legends, fairy tales and dreams, while its Naturalist underpinning derived from the medical community's exploration of the physical causes of visions. Even Catholics were intrigued by the attention Zola had paid to citing the sixteenth-century translation of the *Golden Legend*. *Le Rêve* quickly sold out of its first edition of 44,000 copies.[32]

LE RÊVE, THE GOLDEN LEGEND AND THE SYMBOLIST MOVEMENT

One of the groups most active in representing saints and mysticism in this period was composed of those who would later be called Symbolists. As they reacted against the Naturalist movement and what they considered overblown materialist characterizations of modern life, they called for an examination of the world through suggestion instead of representation.[33] Many writers harshly criticized Zola and his pessimism, arguing that what readers wanted and needed was an ideal, a dream that would help society reform.[34] As one writer put it in an 1894 article for *L'Ermitage*, the movement, "se rejeta vers les sujets de rêve et de légende."[35] The words *dream*, *soul* and *legend* were prevalent, especially in Symbolist journals such as *La Plume* and *Le Mercure de France*.

Medieval texts like the *Golden Legend* thus represented a valuable model for these artists, as did the works of *Primitifs*, medieval painters and stained-glass artisans.[36] As Huysmans put it in his 1894 *En Route*, the seemingly pure language and atmosphere evoked in medieval hagiographies—"le suc dolent et le blanc parfum des très anciennes traductions de la *Légende dorée*"—fascinated the modern poet intrigued by relationships among the arts.[37] In literature, Flaubert was one of the first to attempt to capture this ambience with his "La Légende de Saint Julien l'Hospitalier," which he had conceived in 1846 and rewritten in 1856 and 1875–1876.[38] This tale was widely praised by readers upon publication in 1877.[39] Huysmans lauded his "noble effort" to attempt to imitate the style and approach of hagiography in "Saint Julien l'Hospitalier": "[Ses pages] marchent en un tumulte éblouissant et réglé, évoluent en une langue superbe dont l'apparente simplicité n'est due qu'à l'astuce compliquée d'un art inouï."[40] Maupassant similarly acclaimed Flaubert's attempts to imitate medieval art, comparing the work to "un vieux vitrail d'église d'une naïveté savante et colorée."[41]

In Symbolist circles, Flaubert's "Légende de Saint Julien" and *La Tentation de Saint Antoine* were critical references, widely appreciated and adapted.[42] Indeed, if so many late nineteenth-century Symbolist representations of saints seem to echo Flaubert, it is because he was the primary intertext for a generation of artists' interest in Saint Julian and Saint Anthony. While Flaubert consulted medieval sources in writing his works,[43] many of his peers were more interested in adapting his Naturalist study of Anthony's visions or hallucinations than in imitating medieval texts. Odilon Redon and Henri Rivière's interpretations of the legends, for example, were based nearly exclusively on Flaubert's text.

Part of the attraction of these tales (Flaubert called *La Tentation* his *féerie*), may have been the symbiosis between literature and the visual arts. While the prose of "Saint Julien" called up a series of scenes as vignettes and referred to a stained-glass window in the cathedral of Rouen, *Saint Antoine* included elaborate stage directions that evoked the setting, the lighting and the actions of his characters. Indeed, Flaubert preferred to produce *Saint Antoine* as a play at the Théâtre Saint Martin, but when he could not get it staged, he settled for print.[44] This hybrid production would have consisted largely of hugely colorful costumes and sets against which the characters would intone Flaubert's dialogue; it would probably have been closer to a staged reading than to the kind of theater one generally saw performed on Le Boulevard. In fact, the stage directions were so encompassing (the description of Alexandria in Act II, for example, goes on for six pages and includes precise details about the setting as well as the thousands of people Anthony sees) that it would have been nearly impossible to produce.

Like Flaubert, Symbolist artists of the 1880s and 1890s experimented with form, especially in drama; they attempted new techniques that would avoid the materiality of theater and the referentiality of placing actors on the stage.[45] Accordingly, Symbolist plays tended to prefer staged poetry readings often against a colorful background (like that of *La Tentation*). This background often represented a nebulous otherworld or allworld (like Maeterlinck's Allemonde in *Pélléas et Mélisande*), a pseudo-medieval space of their own creation: a mystical, gauzy, golden world characterized by lost princesses, legends, saints and miracles. Quillard's mystery play, *La Fille aux mains coupées*, for example, was played behind a gauze curtain, with a background painted by Nabi artist Paul Sérusier. Actors recited their lines, while a reader explained their actions in a monotone voice. Similarly, Remy de Gourmont's *Théodat* was performed against a Maurice Denis–designed backdrop formed by red lions on a background of gold.[46] Others, like Henri Rivière, similarly created mystical effects by using technology to evoke the legends of Saint Julian and Saint Genevieve in a form that would remind viewers of the stories of medieval saints told in the stained-glass windows of cathedrals. He, too, used readers to comment on the events taking place on stage.[47]

Although for many Symbolists, Zola's Naturalism was the aesthetic against which they defined their own projects, *Le Rêve* was praised by others as "a reposoir, a temporary altar, a place of mystical encounter for artists

Fig. 4.2. Jules Bastien-Lepage, *Joan of Arc* (1879). Oil on canvas. H. 100, W. 110 (254 × 279.4 cm.). The Metropolitan Museum of Art, Gift of Erwin Davis, 1889. (89.21.1).

and admirers."[48] The book's appeal in Symbolist milieus was most likely related to a hugely successful operatic version of the novel. As early as 1888, Zola was working on the libretto; by 1892, it had been adapted as a Wagnerian-inspired opera, as a Chat Noir production and as the subject of Symbolist illustrations.[49] The novel's mysticism appealed to composer and illustrator for different reasons. Alfred Bruneau, a self-proclaimed "disciple of Wagner," worked closely with Zola and librettist Louis Gallet to produce the work for l'Opéra-Comique. It opened in 1891 to rave reviews.[50] The opera followed the novel closely, except for Angélique's sudden death, which was deemed anticlimactic and comical. The opera thus concluded with the dramatic scene in which Angélique miraculously comes back to life after having been read last rites.

The opera profoundly changed the focus of the novel by giving more weight to the mystical elements of the plot.[51] Through music, Bruneau could represent the saints without having to give them a physical incarnation. While Zola's novel tells us that Angélique hears the saints, the reader does not see a transcription of these voices, and they remain a background element. In the opera, however, the saints are omnipresent. From the first scene, where Angélique leaves her embroidery to read the *Golden Legend* and hears a choir of angels, to her visions of saints in stained glass, Bruneau created musical motifs to refer to the saintly apparitions.[52] As a result, the mysticism that was merely suggested in the book clearly drove the opera, thus shifting emphasis to Angélique's visions and to the conflict she felt between her love for the saints and that for Félicien. The opera was tremendously popular; performances were nearly sold out and it was reprised in 1900, 1914 and 1921. Critics praised this idyll for its novelty, for mixing plain chant with Wagnerian motifs, thus creating an intriguing blend of modern and medieval. Victorien Joncières proclaimed *Le Rêve* the lyrical drama long awaited by "the apostles of the new Wagnerian Gospel."[53]

Joncières' references to the "new Wagnerian Gospel" pinpoint the opera's appeal to members of the Symbolist movement, which was closely affiliated with Wagner's reception in France. Until the 1890s, Wagner's works were shunned in France, except for a small group of writers (later affiliated with Symbolism) who kept them alive in France through the *La Revue wagnérienne*.[54] Bruneau's opera would thus have appealed to the avant-garde, which appreciated Wagner largely for his theories about the *Gesamtkunstwerk*, or total work of art, in which each component complements and improves the others. *Le Rêve*, in which music and lyrics worked together to evoke Angélique's mysticism, thus conformed, in part, to the Symbolist aesthetic.

Zola's novel also appealed to Symbolist artists. Carlos Schwabe, much admired by the Rose + Croix circle, was chosen by the publishers Marpon and Flammarion to produce an illustrated version of *Le Rêve* in 1891. Like Bruneau, Schwabe prominently featured the saintly figures of Zola's novel.[55] Naturalist painter Julien Bastien-Lepage had previously used outlines to represent the vague figures of saints Catherine, Margaret and Michael in his 1870 painting of Joan of Arc's visions (Fig. 4.2), as had Gustave Moreau, whose representations of Salomé sketched mystical elements in outline form. Accordingly, Schwabe chose to portray Angélique's visions as shadowy figures, floating behind the main character (Fig. 4.3). Yet as Laura Morowitz has suggested, Schwabe's figures were so concrete that they often "upstaged" the main characters. He tended to draw attention from

...raidie, tapant des pieds et des mains, prête à déchirer et à mordre (p. 28).

Angélique's personal relationship to the saints (as described by Zola) by creating a mystical sphere where such ghostly figures wandered freely.[56] In "La Crise de folie orgueilleuse," for example, the skulking figure on the left seems nearly as real as the Huberts, on the right. The fact that Hubertine recoils leads one to assume that she, too, has seen him, thus negating the allegorical effect intended.

In fact, Schwabe's quite literal allegorical representation of Angélique's visions appear to have much more in common with contemporary discussions about female visionaries and hysteria than with the plot and medieval mysticism of Zola's novel, a criticism that Zola made clear in his comments about the illustrations.[57] This is not unusual for the time; attempts at representing visions in painting had often produced such effects. Bastien-Lepage's painting of Joan of Arc, for example, was highly controversial, provoking debates about the legitimacy of her visions and calling into question her mental stability.[58] Had she really been a hysteric?

SAINTS, MYSTICS AND MADWOMEN

Critics questioned both Zola's novel and Bruneau's opera, which placed emphasis on a modern woman who sees visions of medieval saints; they compared Angélique to nineteenth-century madwomen. Because of the play's modern setting, J. Weber saw the operatic Angélique as a hysteric:

> Je ne puis voir dans Angélique qu'une hallucinée. Elle se nourrit l'esprit sans relâche avec la lecture de la vie des saints. Elle rêve à sainte Marceline qui est brulée, à sainte Solanges qui est flagellée, à Saint Georges qui terrasse le dragon, à sainte Agnès qui, le cou troué d'un glaive, chante un cantique à Dieu; elle entend même les saints chanter au ciel.[59]

Delectation for the violence of these visions seemed at odds with nineteenth-century ideals about the alleged natural goodness and calm of a healthy young lady. Léon Kerst similarly questioned Angélique's mental stability, but less for the visions themselves than because of the fact that the singers wore modern costumes: "Si l'action du Rêve était au Moyen Age, Angélique ne serait pas comme clinique du Docteur Charcot et serait plus comme Jeanne d'Arc or Jehanne Frollo."[60] This comment underlines a changing nineteenth-century attitude about the nature of religious visions: In the Middle Ages it was perfectly normal to have them, while it was not

Opposite: Fig. 4.3. Carlos Schwabe, La Crise de folie orgueilleuse. Illustration for Emila Zola, Le Rêve (Paris: Marpon et Flammarion, 1893).

in the nineteenth century. A century of positivist scientific studies of the mind by doctors, physiologists and philosophers from Pinel and Esquirol to Hegel and Taine had imposed a new understanding of the origins of visions. Where the Romantic era tended to see them as positive and external—emanating from God or a muse—the positivist era saw such inspiration as deriving from negative and internal forces resulting from genetic and environmental stresses on the body.[61]

Throughout the 1880s and 1890s, doctors and scientists such as Henri Legrand du Saulle and Jean-Martin Charcot studied mental patients in the Salpêtrière Hospital and published their findings. They questioned the status of all those who heard voices or saw ghostly forms, thus linking modern female visionaries to the mentally ill. As a result, they retroactively called into question all mystics: "Many *women Saints* and *Blessed* were nothing other than simply hysterics! It is enough to reread the life of Elizabeth of Hungary, in 1207; of Saint Gertrude, of Saint Bridget, of Saint Catherine of Siena, in 1347; of Joan of Arc, of Saint Teresa ... one will be easily convinced of this truth."[62] Such medicalized reinterpretations of medieval saints' lives were, in turn, critiqued by other doctors or theologians, who accused their colleagues of misreading saints' lives and of applying a modern world view to medieval times.[63]

The medicalization of mysticism had become so prevalent through scientific studies and in Naturalist fiction such as the Goncourts' *Madame Gervaisais* (1869), Zola's *La Conquête de Plassans* (1874) and *La Faute de l'abbé Mouret* (1875), however, that fin-de-siècle writers and doctors asked whether it was possible in the modern world to be a visionary without being insane. Flaubert's *La Tentation de Saint Antoine* prompted similar questions, which are evident in the ways in which his work was interpreted.[64] Was the author interested in the artistic possibilities of adapting the life of a third-century character, as he had been in *Salammbô* (1862)? Or was he curious about exploring hagiography and mystical visions? Perhaps the text was intended primarily as a Naturalistic exploration of the ways in which hunger and solitude brought on hallucination?[65]

These were frequent questions at the time, especially since the second half of the nineteenth century saw a staggering increase in religious visions, notably of the Virgin Mary. From Bernadette of Lourdes to Mélanie and Maxime of La Salette, the Catholic Church created sites dedicated to these visions and pilgrims came to worship.[66] While believers dwelled on the religious inspiration behind these miracles, the scientific establishment quickly rushed to question them. As a result, pilgrimage sites such as Lourdes established medical offices that examined and certified each of the miracles, a phenomenon meticulously described in Zola's 1894 novel *Lourdes*.[67]

This novel, like *Le Rêve*, lay at the heart of the late nineteenth century's debates about saints and madness and revealed Zola's scientific curiosity about the sources of visions. *Le Rêve*, though lacking the overt Naturalist focus characteristic of Zola's other works, still echoed contemporary debates about mysticism and madness, especially in its concentration on female saints, who are depicted disproportionally. While Jacobus de Voragine's *Golden Legend* names only forty or so women out of the two hundred in the volume, Zola clearly favors the female saints, to whom Angélique is attracted.[68] It is no coincidence that Zola sets her mystical experiences at the onset of puberty, nor that her passionate and erotically tinged attraction to Christ is transferred to Félicien, described as "un Jésus."

Zola's preparatory notes reveal that he did intend *Le Rêve* as a scientific study of mystical visions; he wrote it as a "pendant" to *La Faute de l'abbé Mouret*, in which he attributed a priest's nervous breakdown and resultant mystical hallucinations to his family's tendency to madness.[69] *Le Rêve*, as a volume of the *Rougon-Macquart* series, thus implicitly associates Angélique's visions to those of her cousin Serge and to their great grandmother, Tante Dide. Though the narrator does not explicitly criticize Angélique's mysticism, readers familiar with the *Rougon-Macquart* series saw the parallels. As contemporary Jules Lemaître aptly observed, Angélique is pure, mystical and chaste only because of her surroundings: "dans d'autres conditions, elle eût pu aussi bien être Nana ... le mysticisme d'Angélique n'est qu'une forme accidentelle de la névrose Macquart."[70] Zola does hint at this: When Angélique arrives on the Huberts' doorstep, she has a bad-tempered pride that she fights to master; it is her readings of the saints that correct her behavior. Her violent passion for the saints clearly echoes her cousin Serge's adoration of the Virgin Mary in *La Faute de l'abbé Mouret* and her aunt Marthe's prostration in front of the altar in *La Conquête de Plassans*.[71] Zola's idyll thus worked on several levels. For the reader unfamiliar with the *Rougon-Macquart* series, Angélique would seem to be a true believer, permeated with the ideals of the *Golden Legend*. For the connoisseur of Zola's series, however, she was clearly a hysteric, another unhealthy offshoot of the tainted family tree.

IN DEFENSE OF HAGIOGRAPHY: THE CATHOLIC REVIVAL AND ILLUSTRATED LIVES OF SAINTS

Debates about the status of saints—medieval and modern, mystical or hysterical—became even more prevalent during the Catholic revival that swept the end of the nineteenth century. As increased industrialization brought what artists and writers saw as rampant materialism and faltering morals, they were increasingly nostalgic for the idealized Catholicism of their childhood.[72] Frédéric Gugelot has shown that more than 150 intellectuals converted to Catholicism from 1885 to 1935; among the most famous of these were Huysmans, Léon Bloy, Paul Claudel, Louis de Fourcauld and Charles Péguy.[73] The reasons for converting were multiple, often couched as dissatisfaction with the commercial and secular values of fin-de-siècle France, as nostalgia for childhood memories of pure and simple belief, or as an attraction to the faith that inspired medieval art.[74]

As Catholic intellectuals increasingly championed Church traditions, they bristled at the use of religious material for secular use. Indeed, Huysmans' criticism of modern attempts at imitating hagiography with which we began this essay sounded much like that of Catholic leaders, such as Emmannuel d'Alzon, the founder of the Assumptionist movement, who argued that believers needed to reclaim saints for the Church:

> ... les Saints sont un fait, et ils sont en même temps une trop grande gloire pour l'humanité déchue, une trop grande force pour l'Eglise, une trop irréfutable manifestation du surnaturel, pour que les chrétiens doivent jamais consentir à les abandonner aux haines des méchants incapables de les imiter.[75]

At issue was mainstream imitation of saints' lives. The attention that authors and artists had focused on the colorful or mysterious legends of saints tended to secularize them, turning them from their original purpose as examples of the power of faith and appropriating them, instead, for other uses.[76] The use of saintly figures for entertainment or as subjects of paintings or scientific studies objectified saints, reducing their lives, the story of their conversion, to pictures on collector cards or to lists of attributes or sicknesses.

In *Le Rêve*, for example, legend replaces religion: Dorothy was the saint "who was fed miraculous bread in prison," Barbe was "the saint who lived in a tower," and Geneviéve was "the saint whose virginity saved Paris." Angélique, whose story follows that of the saints, becomes an object, in turn: She is described as "little stained-glass virgin."[77] Modern interpretations of the saints created decadent, Naturalist or patriotic versions: Saint Julian is known for the murder of his parents and Saint Anthony for his bizarre hallucinations; Genevieve saved Paris as Joan of Arc had France. In the process, the religious values that these saints originally represented were replaced by their legendary adventures. It was this aspect that Huys-

Fig. 4.4. Collector cards from the late nineteenth century. Sponsored by La Chocolaterie d'Aiguebelle (Drôme) and Ogden's Guinea Gold Cigarettes.

mans had criticized in Zola's use of the *Golden Legend*: the elimination of the religious context. Without the belief that prompted the stories, the vignettes or "small stained-glass figures" that remain are not any different from any other voyeuristic or secular entertainment: going to the opera or theater, watching a puppet show or visiting the Salpêtrière hospital.[78] This trend is clear if one studies the collector cards of the late nineteenth century: Sold with a variety of products, pictures of saints and worshipers mix with actors and famous celebrities (Figs. 4.4 and 0.1).[79]

Such simplified, two-dimensional images of saints produced a backlash among Catholics, who vilified the secular and commercial appropriation of what had traditionally been sacred material. Huysmans' novels and essays are full of scorn for Catholic and secular artists alike, who, he felt, transformed hagiography into "un des lieux communs de la bondieuserie, une transposition dans le livre des statuettes des Froc-Robert, des images en chromo des Bouasse."[80] His reaction reflects the attitude of many Catholics. Indeed, since the 1870s, the Church, especially the Assumptionist order, had waged a campaign to reclaim medieval traditions, and especially saints' lives, for the good of the Church. One of the most striking examples of this campaign to bring people back to Catholicism was the creation, in 1877, of a series of saints' lives to be published in the weekly periodical *Le Pèlerin*, which was directed to the working classes and written in simple French, liberally scattered with stories about pilgrimages, saints' lives and miracles.[81]

Vincent de Paul Bailly, an Assumptionist priest, presented his motives for this series as triple: he was responding to public demand for a popular version of the saints' lives, he wanted to reclaim them from the secular appropriations that cheapened their religious value and he wanted to use them as examples of good Christian behavior, as they were thought to have been in the Middle Ages:

> Contre les iniquités présentes, il n'y a pas d'armes plus redoutables que les traits de la vie des Saints, et il n'y a point d'armes dont les blessures se guérissent mieux; or il faut combattre l'iniquité et guérir les plaies. Le sermon le plus profitable, c'est l'exemple; or les Saints sont par excellence les sources des bons exemples, faisons-les prêcher.... De prétendus sages sont parvenus à rendre la vie très merveilleuse des Saints profondément ennuyeuse, en la dépouillant de l'élément surnaturel et miraculeux dont Dieu lui-même avait pris soin de les orner si abondamment. Le *Pèlerin* restituera le côté traditionnel et populaire de la vie des Saints. Nous voulons en effet préparer une lecture pour les chrétiens et non des travaux d'érudition pour l'école des Chartes.[82]

Like Huysmans, Bailly found that eliminating the faith inherent in medieval saints' lives rendered them boring and trite; they were no different than any other historical narrative.[83] What makes these saints' lives so valuable to the church is their extraordinary nature; the excess of the miracles and the style used to convey them was critical for creating good hagiographies that would bring readers to the Church. While specialists tended to focus on the historical or archeological aspects of hagiography, Bailly and his Maison de la bonne presse wanted to return to the popular and legendary aspects of these lives, those elements that made them beloved to all.

But how could the Assumptionists wrest the saints from theaters, opera and best-selling novels? Bailly's idea of creating the *Vie des saints* series within an extraordinarily popular Christian periodical was a brilliant stroke of marketing. *Le Pèlerin* itself had sought to emulate the medieval practice of using imagery to reach the people; Bailly attempted to reach out to the lower classes of society, which had been neglected by the Church in the nineteenth century. He wanted to "[speak] to the eyes through images."[84] His *Vie des saints illustrée* series would do the same, for it was not just a sequence of lives; above all, it was illustrated. Both the *Pèlerin* and *La Vie des saints* included a wealth of images, many from the greatest Catholic artists: Fra Angelico, Giotto, Fra Lippi and Raphaël, among others. In contrast to the Saint-Sulpice movement, which published hundreds of cheap modern images of saints as little children (Figs. 0.1 and 4.4), the Maison de la Bonne Presse, publishers of both *Le Pèlerin* and *La Vie des saints*, advocated familiarizing the public with great works of art of the past. Perhaps the most impressive example of this tendency was their support of Father J. C. Broussolle's 1904 *Le Christ de la Légende dorée, ouvrage illustré d'un commentaire artistique et de 307 gravures*. This work consisted of a new translation of Voragine's work, divided into the themes "Christ," "The Apostles" and "The Virgin of the *Golden Legend*." Broussole accompanied the translations with 307 engravings, including miniatures from illuminated manuscripts of the *Golden Legend* from the Bibliothèque Nationale and other archives. The work was a labor of love that took him four years, but it was worth it for him:

> A une époque où les croyances catholiques sont aussi vivement ébranlées par le souci exagéré d'un examen critique de toutes nos habitudes de coeur et d'esprit en matière de religion, comme si le chrétien ne devait plus étayer sa piété et sa foi que sur des documents d'archives ou des syllogismes, nous avons rêvé de faire saisir sur le vif la méthode bien différente avec laquelle le moyen âge, et plus particulièrement le XIIIe siècle, songeait déjà, mais de tout autre façon que nous, à ces mêmes problèmes qui nous angoissent aujourd'hui.[85]

As a result of this return to medieval-inspired practices, it was hoped that religious imagery would restore the public's enthusiasm for the saints, thus encouraging believers to see the saints as their friends, their companions and their role models. In fact, although Zola had not meant to advocate Catholicism in *Le Rêve*, the attention he devotes to Angélique's reading of

SAINTE AGNÈS, VIERGE ET MARTYRE

Fête le 21 janvier.

(Traduction libre d'une Vie attribuée à saint Ambroise.)

Sainte Agnès sur le bûcher.

Agnès, l'une des quatre grandes vierges de l'Eglise romaine, triompha par le martyre à l'âge de treize ans.

Elle revenait un jour d'une des écoles où les jeunes filles étaient élevées (il y avait déjà à Rome des écoles pour les chrétiens); rencontrée par le fils du préfet de la ville, celui-ci en fut épris, et pour la séduire, il lui envoya des bijoux; celle-ci les repoussa comme chose très vile. Le jeune homme revint à la charge, lui faisant présenter les pierreries les plus précieuses, et lui proposa, par ses amis, des palais, des villas, une fortune immense.

On dit qu'Agnès lui fit répondre : « Retire-toi de moi, source de péché, entretien de crime, aliment de mort, je suis déjà aimée par quelqu'un dont les joyaux sont autrement beaux que les tiens; il m'a engagée à lui par l'anneau de sa foi, et sa noblesse, sa race, sa dignité l'emportent de beaucoup sur toi. Il a posé son signe

the 1549 version of the Golden Legend did just that. Angélique Rougon was a bad-tempered child, yet her study of the manuscript calmed her. Curiosity about the images led her to read the stories, which she memorized. Eager to imitate the behavior of those in the book, she modified her behavior and emulated the saints; "[elle] se remettait aux mains de Dieu."[86] It was through the beauty of medieval religious art that Angélique was drawn to the Church.

The Assumptionists' *Vie des saints illustrée* series was enormously popular; in fact many read *Le Pèlerin* just for the installment of *La Vie des saints*, which were constantly reprinted.[87] The paper itself was extremely inexpensive (six francs a year), and weekly inserts could be detached from the periodical and reassembled as a volume for private devotion (one could also buy volumes independently). These saints' lives were collected by priests, offered as prizes to children who had successfully completed catechism or given as gifts for saints' days or for funerals.[88] The lives themselves tended to consist of one or two pages of narrative that dwelled on accomplishments of saints from all eras and all countries (Fig. 4.5). They were nearly always accompanied by an illustration and often by a short bibliography (generally Voragine's text, a life cited by an earlier saint, or the Bollandists' works).

The result of the Assumptionists' aggressive marketing of saints' lives as pertinent to the modern Church resulted in an enormous growth in the importance of the saints for everyday life. While lower-class Catholics read the *Le Pèlerin* and its *Vie des saints*, intellectuals, many of whom knew Greek and Latin, returned to the sources. Huysmans' best-selling *En Route* lays out a veritable reading list for those returning to the fold: Saint Denys l'Aréopagite, Saint Bonaventure, Hugues et Richard de Saint-Victor, Saint Thomas d'Aquin, Saint Bernard, Angèle da Foligno and Sainte Térèse, among others.[89] Other writers made their own translations or studies of saints' lives. L'abbé Roze had worked for years on a study of the *Golden Legend*, which was published in 1902, the same year as Symbolist writer and critic Teodor de Wyzewa's new translation of a 1517 manuscript. In the first years of the twentieth century, the *Golden Legend* came into its own again, even in the face of the growing anticlericalism that would separate Catholic Church from French State in 1905. In fact, there were more editions of the *Golden Legend* published in France in the twentieth century than in all other modern languages combined.[90]

Zola's *Le Rêve*, once again, sheds light on such a paradox. Though he

Opposite: *Fig. 4.5. Sainte Agnès, Vierge et Martyre.* Illustration for *La Vie des saints*, a publication of *Le Pèlerin* (829–32). In a volume bound by the Institution des sourdes-muets, Saint-Etienne.

did not emphasize the religious aspects of the work in his novel, he was fascinated by it as a relic from the Middle Ages, as a vestige of an earlier system of thought. He had read about the Bollandists in preparing his novel and although he did not share their beliefs, he was curious about their meticulous research into the saints' lives. He did not agree with the religion of the *Golden Legend*, but he admired it as a work of literature and glorified it as such. This could be said for many of his anti-clerical contemporaries, who, like Anatole France, were fascinated by the literature and the characters while disavowing the religion inherent in the stories themselves. As a result, while the government worked to eliminate Catholic education and to disband religious congregations, the *Golden Legend* took on new importance as a great work of medieval literature.[91] As André Baudrillart put it in a 1902 study of the "Psychologie de la légende dorée," "l'incrédule ne pourra se défendre d'admirer la pureté de cet idéal et de goûter une poésie sincèrement naïve. Et chacun, sans honte et sans ironie, s'abandonnera au charme apaisant et consolateur de la vieille et douce Légende."[92] Popular interest in the potential of saints' lives for entertainment coincided with scientific fascination with mysticism, with scholarly interest for medieval literature and with a grassroots Catholic movement to reclaim saints' lives for the Church. The confluence of these very different movements resulted in a valorization of saints on a number of levels of society—popular and scholarly, religious and secular, clerical and artistic—all of which appreciated the legend itself. Nonetheless, this movement created a rift in the understanding of saints' lives, further emphasizing the divide between legend (amusing entertainment), on the one hand, and hagiography (sacred narrative), on the other. The saints depicted in Voragine's medieval text took on rich new lives at the beginning of the twentieth century: They were cherished both as beloved storybook characters and as sacred historical figures.

Notes

1. "Today, how can one express the doleful essence and the white perfume of very old translations of Voragine's *Golden Legend*? How can one gather in a guileless spray these plaintive flowers that monks cultivated in the confines of cloisters, when hagiography was the sister of the barbarous and charming art of illuminators and stained-glass makers, of the ardent and chaste paintings of the Primitives? One could hardly dream of engaging in studied pastiches, of forcing oneself to ape such works coldly. The question thus remained how to know if, with the resources of contemporary art, one could arrive at capturing the humble and exalted figure of a female saint; and it was at the very least doubtful, since the lack of real simplicity, the overly ingenious cosmetics of style, the

craftiness of an attentive drawing and the showiness of a mottled color would probably transform the chosen into a ham performer. She would no longer be a saint, but an actress who would play the role more or less skillfully; and then, the charm would be destroyed, the miracles would appear mechanical, the episodes would be absurd! ... then...then ...even then one would need to have a truly deep faith and to believe in the saintliness of the heroine, if one wanted to attempt to exhume her and to make her relive in a work." En Route republished in Le Roman de Durtal (Paris: Barthillat, 1999): 329. Unless otherwise indicated, all translations from the French in this chapter are by Elizabeth Emery.

2. For nineteenth-century artists and writers, the term *Primitif* referred to artists of the Middle Ages, specifically the twelfth to fifteenth centuries. For an explanation of this term in the nineteenth-century context, see Michael Paul Driskel, *Representing Belief* (University Park: Pennsylvania State University Press, 1992) and Bruno Foucart, *Le Renouveau de la peinture religieuse en France* (Paris: Athena, 1987). Elizabeth Emery and Laura Morowitz trace the ways it was applied to late nineteenth-century artists and writers in *Consuming the Past: The Medieval Revival in Fin-de-siècle France* (London: Ashgate Press, 2003).

3. "The cry of swooning love, the gift of superhuman exile, the mystical soul." *En Route*, 330.

4. The book had sold 110,000 copies by 1902 and 187,000 copies by 1928. See p. 1619 of Henri Mitterand, "Etude" of *Le Rêve. Les Rougon-Macquart*, Vol. 4 (Paris: Editions Fasquelle et Gallimard [Edition de la Pléiade], 1966): 1610–704.

5. Adolphe Brisson called *Le Rêve* a "poème de grâce" in *Les Annales politiques et littéraires* (21 Oct. 1888), Philippe Gille labeled it an "idylle quasi–Biblique" in *Le Figaro* (13 Oct. 1888), while Gabrielle Mourey, in *Le Parisien*, compared Angélique's story to that of the *Golden Legend* (22 Oct. 1888). Charles Bigot asked whether it was "an appendice à la *Légende Dorée*" (*La République française*, 22 Oct. 1888). For an overview of critical reactions, see Henri Mitterand's "Etude," 1526–35 and 1647–57. Unfortunately, the now indispensable hypertext project of documents related to *Le Rêve*, put together by the Centre d'étude sur Zola et le Naturalisme de l'Institut des textes et manuscrits modernes (CNRS) and the Université de la Sorbonne Nouvelle (Paris III), was not available when this essay was written. It contains nearly every document pertaining to the novel, from preparatory manuscripts to book reviews and adaptations (http://gallica.bnf.fr/ Zola). A great number of contemporary book reviews can be consulted under the "Réception Adaptation" heading.

6. "The Legend and the Cathedral, one helping the other in their work of purification, modifying little by little Angélique's soul, finally stripping her of her hereditary dress to make her like the Legend, like her female saints of flesh and bone." Gabrielle Mourey, *Le Parisien*, 22 Oct. 1888.

7. "A ridiculous religious gewgaw in which this clumsy fool simply forgot mass and the sacraments—A young girl, pure, celestial, dreaming of a Prince Charming but wanting MONEY!!!" Letter 70 to Arij Prins (31 Oct. 1888). *Lettres inédites à Arij Prins* (Geneva: Librairie Droz, S.A., 1977): 145–46. Huysmans certainly would have been more diplomatic in person; one senses his underlying frustration with Zola's aesthetic and with sharing a topic (he was working on a book about the saints that would culminate in *Là-Bas* and *En Route*). It was he who had introduced Zola to *La Légende dorée*. See also the critiques of Charles Bigot and Jules Lemaître, who pro-

claimed it a "conte bleu" (and a poorly written one at that). Charles Bigot, *La République française*, 22 Oct. 1888; Jules Lemaître, *La Revue bleue*, 27 Oct. 1888. Anatole France, too, criticized the book in which, he felt, Zola had sacrificed his talent to write such a "pure" tale. *Le Temps*, 21 Oct. 1888.

8. Zola's preparatory notes, housed at the Bibliothèque nationale (NAF 10.324 fos 103–38), show that the descriptions of these sculptures were inspired primarily by a portal at Vézelay. Its structure was probably copied from the *porte* entry of Viollet-le-Duc's *Dictionnaire d'architecture* (Zola's drawing of the portal he describes in the novel can be consulted on fol. 108). See Mitterand, 1646. Other features of this fictitious cathedral are borrowed from Notre-Dame de Paris, as Zola's notes indicate.

9. *Le Rêve*, 816–17, 825.

10. Zola's notes at the Bibliothèque nationale (MS 10.324 fos 35 to 101) reveal the ways in which he read both Brunet's translation and the 1549 volume, while taking notes and drawings from the sixteenth-century version. See, for example, fol. 67, which reproduces his sketch of the frontispiece's layout. The book he consulted is Bibliothèque Nationale de France RES H279.

11. For the popularity of the *Legenda Aurea*, see note 10 of the introduction to this volume. See also Sherry L. Reames, *The Legenda Aurea: A Reexamination of its Paradoxical History* (Madison: University of Wisconsin Press, 1985): 11–17.

12. Brunet claimed to be the first in 300 years to have translated Voragine's text. His 1843 edition was one of the late nineteenth century's most valuable sources for knowledge about saints' lives. See Mitterand, "Etude," 1644–45.

13. My references refer to the bound copies of *La Revue Illustrée* from 1888. Drawings of medieval woodcuts (with labels identifying their provenance) appeared in Volume 5 on pages 268, 270, 272, 331 and 334.

14. To be fair, credit should also be given to Huysmans, who loaned Zola his copy of *La Légende dorée*. As Henri Mitterand has pointed out, Zola had originally intended to use a generic "Vie des saints" for his work and did not know about the *Golden Legend* until Huysmans spoke to him about it (1640). Jean-Sébastien Macke's "Réception du Rêve de Bruneau dans la presse," included in the hypertext *Rêve* project, lists the hundreds of reviews dedicated to this opera (http://gallica.bnf.fr/Zola/RecepAdap/Opera 2.htm). For more about Zola's religious beliefs, see "Le Jeune Zola et les prêtres," in Pierre Ouvrard, *Zola et le prêtre* (Paris: Beauchesne Editeur, 1986). Philip Walker shows that by the age of nineteen Zola was already beginning to break with Catholicism. By the end of 1864 or earlier, he had lost faith in it entirely. *Germinal and Zola's Religious Thought* (Amsterdam: John Benjamins, 1984): note. 10, p. 103. See also Zola, *Oeuvres complètes* IX (Paris: Cercle du Livre Précieux, 1967): 409, 871–93; X: 881; and *Correspondance d'Emile Zola*, ed. B.H. Bakker, et al. Vol. I (Montreal and Paris: Les Presses de l'Université de Montréal and Editions du Centre National de la Recherche Scientifique, 1978–1995): 223–27.

15. See, for example, Reames, who cites the following early twentieth-century works in support of this claim. Marguerite de Waresquiel, *Le bienheureux Jacques de Voragine, auteur de la Légende dorée* (Paris 1902); André Baudrillart, "La psychologie de la *Légende dorée*," *Minerva* 5 (1902): 24–43; J.-C. Broussolle, "La Légende dorée," *L'université catholique*, n.s. 44 (1903): 321–57; *La Légende dorée de Jacques de Voragine*, trans. J.-.M. Roze (Paris: 1902); *La Légende dorée*, trans. Teodor de Wyzewa (Paris, 1902). As we will see, the phenomenon had begun much earlier.

16. The idea of Mâle as an instigator of this trend is a bit tenuous, as *L'Art Religieux* was Mâle's doctoral thesis and he was not yet widely known outside of art historical circles. It is also likely that it was Huysmans' enthusiastic review of the book in 1899 that made Mâle's work well-known to contemporary readers. This review is republished in "Bouquins: A propos de Barbey d'Aurevilly, Hello, Dom Legeay et Emile Mâle," *Huysmans*, ed. Pierre Brunel and André Guyaux (Paris: Editions de l'Herne, 1985): 345–49. One should also note earlier translations of the *Golden Legend*: the 1890 Latin edition published by Th. Graesse, *Jacobi a Voragine Legenda aurea* (Breslaud); Henri Piazza's 1896 illustrated collector's edition (Paris : G. Boudet, 1896); and an 1896 children's version (Paris-Lille: A. Taffin-Lefort) by A. de Gériolles. France's *Le Crime de Sylvèstre Bonnard* enjoyed great popularity (five months after its publication it was in its third printing of 1,000 copies) and made his reputation as a novelist. See Marie-Claude Bancquart's "Notice" in the Pléiade edition of the novel. Anatole France, *Oeuvres*, Vol. 1 (Paris: Editions Gallimard, 1984): 1109–10.

17. His correspondence clearly reveals his predilection for collecting medieval objects, including pictures of saints. The best indicators of his vast medieval holdings are announcements for the auctions that followed his death. For more about his penchant for the Middle Ages, see Elizabeth Emery, "Bricabracomania: Zola's Romantic Instinct," *Excavatio* 12 (1999): 107–15 and Elizabeth Emery and Laura Morowitz, *Consuming the Past: The Medieval Revival in Fin-de-siècle France* (London: Ashgate Press, 2003).

18. His notes taken from the *Golden Legend* can be consulted in NAF10.324, fols. 1–101. For more on the structural role of saints' lives, see, for example, NAF10.324 fols. 2–7 and NAF 10.323 fols. 20–36, 67–71, 124–25, 146–47, 166–68 in which Angélique's reading of saints' lives is an integral part of her education. He planned to have the saints continue to appear ("revenir sans cesse") throughout the novel (NAF 10.324, fol. 6).

19. See Janine R. Dakyns, *The Middle Ages in French Literature: 1851-1900* (London: Oxford University Press, 1973) and Emery and Morowitz, *Consuming the Past*.

20. "... L'expression la plus naïve et la plus sincère." Gustave Brunet, "Notice préliminaire," *La Légende dorée par Jacques de Voragine* (Paris: 1843), I:1. See NAF 10.324, fol. 35 for Zola's notes from Brunet.

21. "God is debonair and first of all there are men and women saints. They are born predestined, voices announce them, their mothers have radiant dreams. All of them are beautiful, strong, victorious. Great lights surround them, their faces shine.... Their stories are all the same, they grow up for Christ, believe in him, refusing to sacrifice to false gods, are tortured and die full of glory.... Mass conversions occur, forty thousand men are baptized all at once.... Prosperity, health are scorned, joy begins with hardships that destroy the body. And it is thus that they live triumphant, in gardens where flowers are stars, where the leaves of tree sing," 831–32.

22. "Le livre où s'est le plus candidement empreinte l'âme du Moyen Age." *En Route*, 554. Mâle discusses the importance of the *Golden Legend* in *L'Art Religieux du XIIIe siècle en France*. See Dora Nussey's translation, *The Gothic Image: Religious Art in France of the Thirteenth Century* (New York: Harper and Row, 1972), 273.

23. See Mâle, 272–83. Reames analyzes Mâle's comments on pages 16–17. Though Mâle does ascribe democratic aspects to saints' lives, Reames does not

completely place his citations in context. Mâle is very clear in referring to the *Golden Legend* as a "compilation" of earlier material, largely from the oral tradition (272–73). He remarks that most stained glass and sculpture were created before this compilation was set down; the saints' lives had been critical influences for inspiring medieval art (281). For Mâle, like Victor Hugo, the symbolism of medieval art was inherently democratic: It allowed even the lowest members of society to "read" the Biblical stories "written" in stained glass and sculpture. For a discussion of these beliefs, see Elizabeth Emery, *Romancing the Cathedral* (Albany: State University of New York Press, 2001).

24. "They exterminate dragons, they raise storms and calm them, they are transfixed in ecstasy an arm's length from the floor.... Extraordinary adventures happen to them, marvelous stories, as beautiful as novels. And after hundreds of years, when one opens their tombs, sweet scents emerge. Then, across from the saints are devils, innumerable devils ... in this combat of male and female saints against Satan, appalling torture and persecutions take place.... In fact, a continual miracle protects [saints], they grow tired of their torturers.... Continual rescues, apparitions come down from the open heavens, where God shows himself holding a crown of precious stones." 831–35.

25. See pp. 279–81. In the issue of the *Cahiers Naturalistes* dedicated to *Le Rêve* 76 (2002), two scholars underline the sense of the legendary and the marvelous apparent in Zola's use of the *Golden Legend*. See pages 20–24 of Colette Becker, "Le rêve d'Angélique," 7–24 and Jean-Louis Cabanès, "Rêver *La Légende dorée*," 25–65. These articles appeared after my essay was written.

26. William Granger Ryan, "Introduction" to Jacobus de Voragine, *The Golden Legend: Readings on the Saints* (Princeton: Princeton University Press, 1993), xvi–xvii.

27. See Suzanne Fleischman's brilliant and succinct analysis of this phenomenon: "On the Representation of History and Fiction in the Middle Ages," *History and Theory* 22 (1983): 278–310. Saints' lives are the perfect example of this tendency.

28. See Chapter 2, "The Fall of the *Legenda* Reexamined" of Reames, pp. 27–43 and 208–09. There are a number of explanations for the fall into disfavor of Voragine's work in the Renaissance, including, as Reames shows so well, the Protestant Reformation and shifts in the Church from tradition to doctrine. André Vauchez's work on the importance of the saints in the thirteenth century as a reflection of political battles within the Church also supports her claims for a move away from hagiography after the thirteenth century. See *La sainteté en Occident aux dernieres siècles du Moyen Age d'après les procès de canonisation et les documents hagiographiques* (Rome: Ecole française de Rome, 1988). To these arguments, I would add the Renaissance preference for written works as truthful and the increased disfavor of material (such as the many verse saints' lives) stemming from the oral tradition, a movement discussed extensively in Kittay and Godzich's *The Emergence of Prose: An Essay in Poetics* (Minneapolis: University of Minnesota Press, 1987).

29. "Il ressemblait au saint Georges, à un Jésus superbe, avec ses cheveux bouclés, sa barbe légère, son nez droit, un peu fort, ses yeux noirs, d'une douceur hautaine," 873. Because Félicien resembles Jesus, one can ask whether Angélique really betrays her commitment to God by marrying him.

30. See Elizabeth Emery, "'A l'ombre d'une vieille cathédrale romanesque': The Medievalism of Gautier and Zola." *The*

French Review 73:2 (December 1999): 290–300. Indeed, Zola's preparatory notes emphasize Angélique's inability to live in the real world and prove that this conflict between dream and real life lay at the heart of the novel: "L'idée au fond que le monde devrait mourir en ne procréant plus." NAF10.324, fol. 6. His sketches for the novel's conclusion reinforce this tension between dream and reality. See NAF 10.323, fols. 191–94.

31. See, for example, the edition of ten legends edited by Charles Simond for La Nouvelle bibliothèque populaire in 1893 (Paris: H. Gautier), A. de Gériolles' *La Légende dorée, adaptation pour la jeunesse de l'oeuvre de Jacques de Voragine* (Paris-Lille: A. Taffin-Lefort, 1896), Etienne Moreau-Nélaton's *Les Grands saints pour petits enfants: légendes en images* (Paris: L. Chailley, 1896), Madame Mairel d'Eslan's *Nouvelle légende d'orée* (Paris: Desclée de Breuwer et Cie, 1900), and Henri Piazza's deluxe edition with lithographs by Alexandre Lunois, published for G. Boudet in 1896. See also Introduction, n. 4, and nn. 15–16 *supra*.

32. It had sold 110,000 copies by 1902. See Henri Mitterand, 1619.

33. For an excellent analysis of the ways in which the Symbolist movement in art, literature and music developed in France, see Pamela Genova, *Symbolist Journals: A Culture of Correspondence* (London: Ashgate Press, 2002), 158–90. Robert Delevoy's *Symbolists and Symbolism* is also a very approachable work about the movement (Geneva: Rizzoli, 1982), while A. J. Lehmann's *The Symbolist Aesthetic in France* is a classic study of the movement (Oxford: Basil Blackwell, 1968). One has only to open one of the avant-garde journals of the late 1880s and 1890s—*La Plume, Le Courrier Français, Le Chat Noir*, for example—to see the interest in saints, miracles and religious motifs that existed in the poetry, illustration and paintings of their contributors.

34. Ferdinand de Brunetière's famous 1887 attack on Zola announces "La Banqueroute du naturalisme" (a term previously used by Bourget). For a good analysis of this term and its use in science and literature, see Harry W. Paul. "The Debate over the Bankruptcy of Science in 1895." *French Historical Studies* 5 (1968): 298–327. For more about these kinds of debates among literary movements, see Jules Huret's *Enquête sur l'évolution littéraire*, a series of interviews conducted among writers and artists in 1891 (Paris: Bibliothèque Charpentier, 1891).

35. Saint-Antoine, "Qu'est-ce que le symbolisme? *L'Ermitage* v (June 1894): 337. Cited in Dakyns, 243.

36. For a detailed analysis of the ways in which Symbolist writers and artists used medieval painting and stained glass as a model for their works, see Emery and Morowitz, *Consuming the Past*.

37. See the citation that begins this essay, especially the passage "Comment lier en une candide gerbe ces fleurs plaintives que les moines cultivèrent dans les pourpris des cloîtrres, alors que l'hagiographie était la soeur de l'art barbare et charmant des enlumineurs et des verriers, de l'ardente et de la chaste peinture des Primitifs?" For discussion of the importance of Wagner's theory of the *Gesamtkunstwerk* (total work of art) for the Symbolist aesthetic, see A. G. Lehmann, 229–330.

38. For the genesis of "Saint Julien," see Edouard Maynial, "Introduction," *Les Trois contes* (Paris: Garnier Frères, 1961): ii. Interestingly, Stéphane Mallarmé also showed an early interest in saints with his 1865 poem "Sainte," which Théodore Aubanel described as resembling "une vieille peinture de missel..., un vitrail ancien...." Cited in Henri Mondor and G. Jean-Aubry's notes to the poem in Stéphane Mallarmé, *Oeuvres complètes* (Paris: Editions Gallimard [Pléiade], 1945), 1468.

39. See Henri Troyat, *Flaubert*. Trans. Joan Pinkham (New York: Viking Penguin, 1992): 302–03 for some of this praise. Indeed, the tale had such potential for commercial success that Charpentier agreed to publish a deluxe gift edition of "La Légende de Saint Julien l'Hospitalier," replete with an image of the stained-glass window from which the story was inspired. Flaubert's correspondence from 1877–1888 is full of references to this project, which did not come to fruition. See, for example, a letter from 28 Nov. 1878 to Georges Charpentier, wife of his editor, in which he complains about the situation. *Correspondance nouvelle édition augmentée* 8e série 1877–1888 (Paris: L. Conard, 1930): p. 161.

40. "His pages advance in a blinding and ordered tumult, evolving through a superb language whose apparent simplicity owes itself to the complicated trick of an extraordinary art." *En Route*, 330.

41. *La Revue Bleue*. 19 and 26 Jan. 1884.

42. Henri Troyat has described the tremendous reception of *Saint Antoine*: The book sold extremely well, yet critics were painfully negative in their criticism of the seemingly incomprehensible visions, 277–79.

43. See B. F. Bart and R. F. Cook, *The Legendary Sources of Flaubert's "Saint Julien"* (Toronto: University of Toronto Press, 1977). In a letter to his niece, Caroline, Flaubert discusses "Saint Julien" and advises her to read Julian's legend in *The Golden Legend* as well as in *Les Légendes pieuses du moyen âge* of Alfred Maury, a seminal nineteenth-century text for disseminating information about medieval legends (30 September 1875), 265.

44. See his correspondence from 1877–1888. Nearly every letter describes his battles to get his *féerie* published in one form or another. See, for example, a September 1878 letter to his editor Georges Charpentier. *Correspondance*, 1877–1880, 148.

45. For Symbolist theories about the theater, see Frantisek Deak, *Symbolist Theater* (Baltimore: Johns Hopkins Press, 1993), especially the chapter entitled "Mallarmé's Conceptual Theater," 58–93. In "Menus propos," his theatrical manifesto, Maeterlinck clearly preferred solitary readings of plays to staging them. Cited in Deak, 23.

46. See Dakyns, 246–47.

47. See Madhuri Mukherjee's essay in this volume.

48. M. Florentin, "Carlos Schwabe." Quoted and translated by Marla Hand, "The Symbolist Work of Carlos Schwabe," Ph.D. dissertation (University of Chicago, 1984), 90. Cited on p. 100 of Morowitz, "Zola's *Le Rêve*: Symbolism and Medievalism in the Fin-de-Siècle" *Excavatio* 9 (1997): 92–102. This comment was unusual for Symbolists. The *Enquête* with Jules Huret makes the Symbolist antipathy toward Zola clear. Jean Moréas, the author of the 1886 "Symbolist manifesto," was particularly violent in regard to Zola's materialism.

49. A 31 Oct. 1888 letter from Huysmans shows that Zola was working on the libretto. *Lettres inédites à Arij Prins*: Letter 70, p. 146. *Le Rêve* was adapted by Jules Jouy and played at the Chat Noir in 1894.

50. Nearly every critic who reviewed the opera remarked Bruneau's dedication to Wagnerian principles and called him a Wagnerian disciple. See, for example, Bruneau's own interview with *Le Figaro*, 7 Oct. 1900, when he discussed the influence of Wagner in the 1890s.

51. See, for example, an interview between Auguste Germain and composer Bruneau, in which Bruneau identified "mysticism" as the central motif of the opera. Bibliothèque Nationale (Arsenal) manuscript RO2731(2). Similarly, Guillaume Danvers, in an article for *Le*

Monde moderne, criticized the place given to "réminiscences liturgiques." Article contained in Bibliothèque Nationale (Arsenal) dossier RO2731.

52. See Auguste Vitu's 19 June 1891 article for *Le Figaro*, "Premières représentations" and Etienne Destranges, *Le Rêve d'Alfred Bruneau, Etude thématique et analytique de la partition* (Paris: Librairie Fischbacher, 1896): 14–21 for a description of various scenes. Different motifs created by Bruneau included a Golden Legend motif, a dream motif, a mysticism motif, and a miracle motif. See Destranges, 14–21.

53. 7 Sept. 1891, *Revue musicale de liberté*. Joncières's comments were critical of this popularity, which he explained by the melodramatic subject matter.

54. Many of the contributors to this publication, including Paul Verlaine, Stéphane Mallarmé, Odilon Redon and Teodor de Wyzewa, were affiliated with what would come to be known as the Symbolist movement. After the demise of the magazine in 1888, other journals took up the slack, and periodicals such as *La Plume*, *La Revue Blanche* and *La Vogue* consecrated numerous articles to Wagner and his work. In fact, as Richard Sieburth has noted, Dujardin was publishing *La Revue wagnérienne* and the symbolist *Revue indépendante* at the same time, using many of the same authors for both publications. "The Music of the Future" in *A New History of French Literature*, ed. Denis Hollier (Cambridge, MA: Harvard University Press, 1989): 789–98, 794.

55. For more about the collaboration of Zola and Schwabe, see Jean-David Jumeau-Lafond, "Carlos Schwabe, illustrateur symboliste du *Rêve* de Zola," *Revue du Louvre* 5/6 (1987): 410–19, in which he reproduces many of these images, and Laura Morowitz, "Zola's *Le Rêve*." More of these images can be consulted in *Les Cahiers Naturalistes* 76 (2002).

56. Morowitz, 99.

57. See Morowitz, 97–98.

58. This was, in fact, the impression of Zola, who was disturbed by the "literary effect" of Bastien-Lepage's painting. For Zola, its success lay "dans l'étrangeté voulue de cette paysanne hystérique, aux yeux vides et clairs." ("In the calculated strangeness of this hysterical peasant with clear and vacant eyes.") "Le Naturalisme au Salon," *Le Voltaire* 18–22 June 1880.

59. "In Angélique, I can see nothing but a lunatic. She feeds her spirit constantly with readings from saints' lives. She dreams of Saint Marcelina who is burnt, of Saint Solange who is flagellated, of Saint George who slays the dragon, of Saint Agnes who, her neck pierced by a sword, sings a canticle to God; she even hears saints singing in Heaven." "Nouvel opéra." *Feuilleton du Temps* 22 June 1891.

60. "If the action of *Le Rêve* had taken place in the Middle Ages, Angélique would not be like one of Doctor Charcot's patients and would be more like Joan of Arc or like Joan Frollo." "Paris au Théâtre." *Petit Journal* 19 June 1891. Jehan Frollo is the truant brother of archdeacon Claude Frollo in Victor Hugo's *Notre-Dame de Paris*, set in 1482. Jehanne would, presumably, be their sister (the female form of Jehan's name). For a modern comparison of Angélique and Joan of Arc, see Jean-Louis Cabanès, 31–32.

61. See C. J. T. Talar, "(Anti)hagiography and Mysticism in the Work of J.-K. Huysmans," *Excavatio* IX (1997): 73–83 and Elizabeth Emery, "*Le Génie c'est une névrose*: Genius, Society, and the Novels of the Goncourts and Zola." *Excavatio* XVI: 1–2 (2002): 258–73.

62. *Les hystériques: Etat physique et état mental. Actes insolites, délictueux et criminels* (Paris: Baillière, 1891), 224. Translated and cited by Cristina Mazzoni in

Saint Hysteria: Neurosis, Mysticism, and Gender in European Culture (Ithaca NY: Cornell University Press, 1996), 3. See also Charcot's *Nouvelle iconographie de la Salpêtrière* (Paris, 1889); Janet Beizer, *Ventriloquized Bodies: Narratives of Hysteria in Nineteenth-Century France* (Ithaca NY: Cornell University Press, 1994); and Rae Beth Gordon, *Ornament, Fantasy, and Desire in Nineteenth-Century French Literature* (Princeton: Princeton University Press, 1992).

63. See *Saint Hysteria* for discussions of these debates. As Mazzoni points out, Catholic neurologist Antonin Imbert-Gourbeyre was one of those who accused Legrand du Saulle of misinterpreting these texts. See note 11, p. 4.

64. Redon, for example, focused on the scientific leanings of the text, while Rops emphasized the erotic. Rivière brought out the colorful legendary aspects of the text. See Barbara Larson's essay in this volume for an excellent analysis of the ways in which Redon's illustrations emphasized the medicalized aspects of Flaubert's text.

65. See Kitty Mrosovsky's interesting discussion of these questions in the preface to her translation of *The Temptation of Saint Antony* (Ithaca NY: Cornell University Press, 1980): 3–56.

66. See Sandra Zimdars-Swartz, *Encountering Mary from La Salette to Medjugorje* (Princeton, 1991) for more about Marian apparitions of the nineteenth century. For a history of belief in the Immaculate Conception and its resurgence in the nineteenth century see Edwin O'Connor, *The Dogma of the Immaculate Conception: Its History and Significance* (South Bend, 1958). For more about nineteenth-century pilgrimage, see Thomas A. Kselman, *Miracles and Prophecies in Nineteenth-Century France* (New Brunswick: Rutgers University Press, 1983). Emery and Morowitz trace the Assumptionist movement's attempt to attract pilgrims in Chapter 6 of *Consuming the Past*.

67. See Suzanne Kaufman, "Miracles, Medicine and the Spectacle of Lourdes: Popular Religion and Modernity in Fin-de-siècle France" (Ph.D. thesis, Rutgers, The State University of New Jersey, 1996) for an excellent discussion of the scientific and governmental supervision of the site. Ruth Harris' *Lourdes: Body and Spirit in the Secular Age* (New York: Viking, 1999) proposes a thorough history of the site and the effects of the pilgrimage on the area.

68. As Thomas Head has noted, medieval hagiography tended to reflect the misogyny of medieval society; as a result, women saints were a distinct minority. "Hagiography," in the *Online Reference Book for Medieval Studies* (http://the-orb.net/encyclop/religion/hagiography/hagio.htm).

69. See the family tree published in *Le Docteur Pascal*, in which scientist Pascal Rougon characterizes his family and their problems, linking Serge's unhealthy mysticism to his mother's mystical delusions (*La Conquête de Plassans*) and his great grandmother's madness (*La Fortune des Rougon, Le Docteur Pascal*).

70. "In other conditions, she could just as easily have been Nana.... [T]he mysticism of Angelique is merely an accidental form of the Macquart neurosis." 27 Oct. 1888, *La Revue bleue*.

71. Angélique's violent passion for religious images shocks and frightens her adoptive parents. See, for example, p. 829 of *Le Rêve*. Indeed, Zola's notes for *Le Rêve* insist on the soothing effect produced by the legendary "milieu" that surrounds Angélique. See NAF 10.323, fols, 19 and 25.

72. See the citation by Jean Lorrain that begins this volume.

73. *La Conversion des intellectuels au catholicisme en France. 1885–1935* (Paris: CNRS Editions, 1999).

74. Motivations for conversion were obviously much more complex than this and were extraordinarily personal. I offer these themes as examples of what many converts mentioned. For detailed studies of individual converts and their stated motivations, see Gugelot and Griffiths.

75. "Saints are a fact, and they are, at the same time, too great a glory for fallen humanity, too great a force for the Church, too irrefutable a manifestation of the supernatural for Christians ever to consider abandoning them to the hatred of wicked people incapable of imitating them." Cited in a preface to an undated edition of La Vie des saints (Imprimerie et reliure, Institution des sourds-muets, Saint-Etienne). Collection of Elizabeth Emery.

76. See C. J. T. Talar's contribution to this volume for a discussion of the ways in which Prosper Guéranger attempted to defend the legendary aspects of saints' lives.

77. Le Rêve, 824.

78. For a study of popular nineteenth-century activities (such as visiting wax museums, the Morgue and Panoramas), see Vanessa Schwartz, *Spectacular Realities: Early Mass Culture in Fin-de-siècle Paris* (Berkeley: University of California Press, 1988). Rae Beth Gordon discusses the public fascination with hysterics in *Why the French Love Jerry Lewis: From Cabaret to Early Cinema* (Stanford: Stanford University Press, 2001).

79. These collector cards, sold with products as varied as chocolates, wine and cigars, often featured famous celebrities. The saint cards tended to be sold with chocolates. Many of them are on sale, today, on eBay.

80. "A commonplace of kitsch religious trinkets, a transposition in the book of Froc-Robert statuettes, of the Froc-Roberts, chromolithographic images of the Bouasses." (*En Route*, 329).

The images in Figs. 0.1 and 3.19 were produced by the Bouasse family.

81. For more about the history of this publication and its goals, see Emery and Morowitz, "Marketing the Sacred: Medieval Pilgrimage and Catholic Revival" in *Consuming the Past*.

82. "There are no weapons more fearsome against the present iniquities than features of the saints' lives, and there are no weapons whose wounds heal themselves better; moreover, Saints are, above all, the source of good examples, let us preach them. ... So-called wise men have succeeded in making the most marvelous lives of the Saints profoundly boring in stripping them of their supernatural and miraculous elements, with which God himself took care to adorn them so abundantly. *Le Pèlerin* will reconstitute the traditional and popular side of saints' lives. Indeed, we want to prepare readings for Christians and not erudite works for l'Ecole des Chartes." Advertisement for the *Vie des saints* series. First page of the first issue of 1880.

83. This popular movement obviously sought an alternative to the historically and academically driven narratives produced by the Bollandists. This was Huysmans' reaction to their texts, which he described as "une série d'anecdotes ... il est impossible de faire de l'art avec cela" (Letter 188 to Arij Prins, 25 Dec. 1900): 349. For more about the objectives of the Bollandists, see C. J. T. Talar's essay in this volume.

84. See, for example, the explanation given by Bailly of the first illustrated issue of *Le Pèlerin*, in which he explains at length how the Middle Ages used images liberally to inspire religious belief (3 March 1877), 121–22. The clearest document for an understanding of the ways in which the Catholic Church had neglected the lower classes throughout the century is working-class senator Claude-Anthime Corbon's "Pourquoi

nous vous délaissons," a published letter to Bishop Dupanloup, in which he advocates returning to medieval practices to bring the lower classes back to the fold (Paris: Imprimerie nouvelle, 1877).

85. "At a time when Catholic beliefs are so deeply shaken by exaggerated concerns about a critical examination of all our religious habits pertaining to heart and soul, as if the Christian should support his piety and faith on nothing but archival documents or syllogisms, we dreamed of showing in action the very different method with which the Middle Ages, and particularly the thirteenth century, already considered the problems that trouble us today, albeit in another way." J.-C. Broussolle, *Le Christ de la Légende dorée, ouvrage illustré d'un commentaire artistique et de 307 gravures* (Paris: Maison de la Bonne presse, 1904). It would be interesting to see to what extent Huysmans participated in the compilation of this volume. Broussolle was part of his circle in the 1890s. See Robert Baldick, *The Life of J.-K. Huysmans* (Oxford: Clarendon Press, 1955), 275.

86. *Le Rêve*, 836–37.

87. In 1886, La Maison de la Bonne Presse printed 56,000 copies, though some had been reprinted up to three times. See Paul Castel. *Le P. François Picard et le P. Vincent de Paul Bailly dans les luttes de presse* (Rome: Maison Généralice, 1962), 152.

88. A "lettre sur la vie des saints" published in the 13 December 1896 issue of *Le Pèlerin* describes some of these uses. This reader has distributed 14,000 copies in the last three years. "Voici mes moyens de propagande. Récompenses au catéchisme surtout, distribution le dimanche et aux fêtes, aux enterrements pendant l'offrande." Others included having children recite them or giving them as prizes for catechism. Issue 1041, 11.

89. *En Route*, 389. See Gugelot, 75–111, for a summary of the books most often read by intellectual converts at the end of the nineteenth century.

90. See Reames, 23.

91. Both Marcel Proust ("La Mort des cathédrales") and Anatole France (*L'Orme du mail, Le Lys Rouge*) parody this tendency to collect medieval religious artifacts while promulgating laws against Catholicism. The "canonization" of the work itself as literature was reinforced by publications such as Gaston Paris' 1888 *La Littérature française du moyen âge* (1888), which included saints' lives with more secular material. With the establishment of the Société des Anciens Textes Français, the last decades of the nineteenth century witnessed an explosion in the number of scholarly editions of hagiographies produced (many of which we continue to use today). See Charles Ridoux, *L'évolution des études médiévales en France de 1860 à 1914* (Paris: Champion, 2001). Pages 892–96 of this book specifically discuss saints' lives, while the rest describes other scholarly work produced at the time.

92. "A nonbeliever cannot help but admire the purity of this ideal and appreciate a sincerely naive poetry. And each and every one, without shame and without irony, will abandon himself to the soothing and consoling charm of the old and sweet *Légende*." See his article published in *Minerva: Revue des lettres et des arts* (1 Nov. 1903): 24–43.

PART THREE

THE STRUGGLE TO RECONTEXTUALIZE HAGIOGRAPHY

5

Translatio Lidwinae: The Adaptation of Medieval Sources in Huysmans' *Sainte Lydwine de Schiedam*

Laurie Postlewate

> Mult ai usé cum pechere
> Ma vie en trop fole manere,
> E trop ai usée ma vie
> E en peché e en folie.
> Kant court hanteie of les curteis,
> Si feseie les serventeis,
> Chauncuenettes, rimes, saluz
> Entre les drues et les druz ...
> Jamés ne me burdera plus.
> Jeo ai noun Denis Piramus ;
> Les jurs jolifs de ma joefnesce
> S'en vunt, si trei jeo a vuilesce,
> Si est bien dreit keme repente.[1]
>   —Denis Piramus,
>   *La vie Seint Edmund le Rei*

> I will admit that writing St. Lydwina was an act of penance for me. There were few opportunities for the artistic dimension to take off; it is the literary equivalent of fasting ...[2]
>   —J.-K. Huysmans, Letter to
>   Adolphe Berthet, 3 July 1901

For both Denis Piramus, the twelfth-century poet and composer of the life of Saint Edmund the King, and Joris-Karl Huysmans, referring to his recently published rendition of the bizarre story of Saint Lydwine of Schiedam, hagiography was a spiritual exercise, an act of devotion and contrition for the penitent writer. Huysmans' *Sainte Lydwine de Schiedam*[3] was not the only time the author engaged himself in writing as self-reparation: the autobiographical trilogy of *Là-Bas* (1891), *En Route* (1895), and *La Cathédrale* (1898) was also for Huysmans a textual coming-to-terms with his own conversion to orthodox Catholicism.

His life of Lydwine was a different kind of exercise, however, in that the author appears to have modeled his story on the medieval practice of hagiography, a textual form which was, in the Middle Ages, associated with penance and spiritual renewal. An avid student of medieval culture, Huysmans would have known, in addition to the Latin versions of the saints' legends, many of the Old French translations of the same stories that were being published in the late nineteenth century in the savant circle of the *Société des Anciens Textes Français*.[4] Indeed, as the quote which opens Elizabeth Emery's essay in this volume demonstrates, Huysmans was concerned with the problem of how to translate the saints' narratives without losing the essence, "le suc dolent et le blanc parfum" of their stories. Our discussion here will draw examples from the corpus of Old French saints' lives, which in the 1880s and 1890s were being made available to a wider public. The Old French lives would have provided Huysmans with knowledge of the saints dear to the Middle Ages, but also with textual models. We will see that Huysmans, in fact, reproduced many features of the Old French works in his story of Lydwine and that in many ways the authorial persona in his *Sainte Lydwine de Schiedam* parallels that of the medieval composer of the saint's life.

The story of Lydwine of Schiedam, as we know it from contemporary medieval sources of her life, was one of appalling suffering and miraculous courage.[5] Born in Schiedam, Holland in 1380, Lydwine was a young girl of considerable piety and devotion to the Virgin Mary when at the age of fifteen she suffered several broken ribs in a skating accident. From this injury she developed an abscess that eventually burst, spreading infection throughout her body and sending Lydwine's health into a spiraling descent of endless and unbearable torture for the thirty-eight years she lived after her accident. Among Lydwine's many afflictions during this time, as documented by the medieval sources of her life, were excruciating pain in all parts of her body, even to her teeth; constant fever; bouts with the plague; cancer; blindness in one eye and extreme sensitivity to light in the other. After a few years of agony, Lydwine's body was so ravaged by infection and arthritis that she could not move at all except for her left arm. She existed in a state of bodily putrefaction with large chunks of her flesh dropping from her frame, so that when her attendants needed to move her, they had to bind her body together to keep it from falling apart. Eventually Lydwine was unable to eat food and is said to have sustained herself for the last nineteen years of her life solely on the Eucharistic host.

Lydwine's initial reaction to her afflictions was to rebel against God; however, four years after her accident, under the guidance of her confessor, she came to understand her illness as a blessing and a means of meditating on Christ's passion. Lydwine's sufferings came to receive much attention and she had a considerable cult in her lifetime. Lydwine was said to have prophetic gifts and the ability to bilocate; she would frequently enter into a state of ecstasy, her soul leaving her body to travel with her guardian angel and Jesus to view Heaven, Hell, Purgatory and the Holy Land. More importantly, she was able, through the intervention of her own suffering, to relieve her followers—and sometimes even her detractors—of many physical and spiritual ills. Lydwine finally died on Easter Tuesday, 1433, at the age of fifty-three. Her cult was confirmed by Pope Leo in 1890, but she was never canonized, making her only blessed and not actually Saint Lydwine, as Huysmans calls her in his book.

The medieval Latin sources of the life of Lydwine provided Huysmans with the basis for his narrative in French; the way Huysmans used those sources reveals that he followed certain aspects of hagiography as practiced by the medieval vernacular authors. A first indication of this is in the visibility and importance given within the text to the sources of the saint's *vita*. The medieval vernacular saint's life, often in verse and part of a rich tradition of literary works destined for oral recitation, is virtually always derived from a written, Latin source: in the French tradition, the authors often refer to their Latin sources as the *écrit* which they are putting into French, the *romanz*, for the benefit of those for whom the vernacular is necessary or desirable. The examples below from the twelfth-century prologues to the anonymous lives of Saint Catherine of Alexandria and Saint Juliana and the life of Saint Nicholas by Wace reflect the preoccupation of medieval writers with confirming the validity of their texts through the authority of the written source:

> Por l'amitié de ce bon mestre
> Voill je la vie et la saint'estre
> D'une seue amie retraire
> Et de latin en romanz traire,
> Que plus delite a escouter
> A cels qui l'oent raconter.[6]
> (ll. 13–18)

> Une chose vos vulh descrivre;
> Asseiz l'aveiz tuit oït dire,
> Mais vos nel poïstes entendre,
> Si vos en vulh alkes apprendre.
> Le latins vos est mult pesanz,
> Sel vos voldroi dire en romanz.
> Vos ki latin apris n'aveiz,
> Lo plain romanz bien entendeiz;
> Ki l'entendrat parfitement,
> L'anmre en avrat son salvement.
> D'une virgene vos vulh conteir
> Ke l'escriture oi loeir.[7]
>
> (ll. 31–42)
>
> Jo sui Normanz, s'ai non Guace.
> Dit m'est et rové que jo face
> De seint Nicholas en romanz.
> Qui fist miracles bels et granz.
> En romanz dirrai de sa vie.
> Et des miracles grant partie.
> En romanz voil dire un petit
> De ceo que nus le latin dit,
> Qu li lai le puissent aprendre
> Qui ne poënt latin entendre.[8]

For Huysmans also, known from his early days in the Naturalist circle of Zola for painstakingly thorough research on his subjects, source documents were of primary importance. He begins his life of Lydwine with an explanation of the three Latin sources he used, emphasizing their historical precision and authenticity: the testimony of Jan Gerlac, a relative who lived for many years in the same house with Lydwine; Jan Brugman, a Franciscan who added to Gerlac's text details provided by Lydwine's last confessor; and that of Thomas à Kempis, which although a summary of Brugman's version, did include details which Kempis had carefully gathered from those who had known Lydwine. Huysmans assures his reader that the authors of his sources are reliable and credible, "des gens connus et dignes, par leur situation et par leur probité d'âme, d'être crus" and that their works were composed "dans des conditions de bonne foi et de certitude plus sûres" than most historical works.[9] Moreover, Huysmans concludes the *Avant Propos* with eight pages of bibliography citing the works of theology and spirituality that he consulted in the composition of his book.[10] The author's insistence on the verifiable truth of his sources is directed at both those modernist skeptics for whom mystics like Lydwine were nothing more than pathologocial cases of hysteria and to the positivist historians who may have reproached Huysmans with an overly eager credulousness toward his medieval sources. But his concern to reaffirm the authenticity of his sources is also consistent with the strategy of the medieval hagiographer.

The medieval composer of the vernacular saint's life did not, however, see his role as strictly that of translator. The *traductio* of the saint's story meant not only to put it into another language, but also to translate or transfer it, to carry it to different settings and apply it to new purposes; just as the translation of the saint's relics meant taking them from one physical setting to another. The adaptation of the saint's narrative into the vernacular meant taking a rather free hand with the Latin sources; medieval authors readily acknowledge this and justify the additions, omissions and changes they make in their compositions. The fourteenth-century Franciscan poet Nicole Bozon provides us with numerous examples of such commentary in his eleven verse lives.[11] In his *Vie de Seinte Margarete*, for example, Bozon explains why he assumes certain details which the source did not mention:

> Ceo ke avint de celi mal quyn
> Jeo ne ay pas trové en mon latin,
> Ke fit ceu fet aprés la vuewe,
> Meis par cele pleyne de vertuwe
> Jeo crey k'il prist bon fin,
> Me ke trové ne seyt en latin.[12]
> (ll. 303–08)

In his *Vie la Marie Magdalene*, on the other hand, the author justifies omitting entire episodes from the Latin, for fear of boring his audience:

> Si jeo meyse en cest escrit
> Chescun miracle ke le latin dit
> Par long demure en lisant
> Les perceonses serreint trop pesant;
> Kar les perceonses bien se avisent
> Cum bien dure avant ke lisent.
> S'il est court, il unt delit;
> S'il est long, l'unt en despit,
> E lisent tut par fin enu,
> E perdent louer de grant vertu.[13]
> (ll. 483–92)

Huysmans, too, makes a point to justify the way he has treated his sources, especially with respect to the confusing order of events in Lydwine's life which he has reorganized "suivant l'ordre qui m'a semblé être, sinon le plus rigoureux, au moins le plus intéressant et le plus commode."[14] Following the lead of his medieval counterparts in hagiography, Huysmans exploits the mark of authority of his Latin sources, but without allowing that authority to limit his ability to communicate what he sees as the essence of Lydwine's life.

As we have seen, the medieval saint's life was for its author/translator/adaptor a personal act of devotion to the saint and a form of penance. But it was also an opportunity to propose spiritual inspiration and models of holiness to the larger community of believers. The author of the twelfth-century *Vie de Saint Gilles*, for example, offers remission of sins to all those who listen to his work:

>   Gwillame ad nun de Bernevile,
>   Ki par amur Deu e seint Gile
>   Enprist cest labur et cest fès;
>   De ses pechez ait il relès;
>   Deus l'en rende le guerredun
>   E seint Gile le bon barun;
>   Il le conduie ensemble od sei
>   En parays devant le rei!
>   Ki ceste vie funt escrire
>   E ki l'escutent i funt lire,
>   Ki l'escutent pur Deu amur
>   E en lur quers en unt tendrur,
>   Deus lur rende ben la merite
>   E de lur pechez seient quite[15]
>   (ll. 3765–78)

The author of the Old French life of Gregory the Great offers examples of the life of a great sinner who converted, so that his audience may benefit from them:

>   Icil pechié dont parler vuel
>   Ne fait a dire par orguel,
>   Mais por exemple d'autre gent,
>   Qu'il i prendent castïement;
>   Sainte Escripture nos commande:
>   Quand li coupe est onques plus grande
>   Dont le doit on miex anonchier
>   Por l'autre peule castiier.[16]
>   (ll. 9–16)

Huysmans also seems to understand the function of the hagiographic text as twofold; it is at once personal, the "literary equivalent of fasting," and communal, directed to the company of faithful sufferers who can benefit from Lydwine's example. In his conclusion, Huysmans indicates that the saint's story was intended for those "victims of choice" who need a way to make sense of their pain:

> Mais ce livre n'est pas écrit, en somme, pour ceux-là. Il est, en effet, difficile, pour des gens qui vivent en bonne santé, de le bien comprendre; ils le saisiront mieux, plus tard, lorsque séviront les mauvais jours; par contre, il s'adresse plus spécialement aux pauvres êtres atteints de maladies incurables et étendus, à jamais, sur une couche. Ceux-là sont, pour la plupart, des victimes de choix; mais combien, parmi eux, savent qu'ils réalisent l'oeuvre admirable de la réparation et pour eux-mêmes et pour les autres?[17]

The saint's story was, for the Middle Ages, a malleable form which could be shaped to fit the expectations and needs of its audience and the ideological orientation of its composer; this can be seen especially well through comparison of different versions of a single saint's life.[18] Vernacular versions of the saints' stories inevitably communicate the particular idea of holiness that their authors wished to present to their audiences. These models can be motivated by a variety of forces, including the desire to promote the political and theological positions of their writers.[19] The twelfth-century writer Wace, for example, transformed his life of the Virgin Mary into a forceful argument for the Immaculate Conception, at a time when that doctrine was not yet universally accepted in theological circles.[20] Thirteenth- and fourteenth-century versions of the life of Saint Alexis—who lived all of his adult life as a hermit, separated from his wife—insist on the saint's married status, reflecting the contemporary doctrinal emphasis on the indissolubility of marriage.[21] And many vernacular lives pointedly encourage the practice of confession in the period when that sacrament was first being strongly promoted to the laity.[22]

For Huysmans, the one true path to holiness was that of suffering; other types of saintly behavior, while important to Huysmans, were secondary to the ability of the holy to endure tremendous physical pain. The emphasis on vicarious suffering is first seen in an early chapter when Lydwine's confessor explains to her the reasons for her afflictions: "Votre mission est claire; elle consiste à vous sacrifier pour les autres, à réparer les offenses que vous n'avez pas commises; ... Dites à Jésus: je veux me placer, moi-même, sur votre croix et je veux que ce soit Vous qui enfonciez les

cious."²³ The meeting between Lydwine and her confessor is recounted in Huysmans' sources without the element of vicarious suffering. Yet this is the model of holiness on which Huysmans shaped Lydwine's life, allowing him to discuss and promote the somewhat questionable doctrine of mystical expiation to which he was drawn in the later years of his life.

Expiatory suffering, or suffering in reparation for the sins of others and in imitation of Christ, is indeed part of Catholic doctrine and the explicit mission of many saints and holy persons. But Huysmans' brand of vicarious suffering went well beyond that officially sanctioned by the church to include a kind of mechanical substitution by which the sufferer accepts the direct and automatic transference of pain or illness from another person to him or herself. In this way Lydwine took on the toothache of one and the migraine of another (to mention only two of the scores of afflictions she assumed.) Moreover, Lydwine absorbed into her own body not only the physical suffering of others, but also the root cause of that suffering—sin—by assuming the guilt and even the temptations of those too weak to overcome evil themselves. In one of many examples of "mystical substitution" Lydwine takes on the sins of a wicked priest—and even confesses and does his penance for him.

The image of holiness that Huysmans portrays here conforms to the harsh—and even heretical—vision of Christianity the author had personally adopted after his conversion in 1892. As Richard Griffiths has demonstrated, Huysmans, along with Léon Bloy and a number of French Catholic writers, used fictional portrayals of the ideal Catholic to create models of holiness that the average Catholic would find impossible to follow.²⁴ Indeed, Huysmans affirms that very few are suited to the calling of Lydwine; most Christians live in a "zone of tepid piety" and are thus limited to experiencing only "small tortures and joys." The principal source of the particular understanding of expiatory suffering that Huysmans promotes in his life of Lydwine was the defrocked abbé Boullan, a somewhat shady figure with whom Huysmans was engaged in a spiritual friendship between 1890 and 1893. Among the various marginal and outright heretical activities of the abbé Boullan from the 1860s to his sudden death in 1893 was the establishment of an organization called the *Oeuvre de la Réparation*, a league of voluntary vicarious sufferers who agreed to take on the pains, sins and temptations of others—with Boullan acting as their paid broker.²⁵

The reasons for Huysmans' preoccupation—one might even say obsession—with vicarious suffering are multiple and complex, and as biographers and students of his work have demonstrated, they derive both from personal experience (including a fascination with the occult and black magic) and from the author's literary and aesthetic ideas, positions he held from the time of his split from the Naturalist circle of Emile Zola in the 1890s.[26] Pain is an omnipresent motif in Huysmans' *oeuvre*, in which we see a chronological progression toward understanding and acceptance of suffering, just as the spiritual life of the subject becomes more intense. Des Esseintes, the hero of Huysmans' most famous work, the novel *A Rebours* (1884), calls physical pain "a useless, unjust, incomprehensible abomination." For Des Esseintes suffering is incomprehensible and unbearable in that its reason and its purpose are hidden; and it is suffering that drives Des Esseintes to the brink of conversion. In Huysmans' post-conversion works, the author struggles to deal with suffering by giving to it an object on which it can act—the evil of others.[27]

Lydwine, Huysmans' model saint, had to undergo a conversion to understand her pain as an antidote to the world's evil; the interpretation of suffering at which Huysmans arrives through the story of Lydwine's suffering was later to help the author in his own "conversion to pain." Huysmans' correspondence from the final weeks of his life shows that, in excruciating pain from cancer of the mouth, he at first doubted that he could follow the example of suffering provided by Lydwine. He was eventually able to see his situation differently, to the point of refusing morphine in order to suffer in expiation for the sins of others. Indeed, in his last days, Huysmans arranged his own altar table for daily communion with a reliquary containing a relic of Lydwine.[28]

The particular image of holiness that Huysmans communicates through Lydwine is linked to the larger ideological and political interpretation he gives her story. Lydwine's suffering, Huysmans explains, is comprehensible only if we consider her role in history; to this end, the author adds to the narrative an introduction and conclusion which together present an apocalyptic vision of decadent Europe in the late Middle Ages. "L'état de l'Europe, pendant le temps que vécut Lydwine, fut effroyable."[29] Thus begins chapter one of the text, providing an overview, country by country, of the fall of European civilization in the fourteenth and early fifteenth century, including political disasters, schisms and heresies, the incompetence and corruption of the clergy, as well as the numerous epidemics and natural catastrophes that befell the continent. God then sent in troops of saints who, through various combats, sacrifices and sufferings, redressed the balance of Good and Evil and assisted Huysmans' favorite saints of the day—Lydwine, Colette and Françoise Romaine:

> Devant une pareille somme de sacrilèges et de crimes, devant une pareille invasion des cohortes de l'Enfer, il semble probable que,

> malgré tout leur dévouement et leur bravoure, sainte Lydwine, sainte Colette, sainte Françoise Romaine, eussent succombé sous le nombre si Dieu n'avait levé des armées pour les secourir.[30]

The panorama of decadent Europe is taken up again at the end of Huysmans' text where he recounts how Lydwine was shown by Jesus, shortly before her death, a horrific vision of the state of the world; this allowed her to further understand her own role in the great drama of suffering and saintly expiation:

> Jésus lui exhibait, en une épouvantable vision, le panorama de son temps.
>
> L'Europe lui apparaissait, convulsée—comme elle-même l'était,—sur le lit de son sol et elle cherchait à ramener, d'une main tremblante, sur elle, la couverture de ses mers pour cacher son corps qui se décomposait, qui n'était plus qu'un magma de chairs, qu'un limon d'humeurs, qu'une boue de sang; car c'était une pourriture infernale qui lui crevait, à elle, les flancs; c'était une frénésie de sacrilèges et de crimes qui la faisait hurler, ainsi qu'une bête qu'on assassine; c'était la vermine de ses vices qui la dépeçait; c'étaient des chancres de simonie, des cancers de luxure qui la dévoraient vive; et terrifiée, Lydwine regardait sa tête tiarée qui ballotait, rejetée tantôt du côté d'Avignon, tantôt du côté de Rome.
>
> "Vois", fit le Christ, et, sur un fond d'incendies, elle aperçut, sous la conduite de fous couronnés, la meute lâchée des peuples. Ils s'égorgeaient et se pillaient sans pitié; plus loin, en des régions qui semblaient paisibles, elle considéra les cloîtres bouleversés par les brigues des mauvais moines, le clergé qui trafiquait de la chair du Christ, qui vendait à l'encan les grâces du Saint-Esprit; elle surprit les hérésies, les sabbats dans les bois, les messes noires.
>
> Elle serait morte de désespoir si, pour la consoler, Dieu ne lui avait pas aussi montré la contrepartie de ce siècle, l'armée des saints en marche; ils parcouraient sans s'arrêter le monde, réformaient les abbayes, détruisaient le culte de Satan, mataient les peuples et refrénaient les rois, passaient, en dépit de tous les obstacles, dans des tourbillons de crachats et de huées; et tous, qu'ils fussent actifs ou contemplatifs, souffraient, eux aussi, aidaient à acquitter par leurs oraisons et leurs tortures la rançon de tant de maux!
>
> Devant l'immensité de la dette, elle s'estimait si pauvre![31]

The theme of the decadence of society and the expiatory function of the holy in this world is further developed in the following chapter, where Huysmans affirms that in his own fin-de-siècle France, such sufferers as Lydwine are sorely needed:

> Il faut ajouter qu'à l'heure actuelle, les besoins de l'Eglise sont immenses; un vent de malheur souffle sur les régions inabritées des croyants. Il y a une sorte d'affaisement des devoirs, de déchéance d'énergie dans les pays qui sont plus particulièrement les fiefs spirituels du Saint-Siège.
>
> L'Autriche est rongée jusqu'aux moelles par la vermine juive; l'Italie est devenue un repaire maçonnique, une sentine démoniaque, au sens strict du mot; l'Espagne et le Portugal sont, eux aussi, dépécés par les crocs des Loges; seule, la petite Belgique paraît moins cariée, de foi moins rance, d'âme plus saine; quant à la nation privilégiée du Christ, la France, elle a été attaquée, à moitié étranglée, saboulée à coups de botte, roulée dans le purin des fosses par une racaille payée de mécréants. La franc-maçonnerie a démuselé, pour cette infâme besogne, la meute avide des israélites et des protestants.[32]
>
> Le XXe siècle débute donc, ainsi que le précédent fini en France, par une éruption infernale; la luttte est ouverte entre Lucifer et Dieu.
>
> En vérité, il faut espérer que, pour contrebalancer le poids de tels défis, les victimes d'expiation abondent, et que, dans les cloîtres et dans le monde, beaucoup de moines, de prêtres et de laïques acceptent de continuer l'oeuvre réparative des holocaustes.[33]

Huysmans' assessment of his own era contains a virulent, reactionary message, biting in its anti–Semitic fervor and disdain for Protestants, Freemasons and all moderate Catholics.

The saint's life as a beacon of truth from the past, shedding light on the corruption of the present, recalls the *Ubi sunt* motif found in medieval hagiographic texts which frequently express a sense of nostalgia for a time when the holy manifested themselves more clearly and actively in the world:

> Bon fut le secles al tens ancïenur,
> Quer feit i ert e justise ed amur;
> S'i ert creance, dunt or n'i at nul prut.
> Tut est müez, perdut ad sa colur:
> Ja mais n'iert tel cum fut as anceisurs.
> Al tens Noë ed al tens Abraham
> Ed al David, qui Deus par amat tant,
> Bons fut li secles ; jamais n'ert si vailant.
> Velz est e fraisles, tut s'en vat declinant:
> S'ist ampairét, tut bien vait remanant.[34]

The author of the twelfth-century *Vie de Saint Alexis* laments the "declining" era in which he lives and for which the saint's life provides a remarkable counterexample. Indeed, much of vernacular medieval hagiography is either explicitly or implicitly eschatological in vision and in tone, reflecting the apocalyptic thinking which permeates the Middle Ages.[35] Huysmans' eschatology as expressed in *Sainte Lydwine de Schiedam* is more grandiosely cataclysmic and more viciously antisemitic than what one finds in medieval hagiography.[36] However, Huysmans would certainly have found this vision elsewhere in medieval literature, and especially in the painting of the late medieval period—the era of Lydwine—which Huysmans himself knew particularly well.[37]

The fear and dismay presented in this picture of worldly decadence is only comprehensible and bearable with the saint's example of forbearance and faith. The vision of a world in decline is connected to the rhetorical objective of the saint's life, that of exhortation—to move the public by the saint's holiness and to encourage them to engage actively in the ethos of her life. Medieval saints' lives often directly address their audience, calling on them to follow the example of the saint. In this passage from his *Vie de Seinte Marthe*, Nicole Bozon explains to his audience how they can, in very specific and concrete ways, imitate the behavior of the saint:

> Ki cest escrit regardez,
> Quele affiance e quel confort
> Ceste femme out en sa mort.
> Cum sovent ad rehercee
> Ke Jhesu Crist out herbergee
> Par ceo poez entendre
> Ke vus devez estre tendre,
> Tele chose fere en vostre vie
> Ke en vostre morte vus seit aïe.[38]
> (ll. 316–24)

Huysmans too, in his *Sainte Lydwine de Schiedam*, speaks directly to his readers, including himself and his public in the experience of Lydwine's mission. When, for example, Huysmans describes the period of spiritual darkness through which Lydwine passed before she came to understand her suffering as a mission, he compares her experience to that of his readers who have, he is sure, doubted God's existence in their time of affliction:

> L'horizon est noir et les lointains sont clos. Dieu dont le souvenir quand même domine n'apparaît plus qu'ainsi qu'un inexorable thaumaturge qui pourrait vous guérir d'un signe et ne le veut pas. ... On a beau se dire, dans une lueur de bon sens, que l'on a péché, que l'on expie ses offenses, l'on conclut que la somme des

> transgressions commises n'est pas suffisante pour légitimer l'apport de tant de maux et l'on accuse Notre-Seigneur d'injustice, l'on prétend Lui démontrer qu'il y a disproportion entre les délits et la peine....
>
> L'on se reproche alors des contumélies et ses blâmes; l'on implore son pardon et une douceur naît de ce rapprochement; peu à peu, des idées de résignation à la volonté du Sauveur s'inculquent et prennent racine, si le Diable, aux aguets, ne se mêle pas de les extirper.[39]

Huysmans' hagiographic text, as a work of reflection and devotion, presents itself as the catalyst for a new understanding of pain on the part of its readers; but it also aims to incite those readers to participate in the continued celebration of Lydwine's victory-by-suffering over the forces of evil. For medieval writers of saints' lives and for their public, participation in the eternal ethos of the saint came through any act of composing, or hearing or reading—aloud or silently—the saint's story. Nicole Bozon ends his *Vie Seinte Margarete* by reminding the saint of the covenant made to all who involve themselves in the dissemination and reception of her story:

> Margarete, ore pensez
> De moy, cheytif, ke ay translatez
> Vostre vie e vostre passion.
> Ke Dieu me grante sauvacion,
> E a touz cels ke cest escrit
> Orrunt ou lirrunt o delit ;
> Ceo est le covenant avant fet.
> Ore seit gardé, si vus plet.
> Amen.[40]
> (ll. 323–31)

Medieval vernacular lives in verse are typically set in the context of communal prayer through the way the authors conclude the stories. The thirteenth-century writer Rutebeuf ends his life of Mary the Egyptian in a way that is typical of the genre:

> Or prions tuit a ceste sainte,
> Qui por Dieu souffri paine mainte,
> Qu'ele prit a celui Seignor
> Qu'en la fin li fist tele honor
> Qu'il nous doinst joie pardurable
> Avoec le Pere esperitable.

> Por moi qui ai non Rustebuef
> Qui est dit de rude et de buef,
> Qui ceste vie qi mise en rime,
> Que iceste dame saintisme
> Prit Celui cui ele est amie
> Que il Rustebuef n'oublit mie !
> Amen.[41]
>
> (ll. 1295–97)

The anonymous author of the *Vie de Saint Laurent* provides another example of the devotional context of the hagiographic text:

> Prium lui qu'il nous doinst gloire,
> Ou regne en joie parmanable,
> Ke por fait dunt soion copable
> Ne aillum en peril, ne en peine,
> Ne perdun joie soveraine,
> Mais faire nos doinst tel faisance
> Que aveir puissun sostenance,
> Et la floire de parais,
> Jesu, la ou regnes et vis.
> Amen.[42]
>
> (ll. 941–50)

In the Old French lives, the interaction between the narrative and its *destinataire* involves a kind of reciprocity: The believer brings to the saint his or her devotion and prayer, and the saint responds with healing and inspiration. In Huysmans' *Sainte Lydwine de Schiedam*, the same kind of active participation on the part of the reader is suggested not only by the passages directed to the reader, but by the appendices which follow the story: a hymn to Lydwine and an office based on her life. Huysmans stops short of proposing that his readers perform these short liturgies; in fact, he presents the pieces with something of the cold detachment of the scientific *chercheur* who is simply trying to provide an exhaustive account of the documentation on his subject. Yet the inclusion of these paratextual elements further reveals either a conscious decision or a subconscious desire on the part of Huysmans to provide the same kind of devotional context for his life of Lydwine as we find in medieval hagiography.

The parallels we have drawn here between Huysmans' text and the practice of medieval hagiography allow us to appreciate his *Sainte Lydwine de Schiedam* in a new light. Previous studies of the work have focused on its place in nineteenth-century historiography and in the religious controversies of the day, but Huysmans' *Sainte Lydwine de Schiedam* is also medieval.

Lydwine's story, much like the hagiographic texts of the Middle Ages, is a flexible and multifunctional *forme simple*: It furnishes a model which its author and its larger public of readers can use to understand their own lives and deal with their own suffering; it was used by the author to give narrative form to doctrinal points and political opinions; and finally it provides a historical context in which the saint's ethos can be continually present and dynamic. The significance of Huysmans' text, a work of expiation and reparation, coming as it did in the final years of the author's often tortured life and toward the end of a career which saw personal struggles enacted and resolved though literary creation, is understood more completely if we acknowledge the medieval method of hagiography which the author sought to imitate in the strange story of the maid of Schiedam.

Notes

1. "I have lived much of my life as a sinner/ In an unreasoned way,/ I have lived too much of my life/ In sin and folly./ When I frequented the courts/ And for the courtly audience I made lyric poems/ And songs and rhymes/ For ladies and their lovers.../ No more will I play at this./ My name is Denis Piramus/ The tender days of my youth/ Are fading and I draw close to old age,/ And so it is right that I repent." *La Vie Seint Edmund le Rei, Poème Anglo-Normand du XIIe Siècle*, ed. Hilding Kjellman (Genève: Slatkine Reprints, 1974), 3–4. All translations in this chapter, both from the old French and from Huysmans' text, are by Laurie Postlewate.

2. *The Road From Decadence: The Selected Letters of J. K. Huysmans*, ed. Barbara Beaumont (Columbus OH: Ohio State University Press, 1989), 207.

3. Joris-Karl Huysmans, *Sainte Lydwine de Schiedam*, with a preface by Alain Vircondelet (Paris: Maren Sell, 1989). For a full English translation of Huysmans' text: *Saint Lydwine of Schiedam*, trans. Agnes Hastings (Rockford IL: Tan Publishers, 1979).

4. Charles Ridoux, *L'évolution des études médiévales en France de 1860 à 1914* (Paris: Champion, 2001).

5. The sources known to Huysmans are the versions by Jan Gerlac and Jan Brugman found in the *Acta Sanctorum Aprilis, Tomus secundus*, eds. Société des Bollandistes (Paris: Palme, 1866), 270–303; and the life of Lydwine by Thomas à Kempis in his *Opera omnia* (Friburgi Brisigavorum: Herder, 1902–1918), volume 6. The latter is also available in English: *St. Lydwine of Schiedam*, translation and introduction by Dom Vincent Scully, C.R.L., (London: Burns & Oates, 1912).

6. "Out of love for this good Master,/ I want to tell the story of the saint and her life/ Who is a friend to him,/ And to put the Latin into French,/ So that those to whom it is told/ Will delight in hearing it." Henry Alfred Todd, "*La vie de sainte Catherine d'Alexandrie* as contained in the Paris manuscript 'La Clayette'," *Publications of Modern Language Association* 15 (1900), 17–73.

7. "I want to tell you a story/ Which you have heard many times before,/ But you were unable to understand it/ So I will relate it to you now./ The Latin is very burdensome for you,/ So I wish to tell it to you in French./ For you who have not learned Latin,/ You understand the French well;/ And he who will

understand it perfectly,/ Will find salvation for his soul./ I want to tell you of a virgin/ Whose life I heard praised." Hugo von Feilitzen, *Li Ver del Juïse en forfansk Prediken* (Upsala, 1883), Appendix, 7.

8. I am Norman, and my name is Wace./ I was the author of the Rou/ And now I will tell the story of Nicholas in French./ Of the one who worked beautiful and great miracles./ In French I will tell his life story./ And I want to tell a little about/ Some of his miracles, in French/ And of what the Latin tells us/ So that they may know the story/ Who cannot understand Latin." *La vie de Saint Nicolas par Wace*, ed. Einar Ronsjö (Lund: Håkan Ohlssons, 1942), 114.

9. "... people who are well-known and worthy of belief, both because of their status and their total integrity;" "... in all good faith and with more certainty." Huysmans, *Sainte Lydwine*, 10–11.

10. Huysmans, *Sainte Lydwine*, 13–20.

11. *Three Saints' Lives by Nicholas Bozon*, ed. Sister Mary Amelia Klenke (St. Bonaventure NY: Franciscan Institute, 1947); *Seven More Poems by Nicholas Bozon* (St. Bonaventure NY: Franciscan Institute, 1951); A.T. Baker, "Vie de St. Panuce," *Romania* 38 (1909): 418–24; Baker, "An Anglo-French Life of Saint Paul the Hermit," *Modern Language Review* 4 (1908–9): 491–504.

12. "Whatever happened to this hapless fellow/ I have not found in the Latin,/ What he did after this vision,/ But because of she who is full of virtue/ I think he met a good end/ But it is not found in the Latin." Bozon, *Three Saints' Lives*, 41–42.

13. "If I put into writing/ Every miracle that the Latin tells of/ It would take a long time to read/ Which people find a burden;/ For people try to find out/ How long the reading will last before they begin./ If it is short, they are delighted by it;/ If it is long, they dread it,/ And end up bored if they read it all,/ And thereby lose the benefit of the story." Bozon, *Three Saints' Lives*, 25.

14. "Following the order that seemed to me the most interesting and suitable, if not the most precise." Huysmans, *Sainte Lydwine*, 13.

15. "My name is Guillaume of Berneville,/ Whoever for love of God and Saint Gilles/ Undertakes this labor and this deed/ May he have remission of his sins;/ May God repay him/ And may Saint Gilles the good baron,/ Take them with him/ Together into paradise before the king!/ For those who have this life written/ And who listen to it and have it read,/ Who listen to it for the love of God/ And who in their hearts feel tenderness,/ May God grant them the merits/ So that their sins will be forgiven." *La Vie de Saint Gilles*, ed. Gaston Paris et Alphonse Bos (Paris: SATF, 1881), 114.

16. "If I want to tell you here of sin/ I do not do it from pride,/ But to offer an example to other people/ That they take it as a kind of chastisement;/ For Holy Scripture tells us/ That when the guilt is greatest/ Then should we announce it all the more / So that the other one may repent and correct himself." *La Vie de Saint Grégoire*, ed. Eugenio Burgio (Venezia: Cafoscarina, 1993), 3.

17. "But this book was not written on the whole for those people. It is, in fact, difficult for people in good health to understand it; they will understand it later, when they fall upon bad times; on the contrary, the book is addressed more especially to those poor beings stricken with incurable illnesses and confined forever to their beds. They are, for the most part, the victims of choice; but how many are there among them who know that they are carrying out the admirable work of reparation, for themselves and for others?" Huysmans, *Sainte Lydwine*, 279.

18. There is a considerable amount

of scholarship on the changing model of holiness in medieval vernacular hagiography. One would do well to begin with the articles and bibliography in the following volumes: Thomas Heffernan, *Sacred Biography: Saints and Their Biographers in the Middle Ages* (New York: Oxford University Press, 1988); *Saints: Studies in Hagiography*, ed. Sandro Sticca (Binghamton NY: Center for Medieval and Renaissance Studies, 1996); *Images of Sainthood in Medieval Europe*, ed. Renate Blumenfeld-Kosinski and Timea Szell (Ithaca: Cornell University Press, 1991); Bridget Cazelles, *The Lady as Saint: A Collection French Hagiographic Romances of the Thirteenth Century* (Philadelphia: University of Pennsylvania Press, 1991).

19. Many studies in the vast production of scholarly research on Latin and vernacular hagiography deal directly or indirectly with the issue of the saint's life as a vehicle for the expression and promotion of the ideological, theological and political orientation of their authors. See the following: Marie Anne Mayeski, "New Voices in the Tradition: Medieval Hagiography Revisited," *Theological Studies* 63, no. 4 (December 2002): 690–710; Thomas Head, ed., *Medieval Hagiography: An Anthology* (New York: Routledge, 2001); Anne B. Thompson, "Shaping a Saint's Life: Frideswide of Oxford," *Medium Aevum* 63, no. 1 (1994): 34–52; Jacques Dubois, *Sources et méthodes de l'hagiographie médiévale* (Paris: Editions du Cerf, 1993). For issues intrinsic to French vernacular hagiography, see François Laurent, *Plaire et Edifier: Les récits hagiographiques composés en Angleterre aux XIIe et XIIIe siècles* (Paris: Champion, 1998) and Duncan Robertson, *The Medieval Saints' Lives: Spiritual Renewal and Old French Literature* (Lexington KY: French Forum, 1995).

20. William Ray Ashford, *The Conception Nostre Dame of Wace* (Chicago: University of Chicago Press, 1933).

21. James T. Chiampi, "The *Vie de Saint Alexis* and the Weight of Paternity," *Romance Quarterly* 34, no. 2 (May 1987): 131–40.

22. Evelyn Birge Vitz, "The Impact of Christian Doctrine on Medieval Literature" in *The New History of French Literature*, ed. Denis Hollier (Cambridge: Harvard University Press, 1989): 13–18.

23. "Your mission is clear; it consists of sacrificing yourself for others, in repairing offenses that you have not committed; ...Say to Jesus: I want to place myself, by myself, on your cross and I want you to be the one to drive in the nails." Huysmans, *Sainte Lydwine*, 93.

24. On vicarious suffering in Huysmans' *Sainte Lydwine de Schiedam* and in other works, see C. J. T. Talar, "(Anti)-hagiography and Mysticism in the Work of J.-K. Huysmans," *Excavatio* IX (1997): 73–83; Richard Griffiths, *The Reactionary Revolution* (New York: Frederick Ungar, 1965), 149–222, and Joyce O. Lowrie, *The Violent Mystique: Thematics of Retribution and Expiation in Balzac, Barbey d'Aurevilly, Bloy and Huysmans* (Genève: Droz, 1974), 14–17 and 132–57.

25. Robert Baldick discusses at length the influence of the abbé Boullan on Huysmans' life in his *The Life of J.-K. Huysmans* (Oxford: Clarendon Press, 1955.) See also Maurice M. Belval, "Huysmans face à la réparation de Boullan" in his *Des Ténèbres à la lumière: Etapes de la pensée mystique de J.-K. Huysmans* (Paris: G.-P. Maisonneuve, 1968), 125–81.

26. C. J. T. Talar, "A Naturalistic Hagiography: J.-K. Huysmans' *Sainte Lydwine de Schiedam*," in *Sanctity and Secularity during the Modernist Period*, ed. L. Barmann and C. J. T. Talar (Bruxelles: Société des Bollandistes, 1999), 151–81.

27. On directing pain toward a clearly defined object, see Elaine Scarry, *The Body in Pain: The Making and Unmaking*

of the World (New York: Oxford University Press, 1985).

28. Baldick, *The Life of J.-K. Huysmans,* 350.

29. "The state of Europe, during the time of Lydwine's life, was appalling." Huysmans, *Sainte Lydwine,* 21.

30. "Confronted with such an overwhelming quantity of sacrilege and crime, with such an invasion of the cohorts of Hell, it seems likely that, in spite of their devotion and courage, Saint Lydwine, Saint Colette and Saint Françoise Romane would have succumbed, crushed by the sheer number of their enemies, if God had not raised armies to help them," 48.

31. "Jesus showed her, in a frightening vision, a panorama of her times.

Europe appeared to her as in a convulsion—as she was herself—on the bed of its land and she tried, with trembling hand, to draw over herself the cover of the seas, to hide the decomposing body which was nothing more than a magma of flesh, a silt of humors, a sediment of blood; for an internal putrefaction was bursting its flanks; a frenzy of sacrilege and crime made it scream like a beast being slaughtered; the vermin of its vices gnawed it to pieces; the cankers of simony, the cancers of lust that were eating it alive; and terrified, Lydwine beheld its crowned head tossed about, thrown back and forth between Avignon and Rome.

"See this." said Christ, and on a background of fire, she perceived, under the leadership of crowned fools, the abandoned masses. They were pitilessly murdering each other and pillaging their own land; in the distance, in those regions seemingly more tranquil, she contemplated the cloisters traumatized by the scheming of evil monks, by the clergy who trafficked in the flesh of Christ, who sold to the highest bidder the graces of the Holy Spirit; she came upon heresies, ceremonies of witches in the forests, black masses.

She would have died, if, in order to console her, God had not also shown her the compensation of the times which was an army of saints on the march. They traveled continually over the world, reforming abbeys, destroying the cult of Satan, taking into hand the masses and restraining the kings, passing, in spite of all obstacles, through storms of spitting and derision. And they all, whether contemplative or active, suffered too, and helped to pay the ransom of so much evil by their prayers and unbearable suffering! Faced with the immensity of the debt, she judged herself to be poor indeed!" 243–44.

32. "We must add that at the present time, the needs of the Church are immense; a wind of misfortune is blowing across the unprotected lands of the believers. There is a kind of subsidence of duty, a decline of zeal in those countries which are the spiritual fiefs of the Holy See.

Austria is gnawed to the bone by the Jewish vermin; Italy has become a Masonic haven, a harbor for demoniacs, in the strictest sense of the word; Spain and Portugal have also been chewed to bits by the Freemason Lodges; only little Belgium seems less decayed, of a faith less rancid, its soul healthier. As for the privileged nation of Christ, France, she has been attacked, half strangled, boot-kicked, rolled in the dung heap by a mercenary mob of miscreants. In order to accomplish this loathsome task, the Freemasons have unmuzzled the greedy riots of Israelites and Protestants." 274–75.

33. "The twentieth century begins in the same way that the preceding century ended, in an infernal eruption; the struggle has begun between Lucifer and God.

Truthfully, we must hope that to counterbalance the weight of so much challenge, there will an abundance of expiatory victims and that in the cloisters and in the world, many monks, priests and laity will accept to continue the reparative work of the holocausts." 276–77.

34. "The world was virtuous in time of old/ For then there was faith, and justice, and love;/ There was belief which today brings no credit/ The world has changed, it has lost its color:/ Never again will it be as it was in the days of our fathers./ In the time of Noah and in the time of Abraham,/ In the time of David whom God loved so much,/ The world was good; it never again will be worth as much;/ It is now old and frail, it is now in its decline,/ And it gets ever worse, and all virtue is ceasing to be." *La Vie de Saint Alexis*, ed. Christopher Storey (Genève: Droz, 1968), 92. See also Debora Schwartz, "Those Were the Days: The *Ubi Sunt* Topos in *La Vie de Saint Alexis*, *Yvain*, and *Le Bel Inconnu*," *Rocky Mountain Review of Language and Literature* XLIX, no. 1 (1995): 27–51.

35. Medieval eschatology has been the topic of a significant number of interesting studies in recent times. See especially: *The Use and Abuse of Eschatology in the Middle Ages*, ed. Werner Verbeke, et al. (Leuven: Leuven University Press, 1988); *The Apocalyptic Imagination in Medieval Literature*, ed. Richard K. Emmerson and Ronald B. Herzman (Philadelphia: University of Pennsylvania Press, 1992); *Last Things: Death and the Apocalypse in the Middle Ages*, ed. Caroline Walker Bynum and Paul Freedman (Philadelphia: University of Pennsylvania Press, 2000).

36. Elizabeth Emery, "Ecrire la fin: Sainte Lydwine de Schiedam de J.-K. Huysmans," *Les Cahiers Naturalistes* 75 (2001): 203–14.

37. Huysmans, *Sainte Lydwine*, 154–59.

38. "Whoever looks upon this writing/ May draw comfort and reassurance from it/ Just as that woman did in her death./ As you have often heard it told/ That she gave shelter to Jesus Christ,/ By this you must understand / That you must also be generous/ And such a thing as this do in your only life/ So that you may be assisted in your death." Bozon, *Three Saints' Lives*, 58.

39. "The horizon is black and all perspective is cut off. God, of whom the memory remains dominant, appears as an inexorable miracle worker who could cure you by a sign, but He is unwilling. ... It is pointless to tell ourselves, in a gleam of good sense, that we have sinned and that we are expiating our offenses, for one will conclude that the sum total of transgressions committed can never justify the accumulation of so much pain and we accuse our Lord of injustice and we dare to point out to Him the disproportion between our crimes and our punishment....

We then reproach ourselves for our arrogance and for His reprimands; we implore his pardon and a softening comes from this reconciliation; little by little, the idea of resignation to the will of the Savior is instilled in us and takes root—if the Devil, who is ever on the alert, does not intervene to uproot them ...." Huysmans, *Sainte Lydwine*, 85–86.

40. "Margaret, now think/ Of me, poor wretch, who have translated/ Your life and your passion./ May God grant me salvation,/ And that all those who hear or read / This story, may delight in it;/ This is the covenant made before./ Now let it be honored, if you please. / Amen." Bozon, *Three Saints' Lives*, 42.

41. "Now let us pray to this saint,/ Who suffered so much for God's sake,/ That she might petition our Lord/ That in the end he will show her honor/ By granting us everlasting joy/ With the most heavenly Father himself./ For

myself who go by the name of Rutebeuf/ Which is said as 'rude' and as 'beuf,'/ And who put this life into rhyme,/ May this most holy lady/ Pray to Him of whom she is the beloved/ That he not ever forget this Rutebeuf!/ Amen." *Œuvres Complètes de Rutebeuf*, ed. Edmond Faral et Julia Bastin (Paris: Picard, 1977), 2:58–59.

42. "Let us now pray to He that gives us glory,/ Where eternal bliss endures forever/ And that for the deeds of which we are guilty/ We not go into peril or into suffering/ Or lose our share of his sovereign joy,/ But we must accomplish deeds/ That will allow us to share in the sustenance/ And benefits of Paradise,/ With Jesus where he reigns and lives./ Amen." *La Vie de Saint Laurent*, ed. Delbert Russell (London: Anglo Norman Text Society, 1976), 58.

6

Discourse on Method: Hippolyte Delehaye's *Légendes hagiographiques*

C. J. T. Talar

> En ce temps on devient hérétique pour toucher aux légendes.[1]
> —Louis Duchesne, 1877

The nineteenth century was marked by an advance of a critical, historical consciousness in the various theological subdisciplines, primarily in biblical studies. New theories proved foundational—even paradigmatic—to the work of biblical scholarship in Old and New Testaments.[2] Critical methods were also applied by Protestant, Catholic and independent scholars to the study of church history (less threatening, in some quarters, than their use on biblical terrain) and to the closely allied field of hagiography. For some this advance could be construed as progress,[3] yet progress would certainly not adequately describe the fortunes of critical consciousness in nineteenth-century Roman Catholicism. Where hagiography is concerned, the century gives evidence of clear regression when contrasted with the accomplishments of the seventeenth century. This essay retrieves Dom Prosper Guéranger (1805–1875) as an exemplar of a return to a defense of the traditional hagiographical accounts that gathered momentum over the nineteenth century, reacting to the corrosive effects of criticism on those accounts. It examines the work of a group of Jesuit hagiographers, the Bollandists, who were carriers of a critical historical approach to the sources, and focuses on the work of one of their number, Hippolyte Delehaye (1859–

1941). Delehaye's *Les légendes hagiographiques* put forth, for a wider public, working principles and methods utilized by the Bollandists in their work. The hagiographical approaches of Guéranger and Delehaye reflect larger tendencies within nineteenth-century Catholicism, notably, the conflict between the *école légendaire* and the *école critique*.

Prosper Guéranger's *Histoire de sainte Cécile* (1849) may be taken as symptomatic of the change noted above, although he hardly equated an advance of critical consciousness with progress or considered a defense of the traditional accounts of the saints as regression. It is apparent from the book's preface that the revolutionary and anticlerical events of 1848 were very much on Guéranger's mind when composing it: He views the witness of early Christians as a source of instruction and encouragement for mid-nineteenth-century Catholics.[4] But, as the title indicates, he goes beyond the life and martyrdom of the saint to survey the history of devotion to her; nearly two-thirds of the book is given over to the latter. This affords him an opportunity to engage another apparent concern, the corrosive effects of rationalist criticism applied to the lives of the saints. Guéranger traces the roots of this critical approach to the seventeenth century, to the school of Jean de Launoy.[5] His primary target, however, is Sébastien le Nain de Tillemont. Guéranger devotes two full chapters to refuting Tillemont's arguments against the authenticity of the Acts of Saint Cecilia.[6] In doing so, Guéranger is working with one eye fixed firmly on the present. Tillemont's writings are "precursors of modern unbelief."[7] And, while Catholics at mid-nineteenth century may be "less inclined to this tendency toward rationalism which reigned supreme in hagiographical matters over the last two centuries," nonetheless, there remain those for whom lives of the saints are but "innocent fictions of a gracious and holy poetry" and for whom "legend" is accepted in the meaning it has among German Protestants.[8] From Guéranger's perspective, the real peril lies in the broader implications of such an attitude. Invoking a slippery slope argument, he fears that undermining belief in the "miraculous events" narrated in the lives of the saints, "faits annoncés et promis positivement par Jésus-Christ, et à l'aide desquels cette même Eglise apparaît sainte et divine," could well lead to apostasy.[9]

In *Histoire de sainte Cécile* Guéranger was careful to acknowledge the necessity of distinguishing true legends from false. But the *école légendaire*, the school of hagiography he represented, and whose influence he did much to establish, went beyond a tempering of what it regarded as an excessive skepticism by a "sound and impartial criticism."[10] It fostered a credulity which lacked, in practice, the discrimination Guéranger had called for in principle. This tendency is noteworthy in the controversy over the apostolic origins of French dioceses, a debate that pitted defenders of the claim that the Christian faith was preached in Gaul—and churches constituted hierarchically from the first century—against those who argued that Christianity did not really establish itself on any solid basis prior to the middle of the third century. Appeals to the apostolic pedigree of French dioceses were grounded on such legendary accounts as the evangelization of Aquitaine by Veronica and Zacchaeus or the identification of Denis of Paris with Denys the Areopagite. Opposition by critical scholars such as Duchesne to such attempts testified to the presence of an *école critique* as a force the *école légendaire* would need to reckon with.[11] Solesmes played an important role in these exchanges; its campaigns in support of the romanization of the liturgy worked to the community's credit with the Holy See, and Solesmes placed itself at the head of the movement to maintain the legends legitimating apostolic pedigree.[12]

In light of this, given Solesmes' influence and Guéranger's status, his *Sainte Cécile* may be taken not only as symptomatic, but as emblematic of the *école légendaire*. By the end of the nineteenth century, however, there were indications that this type of approach to the genre was losing its appeal, at least in some quarters. In an article taking its inspiration from Henri Joly's *Psychologie des Saints* (1897), George Tyrrell bears witness to this tendency:

> The old time-honoured Saint's Life, with its emphasis on the miraculous and startling features of the portrait, its suppression of what was natural, ordinary, and therefore presumably uninteresting, and consequently its abandonment of all attempt to weave the human and divine into one truthful and harmonious whole, showing the gradual evolution of the perfect from the imperfect, to many minds makes no appeal whatever.[13]

He identified a shift in reception as partially responsible for this change. On the secular side, "an advance in the art of biography in general," responding to the "subjective temper" of the times, reflected a desire to know the process of growth of character, to grasp the individuality of the subject. An exclusively laudatory account of a life, incorporating lists of generic virtues possessed by its subject, would thus lack interest. On the religious side, the lives of the saints served a practical purpose not characteristic of secular biography: It is not only a matter of knowing the saints, but being motivated to follow them. And for that motivation to be effective, the portrayal must be both sympathetic and imitable, at least to some degree.[14]

> We need less than formerly to be dazzled with the wonderful, and more to be drawn to the lovable. We want to be put *en rapport* with the Saints, to feel their humanity, to interpret it by our own, and thereby to realize that no miracle they ever wrought is comparable to the miracle of what they were.[15]

Tyrrell was also aware that there were pressures for change in hagiographical style on the productive side as well. A more scientific study of psychology and the growth of critical methods in history had altered the environment in which lives of the saints were written.[16] It is to this side of hagiography, with its engagement with critical method, that we now turn.

Seeing in the seventeenth century a shift away from the authority of tradition and classic works of the past and toward reliance on experiment, analysis and criticism, some scholars have discerned in it "the authentic beginnings of the modern world."[17] Guéranger's positioning of Launoy and Tillemont as precursors of modern unbelief falls in line with this way of thinking, although he tends to emphasize the negative side of modernity. In this respect, he is solidly in the mainstream of Roman Catholic reaction to modernity throughout much of the nineteenth century. The practice of criticism, however, was not monolithic during the seventeenth century, nor was Guéranger's judgment of it. The period had also seen the founding of the Bollandists, a small group of Jesuits organized for the critical study and publication of the lives of the saints. The initial inspiration came from Héribert Rosweyde (1569-1629), who conceived the idea of collecting hagiographical documents, purging them of the apocryphal and legendary details that obscured the historical figures of the saints and publishing a scholarly *Acta Sanctorum*. His design was realized by Jean Bolland (1596-1665), who shaped the work in collaboration with Godefroid Henschenius (1601-1681).[18] Guéranger had a high estimation of the *Acta*, calling it "... le plus magnifique monument que le génie catholique ait jamais consacré à l'honneur des Saints."[19] His reservations regarding criticism soon reasserted themselves, nonetheless. Two pages later he refers to the "excessive severity" of Henschenius' successor, Daniel Papebroch (1628-1714), which unintentionally contributed to the development of "certain extremely audacious tendencies."[20] Guéranger is able to turn this to his advantage, as Papebroch defended the antiquity and sincerity of the Acts of Saint Cecilia.

The first generations of Bollandists and their successors faced a formidable task. There were the intrinsic difficulties of the subject matter, well suggested by David Knowles:

The hagiographer is plunged at once into the nightmare of early medieval diplomatic and forgery, into all the tangled chronological difficulties of the *fasti* of half the sees of Europe, into the labyrinthine ways of martyrologies, necrologies and calendars, into the linguistic, social and psychological varieties of Christian sentiment—Greek, Persian, Egyptian, Syrian, Slav and Oriental, into the magical mists and colours of the Celtic wonderland, and into the changes and translations that lapse of centuries and popular devotion can bring about in a matter that is of its nature peculiarly dependent upon personal knowledge and popular acclaim.[21]

To which can be added a further level of difficulty stemming from the potential sensitivity of the subject matter as it impinged upon institutional sensibilities. Guéranger makes oblique reference to a case where Papebroch's "excessive severity" made him "the object of sharp recriminations in Catholic Europe."[22] Those sharp recriminations catalyzed by the Bollandist's work extended to the condemnation of the *Acta Sanctorum* of March, April and May by the Spanish Inquisition in 1695 as erroneous, offensive to pious ears, and even heretical. A similar denunciation was sought from Rome, with less success. In 1700 the introductory volume for May found its way onto the Roman Index of Forbidden Books, in view of certain sections on papal elections of the past.[23] Both of these censures stemmed from critical handling of hagiographical legends by the Bollandists. In the first case, in the course of his treatment of Saint Berthold (March) and Saint Albert of Jerusalem (April), Papebroch judged the Carmelite claim tracing the origins of that order back to the prophet Elijah, regarded as its founder, as lacking historical grounding. This unleashed a storm of controversy that lasted over a decade and led to the secret denunciation to the Inquisition and subsequent condemnation. The basis for the censure sought from Rome was more encompassing. The Belgian provincial of the Carmelites drew up a comprehensive catalog of legends that had not survived critical scrutiny in the *Acta* and turned to Innocent XII for redress. The years of controversy and efforts devoted to countering and overturning these measures had the dual effect of diverting Bollandist energies from their primary work and of markedly attenuating the critical edge of the succeeding generation of Bollandists.

To difficulties hagiographical and ecclesiastical can be added those arising from a third source: the political. The Society of Jesus was suppressed in 1773, not to be revived until 1814. This suppression, coupled with the impact of the French Revolution upon Catholicism and the unrest caused by the Napoleonic Wars, had predictably disastrous effects upon the fortunes of the Bollandists. They were able to continue their work for a time but eventually disbanded. They were re-formed in 1837, and volumes of the *Acta* again began appearing in 1845, after a lapse of half a century.[24] When publication resumed, reception was mixed. On the one hand, to some minds the conclusions proffered appeared overly timid when contrasted with the analytical commentary that underlay them. To others, by contrast, they manifested too little respect for tradition and were taken to task for being "too often hypercritical."[25] The second of these perspectives came to dominate perceptions of the Bollandists' work as the century progressed, and their efforts were assimilated into the *école critique*, which engaged in running controversy with the *école légendaire* on a series of issues.

This excursion into Bollandist history has been deliberately selective and is intended to establish a context for examining Hippolyte Delehaye's *Les légendes hagiographiques*.[26] Significant for understanding this work will be factors relating to the nature of hagiographical material and the impact upon it of critical methods refined in the course of the nineteenth century; the continuing sensitivity of such critical work, given the prevailing ecclesiastical climate conditioned by the modernist crisis; and the reinforcement of the defensive posture adopted by the Vatican in reacting to events surrounding the separation of Church and State in 1905.[27]

The nucleus of Delehaye's *Les légendes hagiographiques* (1905) appeared in the form of an article in the July 1903 *Revue des questions historiques*. That initial venue indicates its character as a work for a nonspecialist audience. The introduction to the book version shows that its author was well aware of the types of concerns reflected in Guéranger's *Sainte Cécile* over critical historical approaches to hagiography and took steps to allay them.

> Que de fois on a prononcé le mot de critique destructive, et traité d'iconoclastes ceux qui n'ont d'autres préoccupations que d'apprécier à leur juste valeur les monuments du culte des saints, heureux quand il leur est permis de dire qu'un de ces grands amis de Dieu a trouvé un historien digne de lui![28]

Throughout his introduction, Delehaye took care to emphasize the positive role of the historian. This was doubly prudent, given a genre driven by theological or devotional considerations and marked by a tendency to identify any departure from those with a "lack of faith" and given the nature of a study "mainly devoted to the weak points of hagiographical literature."[29] The aim of the book was consonant with Rosweyde's founding vision, which was to discriminate the apocryphal and the legendary from the historically reliable and provide a formulation of working methods that would meet with twentieth-century standards.[30]

As a work designed for a more general audience, Delehaye's *Légendes* invites comparison with another book of the same period, Marie-Joseph Lagrange's *La Méthode historique, surtout à propos de l'Ancien Testament*. Originally given as a series of lectures at the Toulouse Institut catholique, Lagrange's book was published early in 1903, the same year as the article which formed the core of the *Légendes*. The two books shared more than a style of *haute vulgarisation*; both were concerned with heightening awareness of the necessity of taking literary genre into account in the interpretive process. Both aimed at transcending a binary mentality—evident in both left and right wings of Catholic thought at the time—which equated myth or legend with falsity and history with factual truth. Delehaye begins his study by making a number of distinctions which are designed to position the "hagiographical document" as one "inspired by devotion to the saints and intended to promote it."[31] Hagiography's goal as edification, combined with its possible sources in popular tradition and in literary creation, give it a variable relationship to history:

> L'oeuvre de l'hagiographe peut être historique, mais elle ne l'est pas nécessairement. Elle peut revêtir toutes les formes littéraires propres à glorifier les saints, depuis la relation officielle adaptée à l'usage des fidèles jusqu'à la composition poétique la plus exubérante et la plus complètement dégagée de la réalité.[32]

Taking the pious literature of the Middles Ages as his primary focus, then, Delehaye proceeds to explore, first, how these accounts of the saints were elaborated by the people and, second, the contributions made by the hagiographers themselves to this process of development.

In the popular imagination, the names of saints are magnets that draw to themselves events that belong by right to their secular or other saintly namesakes. To take but one example, the better-known Cyprian of Carthage was the beneficiary of incidents borrowed from the life of his more obscure predecessor, Cyprian of Antioch.[33] Moreover, transposition of names can be further complicated by chronological and geographic confusion.[34]

It is unnecessary to follow Delehaye point by point through his survey of possible effects of the popular mind on the hagiographical legend (understood as "stories or incidents unauthenticated by history"[35]). Two dynamics of this mind set are worth noting briefly, however. On the one hand, saints are subject to a process of typification. The details of period, setting and individual personality recede in favor of an idealized figure, who embodies the requisite virtues and edifyingly overcomes the requisite trials. In contrast to hagiographical documents which preserve a greater measure of historical fact and are necessarily characterized by variation of detail, the legends manifest a repetitive sameness.

> Le martyr en général est partout animé des mêmes sentiments, exprime les mêmes pensées, est soumis aux mêmes épreuves; le saint confesseur qui a gagné le ciel par une vie édifiante doit avoir possédé toutes les vertus de son état, et l'hagiographe, écho fidèle de la tradition populaire, se complaît à les énumérer.[36]

There are floating traditions which, striking the popular imagination, are attached to multiple heroes in classical literature or are linked sometimes to one saint, sometimes to another (and on occasion may be found in both classical and Christian narratives).

Delehaye concludes his survey of the transposition of hagiographic details—of events in one saint's life to another of the same name, of topographical features to unlikely locales, of exemplary incidents shared out among idealized figures—by observing that entire narratives of the saints can become linked with one another, their histories intertwined imaginatively, giving rise to whole cycles of legends, such as those found among the Roman martyrs.[37]

Along with the tendency to abstract, to typify, to idealize, Delehaye identifies a countervailing source of popular elaboration in the desire to localize. It is a sort of "George Washington slept here" preoccupation, applied hagiographically. Beginning with identifications of places and artifacts made on the basis of accounts in both Old and New Testaments, analogous specifications are illustrated from the lives of the saints.[38] The upshot: Attempts to trace the itinerary of a saint by recourse to landmarks that figure in the legends have "not been precisely in the higher interests of history."[39]

If there is a popular propensity to conflate (names, places, events), there is also an inclination to inflate. This is nowhere more evident than in the case of visions, prophecies and miracles which assume so prominent a role in the lives of the saints. For the popular mind, the external manifestations of grace in the miraculous are of greater impact than its interior workings. Certainly, Delehaye is not insinuating a positivist denial of the miraculous *a priori*, but the overall emphasis of his treatment does tend to minimize its presence in the hagiographical narratives.

> L'imagination, surexcitée par la soif du merveilleux et l'ardeur de surpasser les récits extraordinaires par d'autres plus extraordinaires encore, n'a que trop souvent excédé la mesure dans un domaine où des horizons illimités s'ouvrent aux facultés créatrices.[40]

Another mode of inflation has been alluded to earlier, in the treatment of Guéranger and Solesmes. Legendary accounts provided the legitimation for attaching an apostolic pedigree to a number of French dioceses (a trend at work elsewhere in both western and eastern Christianity). Such claims can be said to rest more firmly on a popular desire for honor and self-glorification than on the basis of historical evidence. In short, for Delehaye, "Elles appartiennent à la catégorie des produits de formation légendaire, et ne sont que le développement normal des idées et des aspirations populaires en matière d'origines ecclésiastiques."[41]

Delehaye sums up the effects of the "unconscious mental processes of the people" upon the historicity of hagiographical accounts as leading "to a weakening and obscuring of historical testimony, sometimes even to its almost entire suppression."[42] In moving on to the work of the hagiographer, he again begins by making some careful distinctions. He makes it clear that his study orients him toward consideration of a certain class of hagiographer. Excluded are those who have left actual eyewitness accounts, as well as those writers who possess both talent and training to faithfully discharge the functions of historian—those last representatives of classical antiquity and their medieval imitators. He limits his attention to authors whose writings were composed at some temporal distance from the events they record and whose productions bear little tangible relation to the facts. Since the Acts of the Martyrs composed long after the persecutions (this point is emphasized) comprise the greater part of their literary output, Delehaye makes these his primary object of attention.

There are, first of all, those instances of pious tales composed as fictions to convey a religious truth or moral principle, and as such not intended to be taken as historical accounts. That they may be mistaken for the latter is one more illustration of the popular mind at work. Admittedly, this is a relatively small class of hagiographical productions; most hagiographers intend to write history. But the question immediately arises: What kind of history is understood? Further, how is the historian's task to be construed? Classical antiquity held—and from it, the Middle Ages inherited—no very sharp distinction between history and rhetoric.

> Ce qui est pour nous l'accessoire est mis par les anciens au premier rang. Leurs historiens ont, avant tout, le souci de l'effet littéraire; la vérité des faits les préoccupe un peu moins, l'exactitude à peine, et de la critique ils n'ont, le plus souvent, pas même l'idée. Il s'agit principalement de plaire au lecteur par l'intérêt de la narration, la beauté des descriptions et l'éclat du style.[43]

Less than surprisingly, prefaces to the lives of the saints are frequently preoccupied with style, while questions of historicity are either ignored or glossed over with affirmations of sincerity. Where such lives are perceived to require reworking, they will be improved by paying greater attention to their style, rather than by critically reviewing the evidence. Moreover, this more generalized attitude toward history is, after all, applied to a genre that combines biography with panegyric and moral instruction. This motivates a certain selectivity in such narratives, as the idealization of its subject can lead to the suppression of material which does not serve those ends.

These more general orientations to the subject matter on the hagiographer's part interact with and elaborate further the material supplied by popular tradition. The taste for the marvelous is evident where a simpler version of the acts of a saint (often enough to be found in a single copy) can be compared with multiply attested manuscripts replete with the fantastic and the fabulous. Such comparisons verify the neglect of sober history in favor of those aspects which are continuous with the interest in the extraordinary displayed by the people. What is evident in the choice of sources is confirmed by their mode of employment. The miraculous is not only emphasized; it is enlarged upon. Beasts in the arena exhibit deferential behavior toward those about to be martyred, allusions to actual journeys are elaborated with fairy-tale like details, a saint's assistance to a man rendered unconscious becomes a resurrection from the dead.[44]

If the existence of documentary sources so little checks the hagiographer's imagination, how much more scope is accorded it when the sole basis of a saint's memory is a name, a status (martyr, confessor, bishop or monk) and a shrine? In these sorts of cases Delehaye notes that the hagiographer's task is assisted by the existence of schemas: template outlines which can be peopled with stock characters (the emperor or judge ruthlessly bent on extinguishing the faith), filled in with standard themes (the superiority of Christianity over paganism) and capped off with selections from a standard repertoire of trials and sufferings. Such narratives may even contain wholesale borrowings from accounts of other saints, even to the point of word for word reproduction. The legends of the saints become common property, to be used by convention in good conscience to supplement the silence of the tradition.[45]

In the course of his exposition Delehaye reiterates that he is dealing with a certain class of compositions, to be distinguished—and distinguishable—from those of historical worth. In the case of the Acts of the Martyrs, for example, authentic accounts exhibit clear rhetorical differences from hagiographical fabrications.

Delehaye rounds off his book[46] by using the principles he has established to expose some of the pitfalls and errors to which hagiographers have fallen prey. Attention is given to both insufficiently critical and hypercritical approaches.[47] In the midst of this discussion there emerges a brief statement of the aims of Bollandist labors:

> Ils se sont abstenus, généralement, d'essayer de résoudre les questions insolubles, regardant comme une tâche suffisante de classer les textes hagiographiques, de les publier scrupuleusement, de faire connaître avec toute l'exactitude possible leur provenance, leurs sources, leur allure, et, s'il se peut, de caractériser le talent, la moralité et la probité littéraire de leurs auteurs.[48]

Aims seemingly modest enough, but sufficiently threatening to plunge their work into controversy in the seventeenth century, and more than sufficient to cause difficulties at the end of the nineteenth. Having given a more adequate idea of the first of the three factors complicating the work of the hagiographer raised earlier (the intrinsic difficulties of the subject matter) it is possible to pass on to the second, its sensitivity as it impinged upon institutional sensibilities.

The Bollandists formally claimed Delehaye in 1891, a period of intellectual ferment in French Catholicism. By then Louis Duchesne had already caused unrest by his critical research into church history, and Alfred Loisy had recently begun a long series of publications which would carry critical methods into biblical studies. Two years later, in 1893, the encyclical *Providentissimus Deus* provided early signs of Vatican unease over some of the directions such renewal was taking. More publications of a reformist tenor would follow, as would Roman countermeasures. The story of Roman Catholic Modernism, the intellectual currents that fed it and the ecclesiastical measures taken to check and eventually suppress it has been the subject of a number of recent publications.[49] Here, only a few incidents which have a direct bearing on the work of the Bollandists need be noted.

The critical hagiography undertaken by the Bollandists, especially under the leadership of Charles de Smedt,[50] contributed to the work of intellectual renewal and was affected by a climate it helped create. The application of modern critical methods by the Bollandists, evident in their own publications as well as in their reviews of others, rendered them suspect to some of their fellow Jesuits and to a number of influential cardinals. A presentation made at the International Scientific Congress of Catholics, held in Munich in 1900, proved catalytic in turning suspicion into sanction. In an address calling for a rigorous reexamination of the historical value of popular traditions, the Jesuit Hartmann Grisar, professor at the University of Innsbruck, spoke to a number of matters which bore upon the work of the Bollandists. His main target was a hyperconservatism in the critical evaluation of such traditions, citing the need to reassess both the poetic legends which had supplanted the authentic Acts of Martyrs and more generally the pious naiveté of the Middle Ages—a proposition which led to suspicions of Bollandist inspiration of the Innsbruck Jesuit's discourse. The outcome of *l'affaire Grisar* was to institute a new regime of censorship of the publications of the Bollandists. Beyond the three censors drawn from the ranks of the Bollandists, who had previously surveyed the content of their productions, additional censorship at the provincial level and at Rome itself were inaugurated to pass judgment on whether publication would be opportune. Among the reasons cited for this extraordinary measure were a certain rationalist spirit detectable in their writings, a lack of respect toward directives given by different popes with regard to the study of the lives of the saints and the Roman Martyrology and an excessive severity directed toward works by Catholic authors while overpraising those issuing from heterodox sources.[51] It was in this climate that Delehaye published in 1903 his article in the *Revue des questions historiques*, perhaps in part to counter the unfavorable impressions that had stiffened institutional controls.

The third of the contextual factors bearing upon *Les légendes hagiographiques* engages the political arena, most proximately the events surrounding the separation of Church and State in France. Writing from the perspective of a contemporary observer, Paul Sabatier positioned it as less "a case of two opposing parties" as "two antithetical conceptions of life"—indeed, a clash of opposing civilizations.[52] The Vatican would not have disagreed, although it evaluated those two opposed civilizations differently than Sabatier. At work, from the Roman viewpoint, was the political expression of the theological issues raised by the practice of critical history. The modern spirit of autonomy, evident in Loisy's biblical exegesis, Duchesne's study of Christian origins, Delehaye's hagiography and Maurice Blondel's philosophy of action, was also evident in the French government's insistence that the Church renounce its claims to control political life. Intellectual challenges from within the church were perceived as even more dangerous than the anticlerical attacks coming from without. The implications for the hagiographical work of interest here is well set forth by Harvey Hill.

> Even after the immediate urgency of separation began to wane, ecclesiastical leaders remained in a defensive posture, suspicious of criticism from any source. As a result, when Vatican theologians

returned to the theological questions raised by Loisy and others, they interpreted them in the context of the recent French outrages against the Church.[53]

The ensuing condemnations of Modernism in 1907 were severe and had a chilling effect on Catholic scholarship for decades. While at the time of its publication in 1905 *Les légendes hagiographiques* for the most part received favorable notice, by 1912 it was being denounced to the Roman Index. Although the book escaped this form of censure, the following year it suffered the stigma of being prohibited from use in Italian seminaries.[54] Other hagiographical productions did not fare as well. Henri Bremond's *Sainte Chantal* (1912) was placed on the Index only a few months prior to the prohibition issued against the *Légendes*.[55]

Since we began this study with a discussion of Saint Cecilia in Guéranger's *Histoire*, revisiting hagiographical work on her will allow us to particularize some of the methodological principles surveyed in Delehaye's book and will provide a fitting conclusion to this essay. In his *Histoire de sainte Cécile*, Guéranger accepted the historicity of the events recounted in her Acts, which dated from the fifth century, more than 250 years after the events they describe.[56] In brief outline, Cecilia, a devout Christian of a noble Roman family, had consecrated herself to virginity. She converses with an angel, who serves as her protector. Forced to marry despite her religious convictions, on her wedding night she reveals her secret to her husband, Valerian, promising him the grace and favor of her angel if he respects her promise, and warning him of sanctions if he does not. After receiving baptism from Pope Urban, Valerian, too, sees the angel and with his wife receives garlands of roses and lilies as a sign of their commitment to chastity. Tiburtius, Valerian's brother, calls upon them and is able to smell the miraculously bestowed flowers, but in accord with the angel's words, cannot see them. He is converted by his brother's confession of faith and also receives baptism. The exemplary lives of Valerian and Tiburtius—and above all their assuming the work of burying Christian victims of persecution—attracts the notice of the city's prefect. They are brought before him, interrogated and condemned to death for remaining steadfast in their faith. Their witness converts the soldier Maximus, charged with their execution, together with his retinue. At their martyrdom, Maximus is granted a vision of angels bearing the souls of Valerian and Tiburtius up to heaven. He, in turn, is condemned to death for professing Christianity. The prefect's attention next turns to Cecilia, who is summoned and courageously stands up for her beliefs. He orders that she be scalded to death in a hot bath in her home, but she is miraculously preserved, to the point of exhibiting not even a drop of sweat during the ordeal. The prefect then decrees that she be beheaded, but when Cecilia receives the maximum three strokes specified by law and does not succumb, she is left half dead. In this state she lives three days, edifying the people with her holy teaching and exhorting them to remain steadfast in the faith. Upon her death she receives from Pope Urban the special favor of being buried in the same place as popes. In accord with her wish, Cecilia's home is consecrated into a church and becomes the site of numerous miracles.

Shortly after the publication of Guéranger's *Sainte Cécile*, archaeological discoveries made by Giovanni Battista de Rossi appeared to support claims for the essential veracity of the traditional account. De Rossi's excavations rediscovered the crypt of the popes and, adjacent to it, a crypt ornamented with paintings of Saint Cecilia. According to later tradition, the martyr's body had been removed to the church in Trastevere erected over the site of her house. De Rossi's find substantiated the fifth-century narrative's placement of her burial among the popes, and agreed with other documentary evidence from the sixth and seventh centuries linking it to the cemetery of Saint Callistus. In *Sainte Cécile et la société romaine aux deux premiers siècles* (1873), Guéranger made use of de Rossi's work to renew the assault on the "unprecedented brazenness of German criticism,"[57] both with respect to the saint and the portrait of early Christianity more largely. Though altering his opinion on some matters of chronology and correcting his earlier book in some matters of detail, Guéranger held fast to the fundamental authenticity of the Acts of Cecilia, judging it to incorporate earlier documents that were interpolated into its narrative and confirmed in its minutest details by archaeological facts. Though subject to correction on very secondary points, the Acts are held up as "un document grave, important, accepté par la plus haute autorité, sanctionné par les siècles, et s'encadrant parfaitement avec les événements de l'époque à laquelle se rattache le récit."[58]

In the *Légendes* Delehaye showed himself less accepting. In the sole reference to the Acts of Saint Cecilia made in the course of his exposition he cautions against moving from a discernment of apparently secondary material on the basis of internal comparison of style, to the conclusion that the remainder belongs to really primitive documents of intrinsic value. Such stylistic differences may be more reflective of an ability to reproduce the technical vocabulary and the phrasing of an earlier model than the presence of an original document interpolated by a later compiler.[59] The confidence manifested by Guéranger in *Les actes des martyrs depuis l'origine de l'église chrétienne jusqu'à nos temps* (1856), in which he alleges that fifth- and sixth-century editors, "writing under the very eyes of the bishops, would certainly have abstained from introducing into their narrative any important circumstances up to that time unknown to the people,"[60] cannot be sustained. Delehaye counters, "On suppose, ce qu'il faut démontrer dans chaque cas particulier, que les passions de basse époque dérivent directement 'd'antiques et vénérables récits de l'âge précédent.' Nous savons combien rarement l'hypothèse se vérifie."[61]

In the course of a short review of J. P. Kirsh's *Die heilige Caecilia in der römischern kirche des Altertums* (1910), published in the *Analecta Bollandiana* the following year, Delehaye noted the "insurmountable difficulties" in reconciling the various elements (documentary, liturgical and archaeological) pertaining to Saint Cecilia.[62] In his judgment, the events surrounding the martyrdoms of Valerian, Tiburtius and Maximus originally circulated as an independent tradition and were incorporated into Cecilia's account (consonant with the sorts of borrowings he had illustrated earlier in the *Légendes*). Moreover, he suggested that the basilica in the Transtevere, dedicated to Saint Cecilia, was originally connected with another person of that same name, becoming assimilated into the Cecilia whose martyrdom is recounted in the Acts.[63]

Only in 1936 would Delehaye publish his own attempt to resolve some of the difficulties to which he referred in his review of Kirsh. In marked contrast to Guéranger's confidence the century before, the Bollandist judged the case of Saint Cecilia "peut-être le sujet le plus embrouillé dans toute l'hagiographie romaine."[64] In his discussion he expands upon the brief observations made in the earlier review, raises further problems in need of resolution, and at one point remarks that the double crown of roses and lilies referred to in the Acts has been conferred by an unauthoritative hagiographer rather than an angel.[65] Since this study lies outside the temporal limits of this volume, its details will not be pursued here. But it is worth noting that Delehaye was able to marshal his own archaeological evidence to buttress his contention that the Acts of Saint Cecilia belonged more to the realm of pious fiction than edifyingly retouched history. In 1935 Paul Styger made a convincing case for a revision of de Rossi's dating of Cecilia's crypt in Saint Callistus. It had not been constructed, as had been thought, during the persecutions, but belonged in its entirety to a period after the Peace of the Church. Styger's work played a key role in Delehaye's evaluation of the various elements surrounding Cecilia's cult. Neither the documentary tradition nor the archaeological evidence possessed the factual solidity attributed them by Guéranger. While the material gleaned from the *Légendes* has clarified difficulties with hagiographical documents, Thomas Connolly's remarks address the impact of archaeology:

A historical meditation about Cecilia made at her crypt in St. Callistus is thus hardly likely to be the peaceful reflection one might wish: doubts and questions simply will intrude. The situation is no better at the Trastevere basilica, the reputed site of her house and of the scene of her martyrdom. Recent archaeological judgment has allowed not a single stone from these two monuments, the catacomb and the basilica, to be advanced as evidence for the saint's existence.[66]

The importance of the Bollandists, Delehaye among them, accords his work a certain prominence during the latter portion of the period covered by this volume, congruent with the time of the so-called Modernist crisis in Roman Catholicism. Delehaye's work in hagiography, when coupled with that of like-minded church historians and joined by offerings of critical biblical exegetes, appeared as part of a broader revisionist front, corrosive of Catholic tradition. In his review of Delehaye's *Légendes*, Marcel Hébert observed, "Il est assez piquant de voir un jésuite 'dénicher' des saints."[67] More ominously, he predicted that other scholars would take a step that Delehaye himself had not and would apply the same methods used in exposing the legendary character of hagiographical narratives to the gospel texts. In fact, as he noted, that work had already begun in the efforts of Loisy:

> Après les pages du Père Delehaye, lisez l'Etude de l'Abbé Loisy sur le quatrième Evangile; Loisy fait-il autre chose qu'appliquer à cet écrit des règles de critique identiques à celles du bollandiste? Et le quatrième Evangile apparaît-il alors ce qu'il est en réalité, non pas une histoire, mais une admirable *vision mystique*.[68]

The threats perceived to issue from critical historical methods, augmented by others both intellectual and political, elicited countermeasures which had a notably dampening effect on Catholic scholarship. Although Louis Duchesne was known for possessing a mordant wit, his comment which forms the epigraph to this chapter does not lack force, given the repressive measures applied against those seen to depart from standards of orthodoxy.

Notes

1. "These days one becomes a heretic by questioning legends." Letter of Louis Duchesne to Giovanni Battista de Rossi, 19 June 1877, quoted in Brigitte Waché, *Monseigneur Duchesne (1843–1922)* (Rome: École française de Rome, 1992), 79. Ordained priest in 1867, Duchesne specialized in the history of the early church.

He served as professor at the Institut catholique of Paris (1877–1895) and at the École pratique des hautes études (1885–1895) before becoming director of the École française de Rome from 1895 until his death. A proponent of a critical approach to church history, one of his major works, the *Histoire ancienne de l'église* (3 vol., 1906–1910), was placed on the Index in 1912.

2. Among the "assured results of criticism" subscribed to by biblical scholars were the Graf-Wellhausen theories, after Karl Heinrich Graf (1815–1869) and Julius Wellhausen (1844–1918). This approach identified several distinguishable layers of tradition in the first six books of the Old Testament, with revisionist implications for an understanding of Israel's history. The entire issue of *Semeia* 25 (1982) is dedicated to *Julius Wellhausen and His "Prolegomena to the History of Israel."* In New Testament scholarship the Markan hypothesis argued for the gospel according to Mark as the oldest among the gospels and the dependence of Matthew and Luke upon it. Heinrich Julius Holtzmann (1832–1910) became a prominent exponent of Markan priority. For the story of its reception and significance for the study of the synoptic gospels see Henning Graf Reventlow and William Farmer, eds. *Biblical Studies and the Shifting of Paradigms 1850–1914* (Sheffield: Sheffield Academic Press, 1995).

3. Witness, for example, the title given to the English translation of Albert Schweitzer's *Von Reimarus zu Wrede: Geschichte der Leben-Jesu-forschung*: *The Quest for the Historical Jesus: A critical Study of Its Progress from Reimarus to Wrede*, a judgment on the translator's part that is at variance with the book's actual contents. "Schweitzer's translator, W. Montgomery, and perhaps also Francis Crawford Burkitt (1864–1935), who provided the introduction to the English translation in 1910, might have thought Schweitzer's history of nineteenth century research as 'progress', but for Schweitzer, in 1906, his history of research from Reimarus to Wrede was mostly a series of derailments of the train of scholarship that he wished to get back on track." David Barrett Peabody, "H.J. Holtzmann and his European Colleagues: Aspects of the Nineteenth-Century European Discussion of Gospel Origins" in Reventlow and Farmer, eds., 50–131, citing 122.

4. Dom Prosper Guéranger, *Histoire de sainte Cécile* (Tournai: J. Casterman, 1851), vii–viii. An English translation was published as *Life of Saint Cecilia, Virgin and Martyr* (Philadelphia: Peter F. Cunningham, 1866), which does not include Guéranger's preface. Translations from the *Histoire* are by C. J. T. Talar. On Guéranger see [Dom Paul Delatte], *Dom Guéranger, abbé de Solesmes*. 2 vols. (Paris: Plon-Nourrit, 1909); Cuthbert Johnson, *Prosper Guéranger (1805–1875): A Liturgical Theologian* (Rome: Pontifico Ateneo S. Anselmo, 1984).

5. Through his extensive critical work, de Launoy (1603–1678) earned the reputation of "dénicheur de saints." See *Dictionnaire de théologie* 9 (1926): cols. 2–6.

6. Tillemont gained renown for his monumental *Mémoires pour servir à l'histoire ecclésiastique des six premiers siècles* (16 vols., 1693–1712). The evaluation of the Acts in question is contained in Volume 3. See Bruno Neveu, *Un historien à l'école de Port-Royal: Sébastien le Nain de Tillemont 1637–1698* (Le Haye: Martinus Nijhoff, 1966). Guéranger's counterarguments may be found in *Histoire*, 366–94.

7. Guéranger, *Histoire*, 348. Cf. 385.

8. Guéranger, *Histoire*, xxiii. "Les catholiques d'aujourd'hui sont, il faut l'avouer, moins enclins à cette tendance au rationalisme qui régna en souveraine, sur les matières hagiographiques, durant

les deux siècles qui viennent de s'écouler." And "... ces récits ne sont à leurs yeux que les fictions innocentes d'une gracieuse et sainte poésie."

9. "... notre siècle ... finirait par perdre de vue l'essentiel argument que l'Eglise catholique emprunte de la permanence des faits miraculeux dans son sein, faits annoncés et promis positivement par Jésus-Christ, et à l'aide desquels cette même Eglise apparaît sainte et divine." Guéranger, *Histoire*, xxiii–xxiv. Guéranger amplified these concerns in a series of articles which appeared in *L'Univers* in 1858 and were republished as *Le sens chrétien de l'histoire* (Paris: Librairie Plon, 1945). See especially Ch. III: "Les devoirs de l'historien chrétien."

10. *Histoire*, 361.

11. This controversy is surveyed by Albert Houtin in his *Controverse de l'apostolicité des Églises de France au XIXe siècle* (1901, 1903).

12. See C. J. T. Talar, "Pious Legend and 'Pious Fraud': Albert Houtin (1867–1926) and the Controversy over the Apostolic Origins of the Churches of France" in L. Barmann and C. J. T. Talar, eds, *Sanctity and Secularity during the Modernist Period* (Bruxelles: Société des Bollandistes, 1999): 47–65.

13. George Tyrrell, "What is Mysticism?" [1897] in his *The Faith of the Millions*, 1st series, (Longmans, Green & Co., 1902), 253–72, citing 253. Tyrrell provided the preface to the English translation of Joly's book, *The Psychology of the Saints* (London: Duckworth, 1898), vii–xii.

14. Tyrrell, "What Is Mysticism?" 253–354.

15. Tyrrell, "What Is Mysticism?" 258.

16. Tyrrell, preface to *The Psychology of the Saints*, viii.

17. David Knowles, *Great Historical Enterprises* (London: Thomas Nelson, 1962), 3.

18. The most authoritative accounts of the Bollandists have come from within their own ranks. See Hippolyte Delehaye, *L'oeuvre des Bollandistes à travers trois siècles. 1615–1915* (Bruxelles: Société des Bollandistes, 1959) and Paul Peeters, *L'oeuvre des Bollandistes* [1942] (Bruxelles: Palais des Académies, 1961).

19. "... The most magnificent monument that Catholic genius has ever devoted to the honor of the Saints." Guéranger, *Histoire*, 350.

20. "... Ce critique redoubtable dont la sévérité outrée, nous ne devons pas craindre de le dire, contribua, plus qu'il ne pouvait le croire, à développer certaines tendances trop hardies." Guéranger, *Histoire*, 352.

21. Knowles, 9.

22. "... l'objet de vives recriminations dans l'Europe catholique ..." Guéranger, *Histoire*, 353.

23. Efforts by the Jesuits succeeded in having the decree of condemnation issued by the Spanish Inquisition revoked in 1715—the year following Papebroch's death. The offending volume which had been indexed was not removed until 1900. As a backdrop to these measures it must be noted that the end of the seventeenth century saw the Jesuits involved in multiple controversies over Jansenism, Probabilism, Quietism and Gallicanism, which earned the Society multiple enemies.

24. On these events see Peeters, *L'oeuvre des Bollandistes*, Ch. III–VIII.

25. See Charles de Smedt, "Bollandists" in *The Catholic Encyclopedia* 2 (1907), 630–39, citing 638.

26. Hippolyte Delehaye, born in Antwerp (and thus a fellow townsman of Papebroch), entered the Society of Jesus as a novice in 1876. His early publications brought him to the attention of the Bollandists and after completion of his studies and ordination he was formally assigned to the work in 1891. He assumed

the presidency of the Society of Bollandists in 1912, retaining it until his death. A bibliography of his work can be found in Bernard Joassart, *Hippolyte Delehaye. Hagiographie critique et modernisme* (Bruxelles: Société des Bollandistes, 2000), 23–39. A short account of Delehaye's career appears in Paul Peeters, *Figures bollandiennes contemporaines* (Paris: P. Lethielleux, 1948), republished in English translation in Hippolyte Delehaye, *The Legends of the Saints* Trans. Donald Attwater. (New York: Fordham University Press, 1962), 187–226.

27. Harvey Hill shows the interaction of criticism in relationship to Roman Catholic modernism and French politics as those contexts impacted the career of a prominent French Catholic scholar who promoted the use of critical historical methods in biblical and historical studies. See Harvey Hill, *The Politics of Modernism: Alfred Loisy and the Scientific Study of Religion*. (Washington DC: The Catholic University of America Press, 2002).

28. "How often has not an accusation of destructive criticism been flung, and men treated as iconoclasts, whose sole object has been to appraise at their true value the documents which justify our attitude of veneration, and are only too happy when able to declare that one of God's friends has been fortunate enough to find a historian worthy of his task." Hippolyte Delehaye, *The Legends of the Saints: An Introduction to Hagiography.* Trans. V. M. Crawford (London: Longmans, Green, and Co., 1907), viii. (Since Attwater's translation, referenced in n. 26, was made on the basis of a third, revised edition of *Les légendes hagiographiques*, Crawford's translation, made from the second edition [1906] will be used here.) Hippolyte Delehaye, *Les légendes hagiographiques* (Bruxelles: Société des Bollandistes, 1906), viii.

29. *Legends*, viii, ix. "Il ne sera pas inutile de prémunir, dès à présent, le lecteur contre une impression qui pourrait se dégager d'un travail où l'on s'occupe surtout des côtés faibles de la littérature hagiographique." *Légendes*, viii, ix.

30. "To indicate briefly the spirit in which hagiographic texts should be studied, to lay down the rules for discriminating between the materials that the historian can use and those that he should hand over as their natural property to artists and poets, to place people on their guard against the fascination of formulas and preconceived systems, such has been the aim of this volume." *Legends*, xi. "Exposer sommairement dans quel esprit il faut lire les textes hagiographiques, indiquer la méthode à suivre pour discerner les matériaux que l'historien peut en retirer et ce qu'il doit abandonner, comme leur bien propre, aux artistes et aux poètes, mettre en garde contre l'entraînement des formules et des systèmes préconçus, tel est le but de ce travail." *Légendes*, x–xi.

31. *Legends*, 2. "Il faudra donc réserver ce nom [le document hagiographique] à tout monument écrit inspiré par le culte des saints, et destiné à le promouvoir." *Légendes*, 2.

32. *Légendes*, 2. "The work of the hagiographer may be historical, but it is not necessarily so. It may assume any literary form suitable to the glorification of the saints, from an official record adapted to the use of the faithful, to a poetical composition of the most exuberant character wholly detached from reality." *Legends*, 2.

33. *Legends*, 20. *Légendes*, 23.

34. See *Legends*, 20–21, *Légendes*, 24 for examples.

35. *Legends*, 11. "… le nom de légende s'appliquera toujours à un récit ou à un trait non conforme à l'histoire." *Légendes*, 12.

36. *Légendes*, 28. "Every martyr, as a

rule, is animated by the same sentiments, expresses the same opinions and is subject to the same trials, while the holy confessor who has earned his reward by an edifying life must needs have possessed all the virtues of his profession, which the hagiographer, the faithful mouthpiece of popular tradition, delights to enumerate." *Legends*, 24–25.

37. *Legends*, 38–39. *Légendes*, 44–45.

38. *Legends*, 41–45. *Légendes*, 47–51.

39. *Legends*, 45. "... ce n'a point précisément été au grand profit de l'histoire." *Légendes*, 51.

40. *Légendes*, 58. "The imagination, overexcited by the craving for the marvelous, and possessed by a burning desire to outstrip one extraordinary narrative by another more extraordinary still, has only too frequently overstepped all bounds in a region in which an unlimited field appears to open out before the creative faculties." *Legends*, 51.

41. *Légendes*, 64. "They belong to the category of products of legendary growth, and constitute only the normal development of popular ideas and aspirations in the matter of ecclesiastical origins." *Legends*, 56.

42. *Legends*, 60. "Le résultat de l'élaboration inconsciente des récits relatifs aux saints par le cerveau populaire aboutit, nous l'avons constaté, à affaiblir le témoignage de l'histoire, à l'obscurcir, souvent à le supprimer presque totalement." *Légendes*, 68.

43. *Légendes*, 74–75. "What for us is merely accessory, for the ancients was the very essence. Then historians had regard, above all else, to literary effect; material truth troubled them less, accuracy scarce at all, and of the critical spirit they had, as a rule, no conception whatever. The main thing was to give pleasure to the reader by the interest of the narrative, the beauty of the descriptions and the brilliancy of the style." *Legends*, 65.

44. See *Legends*, 78–91. *Légendes*, 89–102.

45. *Legends*, 91–106. *Légendes*, 103–20.

46. Following treatment of the work of the hagiographer, Delehaye devotes chapters to the classification of texts, to exemplifying how documents are evaluated by examining a particular saint's "dossier" and to the relation between Christian hagiographical accounts and pagan materials (a topical question at the time of his book's writing). Since these lie outside the scope of present interests, they are passed over here.

47. After describing the excesses of both of these approaches, René Aigrain credits Delehaye with working out a judicious median between the two. See his *L'Hagiographie, ses sources, ses méthodes, son histoire* (Paris: Bloud & Gay, 1953), 247–55.

48. *Légendes*, 246. "As a general rule they have abstained from attempting to solve insoluble problems, holding it to be a sufficient task to classify the hagiographic texts, to print them with scrupulous care, to make known with all attainable exactitude, their origin, their sources, their style, and if possible to pronounce upon the talent, the morality and the literary probity of their authors." *Legends*, 218.

49. Pierre Colin, *L'audace et le soupçon: La crise de modernisme dans le catholicisme français (1893-1914)* (Paris: Desclée de Brouwer, 1997) provides extensive coverage of Modernism in France. In English consult Darrell Jodock, ed., *Catholicism Contending with Modernity: Roman Catholic Modernism and Anti-Modernism in Historical Context* (Cambridge: Cambridge University Press, 2000), which extends its scope beyond France, as does Gabriel Daly, *Transcendence and Immanence: A Study in Catholic Modernism and Integralism* (Oxford: Clarendon Press, 1980).

50. Charles de Smedt (1831–1911) was responsible for setting the work of the Bollandists on a firmer critical footing, given advances in methodology made in

the nineteenth century. Greater importance was given to primary sources in the *Acta Sanctorum*, and he inaugurated the periodical *Analecta Bollandiana*. See Peeters, 95–102.

51. For additional background on *l'affaire Grisar* and its aftermath see Joassart, 143–79. This regime of censorship was not lifted until 1920.

52. Paul Sabatier, *Disestablishment in France*, Trans. Robert Dell (London: T. Fisher Unwin, 1906), 59.

53. Hill, 191–92.

54. For particulars of the antimodernist campaign waged against the *Légendes* and the interventions made on its behalf, see Joassart, 261–316.

55. On this episode see André Blanchet, *Histoire d'une mise à l'index: la "Sainte Chantal" de l'Abbé Bremond* (Paris: Aubier, 1967).

56. The preface to the English translation states, "The author has followed with fidelity, the ancient Acts of St. Cecilia, the authenticity of which the reader will find satisfactorily defended in his pages." *Life of Saint Cecilia*, iii.

57. Dom Prosper Guéranger, *Sainte Cécile et la société romaine aux deux premiers siècles* (Paris: Société générale de librairie catholique, 1884), vii.

58. "... a serious, important document, accepted by the highest authority, sanctioned by time, and fitting perfectly with the events of the period to which its narrative refers." Guéranger, *Sainte Cécile*, 430. The substantial accuracy of the Acts of Saint Cecilia still finds twentieth-century defenders. See Warren H. Carroll, "The Reality of St. Cecilia: An Historical Note" in *Faith and Reason* 10 (1984): 36–43.

59. *Legends*, 122–24. *Légendes*, 139–41.

60. Guéranger quoted in *Legends*, 221. "Les nouveaux rédacteurs, écrivant sous les yeux des évêques, se seraient gardés, sans doute, d'introduire dans leur narration des circonstances importantes, qui jusqu'alors auraient été inouïes du peuple fidèle." *Légendes*, 249.

61. Idem. "It is assumed, what has to be proved in every individual case, that the Passions of a debased age were, in fact, derived directly from 'ancient and venerable narratives of an earlier century,' whereas we know how rarely the hypothesis can be verified."

62. "Par quelque côté que l'on envisage l'histoire du culte de Ste Cécile, on se heurte partout à des difficultés insurmontables." *Analecta Bollandiana* XXX (1911): 361–62, citing 361.

63. Delehaye reiterated these judgments, made in the course of this review, in his *Les origines du culte des martyrs* (Bruxelles: Société des Bollandistes, 1912), 324, 340.

64. "... perhaps the most tangled subject in all Roman hagiography." Hippolyte Delehaye, *Étude sur le légendier romain Les saints de novembre et de décembre*. (Bruxelles: Société des Bollandistes, 1936), 74.

65. Delehaye, *Étude*, 86.

66. Thomas Connolly, *Mourning Into Joy: Music, Raphael, and Saint Cecilia* (New Haven: Yale University Press, 1994), 31–32.

67. Marcel Hébert, "Les legendes hagiographiques. A propos d'un livre recent," *Revue de l'université de Bruxelles* 11 (1905–1906): 139–49, citing 139. "It is rather amusing to see a Jesuit demythologize [dénicher] saints." Hébert had left the church in 1903 as a result of the impact of critical philosophy and critical history on his Catholicism.

68. Hébert, 146–47. "After Père Delehaye's pages, read Abbé Loisy's study on the Fourth Gospel; has Loisy done anything other than apply to this writing rules of criticism identical to those of the Bollandist? And thus the Fourth Gospel appears for what it really is, not a history, but an admirable *mystical vision*."

PART FOUR

Hagiography and the Cult of the Nation

7

Polychromatic Piety: Saints According to Anatole France

Christina Ferree Chabrier

Despite his skepticism and antireligious views, Anatole France adapted a surprising number of medieval religious narratives. Exposed at a young age to medieval manuscripts and intellectual discussions in his father's bookstore, France seems to have absorbed some of the nostalgia for the Middle Ages following the *genre troubadour* and the ensuing Romantic movement.[1] Indeed, Romantics such as Victor Hugo and Charles Nodier, whose writings reflect an interest in the Middle Ages, also broadened the uses of medieval imagery in order to influence social change. Anatole France's views of the Middle Ages diverge from those of Romantics, whose works glorified medieval edifices and writings in idealized representations; however, similar to those of Romantic authors, France's adaptations of medieval works and, specifically, his depictions of saints reflect his social beliefs.[2] They also confirm his formidable knowledge of history and his nostalgia for a period when religious faith was possible, before reason destroyed the joy of illusion: "Car il n'y a de joie que dans l'illusion et la paix ne se trouve que dans l'ignorance."[3]

Anatole France's fondness for historical writing is recognizable in many of his works, such as *L'Ile des pingouins* (1908) and *Les Dieux ont soif* (1912). This interest in historiography, a natural effect of the milieu in which he grew up, explains to a certain extent France's familiarity with medieval texts, and hagiography in particular. His gravitation toward the saints is evidenced by *La Légende de sainte Radegonde* (1859), written while he was still at the Collège Stanislas, and the poem "La Légende de sainte Thaïs" (1867); France later reworked this poem into his novel *Thaïs* (1889), in which the protagonist is an actress-turned-saint. In addition, extensive research for his *Vie de Jeanne d'Arc* (1908) led him to focus on medieval religious narratives in particular. France rewrote some of these texts, incorporating them into his own fiction. The most obvious instance of France's liberal adaptation is his rationalization of Joan of Arc's legendary life; in addition, in *L'Ile des pingouins*, France's portrayal of Saint Maël seems to parody medieval accounts of voyaging Irish saints. In fact, France makes passing references to the Middle Ages and to saints throughout much of his voluminous corpus. One collection of short stories offers a particularly strong concentration of representations of saints. *L'Etui de nacre* (1892), which includes "Amycus et Célestin" (1890), "La Légende des saintes Oliverie et Liberette" (1890), "Sainte Euphrosine" (1891), "Scolastica" (1889) and "Le Jongleur de Notre Dame" (1890), will be the focal point of this essay, as these stories offer concise and somewhat typical examples of France's manner of representing saints at the fin de siècle.

L'Etui de nacre comprises seventeen short stories, of which the first six are set either in antiquity or in the Middle Ages. Religious figures are the focus of the five stories named above; they follow the collection's first story, "Le Procurateur de Judée" (see below). The remaining eleven texts are set in more modern times and although they may present certain aspects of religion, the characters are less closely linked with the Church. The characters may be saintly, as is Catherine Fontaine in "La Messe des ombres," but they are not, strictly speaking, saints.

The distinction between long-past Christian figures and modern characters marks a change within the volume. Certain aspects of some of the stories are similar, such as the supernatural, a key element in France's saintly narratives and in some of the subsequent ones. The influence of nineteenth-century interest in spiritualism is apparent in "La Messe des ombres," "Leslie Wood" and "Le Manuscrit d'un médecin de village," for instance. Others are further distanced from religious subjects, despite retaining a minor connection. Religious practices are evoked in "Gestas" (see below). In "Mémoires d'un volontaire" the emphasis is shifted very quickly from an ecclesiastical education to a secular, Revolutionary setting, also found in "L'Aube," "Madame de Luzy," "La Mort accordée," "Anecdote de Floréal, An II" and "La Perquisition." The last story of the collection, "Le petit soldat de plomb," seems the most fantastical, as a toy soldier comes to life and gives an eclectic account of the Battle of Fontenoy.

Unifying all the stories in the collection is, perhaps, France's evocation of irrationality, be it in religious or revolutionary fervor. The title of the collection suggests France's estimation of such strong emotions. France's *étui* keeps souvenirs, memories, safely contained, to be consulted only in moments of nostalgia for irrationality. The changing colors of the *nacre* may signal the variety of the case's contents, while implying that the meanings of the stories change according to one's perspective, just as the colors of the box would change with movement.

The first story of the collection, "Le Procurateur de Judée," sets the tone for the following adaptations of saints' lives. Here, France represents an aged Pontius Pilate conversing with an old friend, L. Ælius Lamia. They discuss many subjects: their failing health, past glories and shames, the Jews, women. Their conversation about women leads Lamia to mention the trial of Christ; he recalls that one of his former lovers disappeared when she decided to follow Christ. Pilate's response, the last line of the story, is striking: "'Jésus?' murmura-t-il, 'Jésus le Nazaréen? Je ne me rappelle pas.'"[4] Marie-Claire Bancquart aptly notes that "... la fin du conte frappe le lecteur contemporain de stupéfaction, parce qu'elle va à rebours de la connaissance que, lui, il possède de Pilate: cette connaissance n'existe que par rapport à Jésus."[5] The reader, expecting confirmation of the importance of Christ, is left to wonder at his merely peripheral presence. Is Christ's prosecution, one intrinsic element of Christianity, so easily forgotten? What does Pilate's poor memory reveal regarding documentation of religious figures?

The reader presumably knows of Christ through his or her familiarity with religious writings, whether direct textual studies or by way of the Church's indoctrination. Pilate's forgetfulness indicates a lack of records concerning Christ; he would not fail to remember if there were accounts circulating. France thus suggests the importance of texts. Indeed, for the modern believer, Christ's significance depends on writing rather than on spoken testimony of eyewitness. At the same time, however, Pilate's response raises the question of the veracity of writing. If seeing implied truth, as confirmed by the etymology of *vrai*, what conclusion can be drawn from the absence of this key eyewitness' testimony? The importance modern Christianity attributes to Christ's prosecution is established without seeing, but based on texts; yet here, *le voir*, or *le vrai*, is distanced from writing, suggesting its falseness. This first story serves as a caveat, then, that all that is written does not represent reality, an appropriate sentiment to introduce France's saintly tales.

Although France's stories imitate the style of their medieval counterparts, saints seem to be diminished in worth throughout France's works. In *L'Etui de nacre*, France's pastiches of medieval saints' lives represent holy men and women as simplistic and irrational. These may also be characteristics of medieval narratives, yet France's tone is playful, making his accounts seem more like charming fiction than realistic representations of saints whose examples should be followed.[6] Additionally, throughout France's corpus references to saints in stories set in the nineteenth century often depict them playing a purely popular role, having little to do with religion and more with folklore. In *L'Orme du Mail* (1897), for instance, Saint Anthony of Padua is reduced to a finder of lost baubles[7] and two clergymen discuss a girl's visions of Saint Radegonde as a means of influencing politics.[8] Such representations of saints convey France's view that true faith is a thing of the past and religious practices are the modern-day remnants of medieval belief.[9] France's wariness of faith is echoed in his critique of Zola's *Le Rêve*, where France posits that such a story is misplaced in the nineteenth century and belongs, rather, in a medieval setting:

> [L]es légendes des vierges martyres, telles qu'elles fleurirent au XIIIe siècle, sont autant de joyaux dont il faut goûter à la fois la richesse éblouissante et la naïveté barbare. Ce sont les chefs-d'œuvre d'une orfèvrerie enfantine et merveilleuse. Le bon peuple en resta longtemps ébloui et ce fut jusqu'au XVIe siècle la poésie des pauvres. Mais M. Zola se trompe fort s'il croit que la religion d'aujourd'hui en a gardé le moindre souvenir.[10]

Naïveté, be it that of believing in legends or that of religious faith, has no place in France's ideology. Furthermore, in modern France true faith is questionable, as piety and faith are overshadowed by religious formalities: "En réalité, ce qu'apprend une petite fille élevée comme Angélique, dans la piété, à l'odeur de l'encens, ce n'est point la légende dorée, ce sont les prières, l'ordinaire de la messe, le catéchisme; elle se confesse, elle communie. Cela est toute sa vie. Il est inconcevable que M. Zola ait oublié toutes ces pratiques."[11] The crux of France's criticism is Zola's representation of a mystical world that no longer exists, giving a false impression of contemporary realities of religion.

The distinction between religion past and present pervades France's works.[12] Indeed, in several works France mocks those who practice modern religion, and quite strikingly in "Gestas" (1891), from *L'Etui de nacre*. The title character is no saint, but rather a drunkard who conceives a strong desire to confess and who is "prédestiné à la béatitude éternelle," as France notes at the end of the tale.[13] It is at the beginning, however, that the caricature of the believer comes into play, first with Gestas' naïveté: "... il est ingénu et il a gardé la foi naïve de son enfance." This echoes the portrayals of saints in the stories treated below, but Gestas' actions are a parody of those of a religious man: "... une de ces ruelles est selon son cœur, car bordée de mastroquets et de bouges, elle porte à l'angle d'une maison, une Sainte Vierge grillée dans sa niche bleue. Il va le soir de café en café et fait ses stations de bière et d'alcool dans un ordre constant: les grands travaux de la débauche veulent de la méthode et de la régularité."[14] In a quasi-religious state, he frequents bars as a Catholic would move about the Stations of the Cross. As if observing traditional Catholic devotional practices, Gestas goes about his tasks with determination, the act of getting drunk likened to the celebration of the passion of Christ.

Contrasting with this somewhat jaded view of contemporary practices are stories set in the remote patristic era; ritual has not yet superseded the pure belief of early Christianity. Despite their seeming simplicity, the saints' stories in L'Etui de nacre are interesting examples of how France questions the veracity of religion and the authenticity of belief as practiced in his own time. This criticism of nineteenth-century faith, predating France's condemnation of the Church's role in the Dreyfus Affair, foreshadows what would be his active support of the separation of Church and State.

"Amycus et Célestin" is the first in a series of stories depicting the Christianizing of pagan Gaul. Célestin, a hermit, befriends a faun called Amycus. Once the creature has proven to Célestin that he is not a demon, Amycus helps the hermit decorate the chapel, saying that because he is familiar with the land, he is better able to find the prettiest foliage. Célestin accepts Amycus' aid, for he wishes to attract worshippers away from the "arbre des fées," a decorated tree to which local girls bring offerings, to Célestin's great chagrin.[15] Presumably, the chapel's beautification increases its profitability, which is why Célestin baptizes Amycus. In fact, after their deaths, a church is built on the same site, becoming "un lieu de pèlerinage" where "les fidèles y vénèrent la mémoire bienheureuse des saints Amic et Célestin."[16] Remarkably, both the hermit and his faun companion are canonized.

Bancquart suggests that this text likely evolved as a result of France's research for *Thaïs*: "Dans la vie de saint Paul contée par Michel-Ange Marin, se trouve ... l'épisode du satyre qui confesse à Antoine l'existence de Dieu, puis s'enfuit. Saint Jérôme est le premier à conter ces aventures sur lesquelles brodèrent les hagiographes."[17] Saint Jerome's work was a source for hagiographers and Anatole France alike, for in "Amycus et Célestin," Célestin welcomes the faun because the hermit is familiar with Saint Jerome's life of Saint Paul: "Il lui souvint à propos que saint Jérôme avait eu pour compagnons de route, dans le désert, des satyres et des centaures qui avaient confessé la vérité."[18] France subtly alters the story by making Célestin's recall faulty; he mistakenly attributes events from Saint Anthony of Alexandria's life to Saint Jerome, the composer of Saint Anthony's life.

Célestin's memory may very well be imperfect, as he is quite old, but France's own reading of Saint Jerome can be seen in some of the details of the short story. Both Anthony and Célestin are walking when the fauns appear in the respective accounts, and the descriptions of the fauns have some common characteristics. Saint Jerome's faun is "un fort petit homme qui avait les narines crochues, des cornes au front et des pieds de chèvre."[19] France mentions some of the same features, particularly the faun's stature, his nose, and the obviously distinguishing horns and hooves. Even so, France's description is more elaborate and differs in details such as the shape of the faun's nose: "... un jeune garçon lui barra le passage. Il était à demi vêtu d'une peau de bête, et c'était plutôt un faune qu'un garçon; son regard était perçant, son nez camus, sa face riante. Ses cheveux bouclés cachaient les deux petites cornes de son front têtu; ... ses pieds forchus se dissimulaient dans l'herbe."[20]

Similarly, France's wording subtly echoes that of Saint Jerome when the faun introduces himself to Saint Anthony. The faun in Saint Jerome's text explains: "Je suis envoyé vers vous comme ambassadeur par ceux de mon espèce, et nous vous supplions tous de prier pour nous celui qui est également notre Dieu, lequel nous avons su être venu pour le salut du monde, et dont le nom et la réputation se sont répandus par toute la terre."[21] France's faun, like that of Saint Jerome, seems to emphasize their common beliefs when he mentions that Easter is a day of celebration for him: "Ce jour est pour moi comme pour toi un jour de fête."[22] Nor can the reader forget that Easter symbolizes the resurrection of Christ and the salvation of mankind, for Célestin tests Amycus' knowledge of Christianity by asking him to repeat "il est ressuscité."[23]

This parallel is strengthened by the correspondence of Easter with the traditional decoration of the fairy tree, raising the question of the Church's appropriation of dates already celebrated in pagan ritual. France puts it plainly in the "De Carnac" (1891) section of *Pierre Nozière* (1899), where he recounts the story of Saint Cornély: "Sa fête tombe le 13 septembre, et ... cette date coïncidant avec l'équinoxe d'automne, la fête du saint a dû se substituer à quelque féerie agricole des païens. ... Comme le dieu rustique dont il a pris la place, il reçoit des victimes; on lui offre des vaches, mais on ne les immole pas. Elles sont vendues au profit de l'église."[24] France distinctly relates paganism with nature and Christianity with material gain. He also specifically emphasizes Christianity's appropriation of pagan feast days.

In "Amycus et Célestin," despite the substitution of Christian for pagan celebrations, the reader never learns definitively that the faun has been converted. It is clear, however, that he acquires the language of

Christianity, for he asks Célestin not to exorcise him: "Bon ermite, lui dit-il, ne m'exorcise pas. Ce jour est pour moi comme pour toi un jour de fête. Il ne serait pas charitable de me contrister dans le temps pascal."[25] Moments later, Célestin is convinced that Amycus is no demon because the latter knows the right response to Célestin's liturgical discourse: "Faune, sois un hymne de Dieu. Dis: il est ressuscité." Amycus gives the proper reply, "Il est ressuscité, répondit le faune. Et tu m'en vois tout réjoui," thereby convincing the hermit of his conversion.[26] Soon after, however, it becomes apparent that Amycus never understands the mysteries of Christianity, nor has he abandoned pagan rites. He continues to worship the sun and the earth, even as Célestin says Mass: "Et pendant que Célestin célébrait le sacrifice de la messe, le capripède, inclinant jusqu'à terre son front cornu, adorait le soleil et disait: 'La terre est un gros œuf que tu fécondes, soleil, soleil sacré.'"[27]

This juxtaposition of Christian and pagan figures recalls Flaubert's *Tentation de saint Antoine*.[28] Indeed, France's *Thaïs* was greatly inspired by Flaubert's work, whose considerable influence can be seen in many later representations of saints. Further, in "Amycus et Célestin" the faun's evocation of a sacred sun suggests the final image of the 1874 *Tentation*: "Tout au milieu et dans le disque même du soleil rayonne la face de Jésus-Christ."[29] In "Amycus et Célestin," the contrast of pagan and Christian characters goes hand in hand with their representation as physical or spiritual figures. This distinction between physicality and spirituality again seems to echo Flaubert's *Tentation*, and particularly the 1849 version, where the saint's porcine companion exhibits mostly physical characteristics while the saint is more concerned with spiritual matters. Like Amycus, Antoine's pig remarks the goodness of the sun and its physical merits: "Quel bon soleil! cela vous chauffe. Ah! le bon soleil! quel bon soleil!"[30]

In addition to its similarities with Flaubert's text, "Amycus et Célestin" bears a striking resemblance to another tale in France's own corpus, "Saint Satyre" (1893), where the grafting of Christianity onto extant pagan systems is particularly evident. This first story of the collection *Le Puits de sainte Claire* (1895), is an account of a satyr canonized for his good deeds. After death, wishing to preserve his own pagan religion despite his assimilation into the Christian tradition, he offers his tomb to house the last vestiges of nymphs and satyrs. Because these creatures cause provocative visions for those who approach the tomb, the Church exorcises it, ridding the region of its pagan history. The similarities linking the two texts are evident, but Bancquart cautions, "Il ne faudrait pas en effet considérer "Saint Satyre" comme un simple doublon du conte "Amycus et Célestin" du recueil *L'Etui de nacre*; celui-ci n'en est que l'ébauche.... ['Saint Satyre'] voit honorer les figures du désir, satyres et nymphes. Puis la venue du Christ tue lentement les anciens dieux."[31]

Indeed, the later work is more detailed and explicit in its depiction of the Church's effort to rid the countryside of pagan superstition, but "Amycus et Célestin" already provides several illustrations of the superposition of Christianity onto established belief systems. Here, the chapel provides a particularly clear example of the Christianizing of pagan lands. As the two make their way to the chapel to celebrate Easter, the building is described as "petite et de structure grossière; Célestin l'avait bâtie de ses mains avec le débris d'un temple de Vénus."[32] Erected from the ruins of a pagan temple, Célestin's chapel later undergoes another transformation. Just as the Church itself gains strength, so the chapel is rebuilt as a church: "Sur la colline où Célestin avait construit l'étroite chapelle qu'Amycus ornait des fleurs des montagnes, des bois et des eaux, s'élève aujourd'hui une église dont la nef remonte au XIe siècle, et dont le porche a été réédifié sous Henri II, dans le style de la Renaissance."[33]

The faun and the hermit represent their respective religions; one is a symbol of pagan sexual freedom, while the other is a Christian ascetic. Yet there is a certain parallel of the two in the story.[34] There is, first, the aforementioned similarity vis-à-vis the holy day of Easter, but the text presents another perspective when Amycus explains why he has chosen to reveal himself to the hermit: "Je suis venu à toi, mon père, parce que tu as l'air assez bonhomme sous ta longue barbe blanche. Il me semble que les ermites sont des faunes accablés par les ans. Quand je serai vieux, je serai semblable à toi."[35] According to Amycus, then, the only difference between them is their age. In other words, when age diminishes the faun's inherent sexuality and he descends from his sexual peak, he will be an appropriate candidate for Christian living.

The faun is prematurely pushed into a Christian role by Célestin's decision to baptize him, based on the hermit's belief that Amycus has made the church more attractive than the fairy tree. The baptism paves the way for the canonization of this creature, still pagan at the end of the story, and may be understood as a reward given to the faun for his part in the advancement of the Christian rites. Because Amycus gives no sign of having adopted Christianity, however, Célestin's deed is misguided. In portraying the baptism and subsequent canonization of the faun, France seems to make one final acknowledgement of the text written by Saint Jerome. Here, Saint Anthony reproaches Alexandria for its deification of animals such as the faun: "Malheur à toi, Alexandrie, qui adores des monstres en qualité de dieux! ... Les bêtes parlent des grandeurs de Jésus-Christ et tu rends à des bêtes les honneurs et les hommages qui ne sont dus qu'à Dieu seul!"³⁶ Although Célestin does not deify Amycus, he does treat the faun as a pious, converted human being rather than as a creature born of pagan beliefs.

Moreover, Célestin's decision to baptize the faun actually works against the establishment of the Church; Amycus' manner of decorating the chapel paganizes the sacred space by introducing elements previously associated with pagan rites. His actions, which Célestin sees as profitable, emphasize similarities of the church and the fairy tree and attenuate the competition between the two rather than resolving the issue. In short, Amycus ensures the survival of aspects of paganism by incorporating them into Christian tradition instead of trying to exorcise them as Célestin would the fairy tree and the faun himself. Bancquart notes, "Sans cesse vaincu et tenté par [les divinités], [Célestin] finit par instaurer lui-même le malentendu qui les fait entrer dans le culte orthodoxe. Il est pris à leur piège gracieux, et cette maldonne emplit de malignité tout le récit d'Anatole France."³⁷ Once baptized, Amycus exploits the Church's own practice of founding new traditions based on established ones in order to reinstate elements of paganism; yet, the faun's insertion of pagan decorations into Christian space represents an attempt to preserve paganism from within the Catholic tradition, rather than obscuring it by overwriting the extant system.

"Amycus et Célestin" seems like a charming retelling of the confluence of paganism and Christianity, but upon examination less innocent features become apparent. Among these are the Church's attempt to efface history by exorcising ancient beliefs and the very depiction of the two saints in the text. Amycus is clearly not even converted and Célestin nevertheless baptizes him; one saint is a confirmed pagan, while the other is no longer very perceptive or willfully ignores Amycus' persistent paganism. The Church's conferral of sainthood to the unconverted faun suggests that the institution will recruit even creatures whose existence goes against its principles, as long as the results are to its profit. Saint Amic is the embodiment of the Church's hypocrisy. Furthermore, France represents Christianity, through these two saints, as a fraudulent religion, built upon existing systems. Accordingly, to reject paganism would be, in effect, to deny an integral element of Christianity. Finally, Amycus' designation of the hermit as an aged faun raises the question of the physical and spiritual changes that occur with age; Célestin's loss of memory, his naïveté and his celibacy seem to suggest that Christianity is not a religion for those of sound body and mind.³⁸

Like "Amycus et Célestin," "La Légende des saintes Oliverie et Liberette" begins with a description of the spiritual atmosphere of the fourth century after Christ and the pagan practices of the era. France then introduces Saint Bertauld, a Scottish nobleman-turned-missionary, and narrates his arrival in the Ardennes. He has little success in converting the inhabitants to Christianity, however, and they chase him from their villages. In the second part of the short story, Bertauld meets Oliverie and Liberette, two sisters whose father is a rich seigneur. Bertauld sees great Christian potential in them, especially in Liberette who is ready to accept the new religion on his word; her sister, on the other hand, asks for a sign that the Christian God is truly the only one. Bertauld decides to become a hermit and says that Oliverie will receive a sign and that God will send a guide to lead them to his hermitage.

In the third chapter, a unicorn appears to Oliverie, but not to Liberette; the latter would rather believe based on faith alone. The creature leads them to Bertauld, who instructs them for a year, and they, in turn, convert their father during a visit to him. On their return to Bertauld's hermitage, Oliverie is unable to cross a river, though her sister succeeds, aided by her faith in God's power. Stranded, Oliverie becomes a hermit, building a hut next to a nearby brook, which is then named for her. In the last section, Liberette, returning alone to Bertauld, finds him dead. After burying him, she, like her sister, becomes a hermit beside a stream. It likewise bears her name, but unlike that of her sister, Liberette's possesses miraculous healing properties. Meanwhile, Valfroy converts the rest of the region.[39] Liberette dies first, as a reward for her unquestioning faith, and Oliverie follows ten years later in A.D. 364, according to France.

Marie-Claire Bancquart's notes to the story reveal that Bertauld's popularity was at a high point in the twelfth century, when an anonymous life appeared. France apparently also consulted a seventeenth-century version by Jean Liétau. France's adaptation differs considerably from these accounts of Bertauld's life; he omits Bertauld's companion Amand, situates the story a century earlier and leaves out the tame lion that accompanies the two missionaries in the other versions. In addition, the medieval account mentions that Oliverie's spring is the miraculous one, not Liberette's.[40]

Several aspects of France's text invite commentary. Perhaps the most pertinent feature of France's story is the juxtaposition of pagan rites and supernatural creatures with Christian imagery and saints. Though an aspect already noted in regard to "Amycus et Célestin," in "Oliverie et Liberette" France seems to insist on the similarities of pagan and Christian myths, again suggesting a correspondence with Flaubert's *Tentation*—the mixing of beings born of Christian and pagan origins. Indeed, France views the invocation of the saints as a legacy of pagan beliefs in *Sur la pierre blanche* (1905): "Les Italiens ne demandaient à leurs dieux que des biens terrestres et des avantages solides. A cet égard, en dépit des terreurs asiatiques qui ont envahi l'Europe, leur sentiment religieux n'a pas changé. Ce qu'ils exigeaient autrefois de leurs dieux et de leurs génies, ils l'attendent aujourd'hui de la Madone et des saints."[41]

Similarly, in "Oliverie et Liberette" the correlation of paganism to Christianity accents the irrationality of Christian belief and those who represent religion; France chooses to emphasize the supernatural aspects of Christianity as well as those of paganism, making them appear equally fictional. He sets up the parallel of paganism and Christianity by evoking several legendary creatures living in the Ardennes. First, he lists a basilisk, a unicorn and a dragon. Then a few lines down, he mentions nymphs, satyrs, centaurs and Ægipans.[42] The textual division of these creatures may be seen as an indication of tension between Christian and pagan belief systems; the first three creatures all figure prominently in medieval religious imagery and in the Bible. While the basilisk and dragon are usually associated with evil and the unicorn with purity and goodness, in this context their importance is related more to their supernatural aspect than to their allegorical meaning. France raises the question of the irrationality of Christianity, underlined by the juxtaposition of these biblical creatures with others that are more closely related to paganism (nymphs, satyrs, centaurs and Ægipans), thus blurring the line separating Christian and pagan belief systems. Furthermore, France attributes to God's power man's ability to perceive even the pagan creatures: "Parce qu'alors la nature mystique était révélée aux hommes et que les choses invisibles devenaient visibles pour la gloire du Créateur, on rencontrait dans les clairières des nymphes, des satyres, des centaures et des égipans."[43]

The images associated with these creatures also reflect the atmosphere of mixed systems that France suggests. Among these beings, four of the seven are hybrids. The basilisk (or cockatrice) is, at least in medieval imagery, a mixture of cock and serpent; satyrs are part goat and part man; centaurs combine horse and man; Ægipan was part goat and part fish according to some accounts, but his namesakes retain only his goat characteristics, combined with man instead of fish. In this text, these composite creatures may be understood as symbols of the hybridization of religions, undermining the Church's plan to replace the pagan system with the Christian one. Once more, France seems to point the finger at the truth of the matter: Pagan religions did not disappear; the Church simply grafted its system onto the existing ones.

France furthers the comparison of Christianity and paganism in the reaction Bertauld encounters when he preaches that "Le Dieu que je vous enseigne ... est le seul véritable. Il est unique en trois personnes, et son fils est né d'une vierge."[44] Although the inhabitants of the Porcin region deny that there can be only one god, they too claim to worship a statue that they think bears some resemblance to the Christian Virgin:

> Mais ce que tu dis d'une vierge divine n'est pas sans vérité. Nous connaissons une vierge au triple visage.... Elle se nomme Diane, et son pied d'argent effleure, sous les pâles clartés de la lune, le thym des montagnes. Elle n'a pas dédaigné de recevoir dans son lit d'hyacinthes fleuries des bergers et des chasseurs comme nous. Pourtant elle est toujours vierge.[45]

The tone of this paragraph, along with their paroles railleuses as they chase Bertauld from their town, clearly marks their disdain for the irrational Christian beliefs that Bertauld represents. Of course, for a skeptic like France, the pagan belief in multiple gods seems no more rational than the Christian doctrine. So even though he calls the pagans "ces hommes ignorants," France's juxtaposition of the two systems raises the question of any real difference between them since, according to this representation, both are equally founded on irrationality.[46]

Saints embody this rejection of reason in France's works; one illustration of this is his portrayal of Oliverie's punishment for requesting a sign that the Christian God is the true God, and for not possessing the irrational faith that characterizes her sister's belief. In addition to Oliverie's initial lack of faith, she again disappoints the Christian ideal when she tries to use a staff to help cross the swift river that her sister has miraculously traversed. Because she does not exhibit the same blind faith as her sister, Oliverie is unable to cross the stream and must establish her residence on the side of the impassable river opposite her sister. This is her punishment for not trusting God's power: "[Oliverie] comprit qu'elle était justement punie pour avoir douté de la puissance céleste et pour n'être pas allée à la grâce de Dieu, comme avait fait sa sœur Liberette."[47] At the end of the tale, Oliverie is again penalized for this and for her initial lack of faith. When her sister dies, Oliverie learns in a revelation why she will live longer: "Parce que tu as demandé un signe afin de croire et pris un bâton pour appui, l'heure de ta mort bienheureuse sera retardée et le jour de ta glorification reculé."[48]

Liberette, on the other hand, is marked by unquestioning faith from the moment she first hears Bertauld preach. Because she prefers to have no proof of God's validity, "Liberette était née pour être une grande sainte."[49] In addition, the spring beside which Liberette builds her hut possesses miraculous healing properties, contrasting with Oliverie's commonplace stream. The rewards and favoritism accorded to Liberette, not to the skeptical Oliverie, establish Christianity's appreciation of irrationality; Oliverie's punishments represent the outcome of attempting to reason about religion.

From a rationalistic perspective, France's story questions the merits of blind faith. Liberette's devotion results in her finding Bertauld's dead body when she returns alone to his hut, and she herself dies ten years earlier than her sister. Although premature death, like martyrdom, is to be seen as a reward in traditional saints' lives, in France's adaptation the omnipresent conflict of reason and faith invites the interpretation that even Oliverie's slight attempt at rationalism might actually be a better choice. France's failure to differentiate Christianity from paganism lends additional support to this stance; if both are equally irrational, there is no clear advantage to choosing one over the other.

A later work, "Le Miracle du grand saint Nicolas" (1908), from *Les Sept Femmes de la Barbe-bleue* (1909), also emphasizes the naïveté associated with saintliness and seems to indicate that religious legends carry no more significance than any other fairy tale.[50] Because France situates "Saint Nicolas" between two adaptations of fairy tales, this fanciful account of the saint appears to be classified in the same genre. This story is far from innocent, however, in its representation of the saint. Nicolas, typically associated with generosity, here is transposed as a "moins ancien" bishop, as France distances his story from the account given by the Church.[51] According to France's version, Nicolas is a rich, yet naïve bishop whose miraculous resuscitation of three boys leads to his ultimate excommunication; after they are brought back to life the boys create financial, military and religious problems for the region. The latter result in Nicolas' excommunication after one of the boys spreads heresies and Nicolas takes no strong action to stop him. In fact, the saint's naïveté prevents him from understanding that the boys' many destructive and anti–Catholic actions damage him, the Church and the country. If he were not naïve, the saint would not face the punishment of excommunication; this story is thus another illustration of the incongruity of the medieval religious figure's innocence with the modern world.

Reason and religion are also at the heart of "Sainte Euphrosine." Euphrosine is the young, well-educated daughter of a rich man of Alexandria. She proves her intelligence by answering three questions in a contest; the first two are riddles, and the third is a question of logic. None of the men competing are able to solve these problems, but when Euphrosine succeeds, she modestly deflects praise from herself, praising Christ as "principe et fin de toute connaissance."[52] Many suitors present themselves to Euphrosine's father. Having spent his wealth on a collection of curious mechanisms, he encourages one of the richest admirers, Longin, to court his daughter and likewise urges her to consider Longin's proposal. Euphrosine, however, has other plans for her future and reveals to her father that she would like to devote herself to Christ. Her father does not approve her wish, declaring that he will force her to marry Longin. Nor will Longin accept her argument; he announces that he intends to satisfy his desire rather than cede to any reasoning that might convince him to renounce the union. Consequently, Euphrosine plans to escape by disguising herself as a man. In this way, she successfully leaves the city and presents herself as an orphan named Smaragde at a monastery headed by Saint Onuphre. She is safe here, for she knows that her father and fiancé will not look for her in a monastery, but rather would expect her to seek refuge in a convent.

Five years pass, until one day Longin seeks entry to the monastery in order to be cured of "un mal mortel," which turns out to be his love for Euphrosine.[53] He does not recognize his former fiancée, who counsels him, and he leaves, only to return later and become a monk. Euphrosine's father also appears at the monastery, as a beggar. He, like Longin, does not recognize Euphrosine and recounts the sad story of the loss of his daughter and his material possessions. Upon hearing her father's account, Euphrosine reveals her identity to him and he decides to become a monk as well. Euphrosine's father alone knows of her disguise, and she, her father and Longin live together in the monastery for some years, until they all die within a two-month period. At the age of 132, the abbot Onuphre dies soon after (in A.D. 395).

The most salient aspect of France's adaptation of the *Life of Saint Euphrosyne* is perhaps the mix of reason and passion that pervades the story. France's initial depiction of the young Euphrosine emphasizes her logical mind. When, after correctly answering all three questions, she chooses to devote herself to the Church, France's story represents the application of reason to religion:

> Mais comme elle était chrétienne et d'une piété peu commune, loin de s'enorgueillir de ces honneurs, elle en conçut la vanité et se promit d'appliquer, à l'avenir, la pénétration de son intelligence à résoudre des problèmes plus dignes d'intérêt, comme, par exemple, à faire la somme des nombres représentés par les lettres du nom de Jésus et à considérer les propriétés merveilleuses de ces nombres.[54]

As a Christian, Euphrosine would like to use her abilities to celebrate her beliefs. France, however, as a nonbeliever, seems to be using his own capacity for irony in his depiction of the use of reason to decipher the "marvelous properties of the numbers represented by the letters of Jesus' name." Certainly, France's evocation of such a task may imitate medieval hagiography, as do many of the stories in *L'Etui de nacre*. France's views are far from the medieval hagiographer's religious sentiment, however, and he is well aware that much of his public no longer holds religion in high regard. So although Euphrosine's application of logic to the contemplation of Christ may be in imitation of medieval texts, France only emphasizes the futility of logic in religious matters by calling attention to his medieval models, thereby associating religion, irrationality and the Middle Ages.

The conflict of reason and passion again becomes manifest when Euphrosine asks Longin to release her from the planned union. Longin, like Euphrosine, feels compelled to follow his feelings rather than attempting a logical examination of Euphrosine's wishes: "Clarissime Euphrosine, l'amour est plus fort que la volonté; c'est pourquoi il convient de lui obéir comme à un maître jaloux. Je ferai à votre égard ce qu'il m'ordonne, qui est de vous prendre pour ma femme."[55] Longin's passion, not reason, inspires his resolution. Both Euphrosine and Longin would base the rest of their lives on irrational decisions; they differ only because Longin's feelings are not condoned by the Church. Indeed, Longin's passion causes him to threaten Euphrosine's sanctity. By making Longin's passion a carnal counterpoint to Euphrosine's religious impulse, France subtly illustrates the lack of fundamental difference between the two; the only real distinction is the Church's norms.

France extends Euphrosine's connection to irrationality when he refers to the legend in an article appearing in *L'Echo de Paris* on January 31, 1899. Here, France relates the story of the Alexandrian saint to the history of Compiègne, as M. Bergeret recounts the translation of the saint's relics to Reims, with a brief stop in Saint-Jean-au-Bois, where the narrator is staying. By trickery, he explains, the abbess prevented the transporters from continuing the journey to Reims, thus keeping the relics in her abbey. Her reason for this was to gain renown and donations through the celebrity of the relics: "Car les reliques de sainte Iphraise guérissaient diverses maladies tant des hommes que des bestiaux."[56] France presents the saint only in terms of the belief that her relics produce miracles, reinforcing the correlation between medieval religion and irrationality. This anecdote also portrays the greed of the clergy through the contrast of the saint's simple faith and the abbess' profitable cunning. Here, money is clearly linked to Church leaders. While saints may be simple and illogical and therefore outdated according to France, his frequent association of Church leaders to riches and trickery identifies the institution as a more powerful threat than its simple constituents.

The last section of "Sainte Euphrosine" consists of the narrator's playful assurance to the reader that his source is a medieval text written between the seventh and fourteenth centuries. In this pastiche of medieval hagiography, the narrator explains that he has attempted to remain faithful to the original; he also deplores medieval stylistics: "Le diacre Georges contait avec moins de grâce qu'Hérodote et même que Plutarque."[57] He then anticipates the various criticisms that his work will generate, which he supposes will be based on details in his story that do not appear in known versions of the legend, most notably in the works of Rufinus and Saint Jerome. He counters these imagined protests by arguing the validity of his source, albeit one which is (conveniently) known only to himself. France's narrator is clearly poking fun at the seriousness of medieval hagiography while again raising the question of the veracity of written sources.

Though his narrator's source for "Saint Euphrosine" is probably imaginary, it is likely that France's story is based on the Oxford manuscript of the saint's life, as it appears in Paul Meyer's *Recueil d'anciens textes bas-latins, provençaux et français* (1874), where it is placed immediately following the life of Saint Thaïs.[58] It is perhaps not coincidental that France chose to adapt the legends that he did. He freely admits that his well-known "Jongleur de Notre-Dame" (1890) was inspired by Gaston Paris' account of the legend in his 1888 work, *La Littérature française au moyen âge*. Paris' documentation of medieval literature greatly influenced writers of France's generation, and Gaston and his father Paulin Paris were among those erudite scholars who frequented the same intellectual circles as France.[59] Gaston Paris' *La Littérature française au moyen âge*, and specifically Chapter Five, offers a rather heavy concentration of elements also present in France's corpus. Paris first mentions the *Vies des Pères du désert*, in particular the writings of Saint Jerome. Recall that in addition to the reference to Jerome in "Sainte Euphrosine," France's "Amycus et Célestin" echoes aspects of Saint Jerome's life of Saint Paul. Next, Paris cites the life of Saint Thaïs, then that of Saint Euphrosyne and, two pages later, writings on Saint Nicolas of Myra. Paris' work is meant as an instructive presentation of medieval literature and therefore lacks the playful tone of France's adaptations of the legends, but this text is fundamental for any study of late nineteenth-century rewritings of medieval narratives. Indeed, because France himself acknowledges the inspiration he derived from Paris' account of the "jongleur," it is possible that he was similarly influenced in writing "Amycus et Célestin," "Sainte Euphrosine" and "Le Miracle du grand saint Nicolas." His research for *Thaïs* was already well underway by the 1888 publication of Paris' work and probably owed less to it.

In addition to the conflict between reason and passion, a significant aspect of France's adaptation of the *Life of Saint Euphrosyne* is the manner in which he depicts the Church and its adherents. When Euphrosine, disguised as Smaragde, arrives at the monastery, the abbot Onuphre welcomes an ostensibly male orphan with these words:

> Heureux l'enfant qui fuit le siècle dans sa robe d'innocence! Les âmes des hommes sont exposées à de grands périls dans les villes, et particulièrement à Alexandrie, à cause des femmes qui y sont en grand nombre. La femme est un tel danger pour l'homme, que la seule pensée m'en donne encore à mon âge un frisson qui secoue toute ma chair. S'il s'en trouvait une assez effrontée pour entrer dans cette sainte maison, mon bras retrouverait soudain sa vigueur pour la chasser à grands coups de cette crosse pastorale.[60]

This humoristic depiction of the excess of fervent belief, compounded by the irony of the abbot's statement, is belied by Euphrosine's own experience, since the danger posed to her sanctity was by a man, Longin. France emphasizes Saint Onuphre's misogynist viewpoint when the abbot tells Euphrosine that woman is "impure, et la seule trace de ses pas est une souillure infecte."[61] Because Euphrosine's very presence in the monastery contradicts this opinion, France's insistence on Onuphre's sexism only serves to better illustrate the abbot's erroneous belief.

By invalidating the authority of one of the Church's saintly representatives, France destabilizes the very institution that the medieval *Life of Saint Euphrosyne* meant to promote. In so doing, he reveals his own anticlerical tendencies; he is haunted by the Church's power: "ce qui occupe et inquiète France ... ce sont les rapports des intellectuels et du gouvernement avec L'Eglise catholique."[62] Anticlerical, irréligieux and anti–Ralliement, France exemplifies his views in l'*Histoire contemporaine* "en mettant en scène, dans une suite de nouvelles, des personnages de prêtres dangereux pour la République."[63] The religious figures represented in *L'Etui* are generally less obvious illustrations of France's concerns regarding the Church, but the stories nevertheless retain a certain degree of acrimony toward the institution.

"Scolastica" is a tale that bears some resemblance to "Sainte Euphrosine," as the two revolve around the same conflict: a young woman who has made a commitment to Christ, disregarding the worldly pressure to marry and produce offspring. In this story set in fourth-century Auvergne, the title character, a young girl, marries her fiancé, Injuriosus. Before consummating the union, however, she tells him of her wish to preserve her virginity for Christ. Despite his argument that the main reason for their marriage was precisely to procreate, each being the last of his or her family, Scolastica remains firm in her resolution. In fact, she argues so passionately for the merit of religion that Injuriosus decides to remain celibate with her.

They live together for ten years before Scolastica dies, coming back to life only briefly to chide Injuriosus for his prayer: "Je te rends grâce, Seigneur Jésus, de ce que tu m'as donné la force de garder intact ton trésor."[64] Injuriosus dies soon after Scolastica, and a miraculous climbing rosebush springs up during the night, uniting the two tombs. While the Christians who see this recognize it as a sign of God, France reminds the reader that the countryside was still inhabited by pagans and then mentions a certain Silvanus, who, upon seeing the rosebush, interprets this sign according to his pagan viewpoint: "La triste Scolastica, se dit-il, maintenant qu'elle n'est plus qu'une ombre vaine, regrette le temps d'aimer et les plaisirs perdus. Les roses qui sortent d'elle, et qui parlent pour elle, nous disent: Aimez, vous qui vivez. Ce prodige nous enseigne à goûter les joies de la vie, tandis qu'il est temps encore."[65] France then refers to a poem by Silvanus, supposedly found by chance in a Bible in the collection of Michel Chasles, a physicist who erroneously believed he possessed many ancient documents, which were later recognized as forgeries.[66] Bancquart notes that the two verses that France cites as the first and last of Silvanus' poem are, in reality, an adaptation of verses drawn from two separate works by Ausone, a fourth-century Bordelais poet.[67]

According to Bancquart, France's source for "Scolastica" was Grégoire de Tours' *Histoire des Francs*, at least for the basic story of the saints.[68] In France's version, there is a rather clear juxtaposition of pagan and Christian belief systems, such as those encountered in "Amycus et Célestin" and at the beginning of "Oliverie et Liberette." "Scolastica" presents a somewhat more explicit contrast, however, as the evocation of Silvanus and his interpretation of the rosebush is a clear reminder of the differences of the systems vis-à-vis sexuality.[69] While the two systems can thus be seen as divergent, the juxtaposition of Christianity and paganism creates a hybrid image of the Christian religion, as in the two other stories. Instead of the composite creatures present in "Oliverie et Liberette," however, in "Scolastica" Christianity envelops pagan beliefs. In a more conspicuous illustration than in "Amycus et Célestin," France shows that despite Christianity's seeming victory over paganism, it also serves to protect certain aspects of the older beliefs, represented by the pagan poem preserved in a Bible. In fact, France chooses to close the tale with Ausone's poetry, disguised as the imaginary Silvanus' pagan poetry; by finishing on a pagan note, France ensures that non–Christian aspects of the story remain in the reader's mind. The pagan ending eclipses the Christian legend, valorizing pagan love over the moral example of a medieval saint's Life.

A similar story, "Histoire du bienheureux Longis et de la bienheureuse Onoflette" (1887) appears in *Pierre Nozière*. Here, however, the roles of the characters are reversed, as it is the male character, Longis, who persuades Onoflette to devote herself to the Church. As in "Scolastica," there is a juxtaposition of pagan aspects with the retelling of this legend when the ending leads into a detailed description of the remaining pagan traditions of the region where the pious story originated, merging Christian folklore and pagan superstition.

France's allusion to the Bible and to pagan poetry in "Scolastica" is just one manifestation of the codependency of Christianity and paganism. Although they differ in form, the one aspect that both systems share is their irrationality; for a rational skeptic like France, then, there can be no clear valorization of one over the other. Furthermore, because the religions are equally irrational, the characters' beliefs seem to be merely a question of their frame of reference. Thus the Christians rightly attribute the rosebush to Scolastica and Injuriosus' saintliness, and Silvanus aptly explains it as a sign of Scolastica's sexual frustration.

In France's works there is no discrimination between miracles. Republican, pagan or Christian, they are all illusions; depictions are charming and dubious, whether it is an *arbre des fées*, a miraculous rosebush or a posthumous act attributed to a saint. This is the case in the description of Saint Adjutor from *Pierre Nozière*. Linked to the town of Vernon, like Longis and Onoflette, Adjutor is a Crusader imprisoned by the Infidels. Before expiring, he is miraculously transported back to Vernon where he contacts his mother and then dies. Popular legend retains another miraculous act involving this saint, who became known for saving sailors from a whirlpool in the river. According to legend, Adjutor threw the chains remaining from his captivity into the abyss that was causing the whirlpool, filling the hole and stopping the wreckage. France, ever the logician, playfully reconciles the event of his miraculous return with his saving the sailors: "Il ne me reste qu'à expliquer comment saint Adjutor, qui passa de ce monde à l'autre le jour même de son retour à Vernon, put jeter ses chaînes dans le fleuve pour combler le gouffre. Cette difficulté n'est qu'apparente. Le saint revint sur la terre pour opérer ce miracle."[70] France may well be imitating medieval writings. On the other hand, his wording, indicating his intent to use a miracle to explain another miracle, accents the lack of reason in religion, and particularly in medieval religious narrative. In addition, by emphasizing the folkloric qualities of the saint, France undermines his own pseudo-historical account of the saint's feats and imprisonment, implying that saints' lives are no more trustworthy than folklore; the stories that promoted the foundation of the medieval Church are to be preserved as mementos, for nostalgia's sake, but not as Christian models.

Innocence, naïveté and the incapacity to reason are recurrent themes throughout France's corpus, establishing his desire for rationality, whether in religious or revolutionary contexts.[71] In his portrayal of religion and of the saints that he uses as the embodiment of religious values, there is a strong association between the Middle Ages and this lack of reason, as the stories from *L'Etui de nacre* illustrate. Not coincidentally, women are depicted as particularly suited to the religious life, as is evidenced by the number of female saints that France depicts: Jeanne d'Arc, Thaïs, Euphrosine, Scolastica, Oliverie and Liberette, among others. "Euphrosine" represents the Church's influence on women, for even in the face of the abbot's misogynistic views Euphrosine embraces a doctrine that would seem to exclude her sex from grace. Yet Euphrosine's extreme attraction to faith only serves as a reminder of France's fundamental beliefs about women. According to Lahy-Hollebecque's study, *Anatole France et la femme*, France rarely accords women the ability to reason, as the author notes regarding France's *Thaïs*: "Mais hélas, Thaïs n'est qu'une faible femme, à qui la grâce du raisonnement est refusée. Elle essaye bien de lire les philosophes, mais elle ne les comprend pas; et, quoi qu'elle fasse, il lui faut retomber aux puériles explications du mythe chrétien que lui présente un diacre obscur."[72] Depictions such as this support Lahy-Hollebecque's statement that "pas une seule fois dans toute l'œuvre d'Anatole France le mot intelligence ne se trouve appliqué à la femme."[73]

Euphrosine is perhaps the exception that proves the rule, for she possesses "un esprit subtil et curieusement orné."[74] In addition, the very term *intelligence* is indeed used to describe her mind: "[Elle] se promit d'appliquer, à l'avenir, la pénétration de son intelligence à résoudre des problèmes plus dignes d'intérêt, comme, par exemple, à faire la somme des nombres représentés par les lettres du nom de Jésus...."[75] France's observation of her application of reason to mystical problems, however, does suggest that whatever intellectual potential Euphrosine exhibited is eclipsed by her own blind faith, to which she is particularly susceptible because of her sex.

Men and women throughout *L'Etui* are equally vulnerable to irrationality; the collection is, after all, a showcase of past illusions. Women seem particularly suited to religious belief, however, while men are depicted as irrational in other contexts, such as love or the Revolution. In cases where male characters hold strong religious convictions in *L'Etui*, they are feminized through allusions to their diminished virility caused by age (Célestin), by lack of interest in women (Barnabé the juggler) or by their vows of celibacy (Injuriosus, Scolastica's husband).

Célestin's failing memory and his white beard indicate his old age. As seen above, his age is linked to diminished libido when Amycus tells him that hermits are like old fauns. In addition, Célestin tries to suppress aspects of paganism that are associated with sexuality, such as the fairy tree, whose fairies "répandent des charmes sur les jeunes garçons et sur les jeunes filles."[76] Barnabé, in "Le Jongleur de Notre-Dame," also lacks desire, at least for women, being more tempted by drink than by lust: "A la vérité, il n'avait pas l'esprit tourné aux désirs charnels, et il lui en coûtait plus de renoncer aux brocs qu'aux dames."[77] It seems that the ease with which he accepts a place in the monastery is partly due to his lack of "carnal desires." The last male character cited above is Injuriosus, who marries Scolastica and then is persuaded not to consummate the union. In this case, it is not lack of desire that influences his decision, but Scolastica's own persuasive words. In fact, the impression that France gives the reader is that Injuriosus allows himself to be cuckolded.

Scolastica secretly pledged herself to Christ before marrying Injuriosus, but according to her own words, her union with Injuriosus nullifies the previous one: "Voici que, divorcée d'avec l'Epoux céleste qui me promettait le Paradis pour dot, je suis devenue l'épouse d'un homme mortel...."[78] When Injuriosus agrees not to consummate the marriage, Scolastica once again dedicates her virginity to Christ. Now, however, she is technically married to Injuriosus by the Church's own ceremony, so when she reinstates her union with Christ, she seems unfaithful to her husband, Injuriosus. Despite her wedding vows to Injuriosus, she continues to refer to Christ as her husband: "Injuriosus, dit-elle, il est difficile à un homme d'accorder une pareille chose à une femme. Mais si tu fais que nous demeurions sans tache dans ce monde, je te donnerai une part de la dot qui m'a été promise par mon Epoux et seigneur Jésus-Christ."[79] In fact, the sole marital privilege that Injuriosus enjoys is that of being nagged by his dead wife when he offers thanks to Christ for being able to preserve Scolastica's purity. Chaste, cuckolded and henpecked from beyond the grave, Injuriosus, like Célestin and Barnabé, lacks virility. Comparable to women, then, these saintly male characters are entirely consistent with France's representation of the Church's most faithful adherents—irrational and outdated by his modern, rational standards. France's characters may represent nostalgia for simpler times; however, his insistence on the illogicality of faith implies the impossibility, even the undesirability, of a return to simplicity, as this could only result from the loss of reason.

Fin-de-siècle representations of saints have been informed by centuries of rewritings: anonymous medieval lives, Jacobus de Voragine's *Golden Legend*,[80] Bollandist documentations and secular Romantic adaptations. The Romantic movement seems particularly important in Anatole France's case. In a manner consistent with the Romantic espousal of historical preservation, France transcribes and adapts medieval lives as a means of saving a disappearing legacy and reinforcing a sentiment of nationalism. In the lives that France presents in *Pierre Nozière*, for instance, the texts exhibit a preoccupation with the relationship of medieval saints to regional folklore and with the part that this folklore plays in the formation of a region's collective identity. The narrator's claims regarding the veracity of his sources are nevertheless undermined by his avowal: "... Il est temps de me rappeler que je ne suis point un hagiographe."[81] As a storyteller, Pierre's reasons for depicting saints do not include the transmission of moral truths, but a sort of national history. France's own techniques prevent his stories from being mistaken as hagiographic, as true examples of Christian morals; by incorporating paganism and citing false sources, France avoids masking his fictions in the cloak of truth. Irony and cynicism counter the nostalgia of the stories and distinguish his writings from the idealized Christianity for which he reproaches the Romantics, as the gardener in *La Révolte des anges* (1914) explains: "Le pis est que les enfants du siècle, tombés dans le dérèglement le plus affligeant, conçurent un christianisme pittoresque et littéraire, qui témoigne d'une débilité d'esprit vraiment incroyable et, finalement tombèrent dans le romantisme. La guerre et le romantisme, fléaux effroyables!"[82] France places his stories in an *étui* for safekeeping, echoing Romantic goals; the title of the collection also implies that by containing the stories in a box he limits the effects of their irrationality.

As in some Romantic works, France's legends of saints seem to represent nonreligious purposes, in contrast to those of a medieval Life. Rather than religious edification, France's depictions of saints emphasize the collective knowledge of the nation; these works can be seen as a documentation of popular history, exemplified in France's addendum to "LÆta Acilia" (1888), from the collection *Balthasar* (1889). At the end of this story involving Marie-Madeleine, France justifies the confounding of two Maries who might be seen as separate people according to some critics: "... La poésie populaire est plus subtile que la science.... Par un tour heureux de son imagination, le populaire fondit ensemble les deux Marie et créa ainsi le type merveilleux de la Madeleine. La légende l'a consacré, et c'est de la légende que je m'inspire dans mon petit conte. En cela, je me crois absolument irréprochable." As if popular legend were not authoritative enough, France offers further basis for his character: "Je puis encore invoquer l'autorité des docteurs. Sans me flatter, j'ai pour moi la Sorbonne. Elle déclara, le 1er décembre 1521, qu'il n'y a qu'une Marie."[83] While France seems to mock all authoritative assertions, by presenting the Sorbonne as a source secondary to folklore, France proposes that the legacy of legends is not necessarily based in historical fact, but rather on a common perception.

Accordingly, popular legend represents truth as documentation of the nation's heritage, but not because the tales can be proven through historical references. For France casts doubt on the validity of history in "M. Pigeonneau" from *Balthasar*, when the title character muses: "... l'histoire n'est qu'un art, ou tout au plus une fausse science. Qui ne sait aujourd'hui que les historiens ont précédé les archéologues, comme les astrologues ont précédé les astronomes, comme les alchimistes ont précédé les chimistes, comme les singes ont précédé les hommes?"[84] History is no more than the art of storytelling under the guise of truth.

On the other hand, popular legend can be associated with the identity of a region, such as that of the town of Saint-Valery-sur-Somme. In "L'Histoire de saint Gualaric ou Valery," Pierre Nozière states: "Si j'ai ... dessiné de mon mieux la figure du grand apôtre de Vimeu, c'est que cette figure ressemble, dans ses traits essentiels, à celles de tous les vieux évangélisateurs des Gaules. Par là, elle mérite d'être considérée avec attention par tous ceux qui s'intéressent à l'histoire de notre pays."[85] Saints in France's corpus may not seem significant from a religious perspective, but as they relate to the region's identity, they certainly play an important role: "Il reste dans le patrimoine de chacun de nous quelques parcelles des biens qu'ils ont légués à nos pères. Ils ont lutté contre la barbarie avec une énergie féroce. Ils ont défriché la terre; ils ont apporté à nos aïeux sauvages les premiers arts de la vie et de hautes espérances."[86]

In France's works, saints and religion sometimes have value as actors in the development of the country's identity. Yet even in texts where the merits of religion are discernible, France emphasizes that the time for saints, belief and the Church has passed, thus excluding religion from his vision of the future. France's perception of the Church echoes ideals expressed by Saint Jerome, although in the saint's case the belief system represented as outdated is paganism, not Christianity. Unlike France, Saint Jerome, a fervent advocate of Christian asceticism, never questioned the truth of Christian faith. Yet in the period of Roman decadence, he contemplated pagan philosophers, saints and satyrs and wrote satires of the Church's excesses. In the fourth century after Christ, Jerome already cried out for the Church's reform by suppressing practices inherited from pagan debauchery: "Jerome believed that the Church, whose task had been to purify by its doctrines the whole mass of society, had instead been corrupted by its rise to wealth and power until it stood no higher than the surrounding paganism."[87]

Jerome's influence is greatly felt in many aspects of France's corpus. The saint is mentioned in passing in several works, as in "Amycus et Célestin." Additionally, Jerome may be a model for the abbot Jérôme Coignard, whose knowledge of ancient pagan philosophy often outshines his Christian vocation. Also, for Epiphany in 1884, France submitted "L'Histoire de Gaspar et de la reine de Saba," a story about one of the three wise men, signed "Gérôme."[88] Finally, and most strikingly, Saint Jerome's influence is notable in France's satirical tendencies; France's works illustrate his opposition to irrationality and obsolete practices just as Jerome wrote to denounce practices he considered outmoded in his time.

In the midst of the French Decadent period and struggles between Church and State, fifteen centuries after Roman decadence and the writings of Jerome, Anatole France likewise finds fault with the Church. One of Jerome's main objectives was to promote conversion from paganism to Christianity. In a parallel move, France's devaluation of the modern Church seems to endorse the national conversion from a government heavily influenced by the Church to a secular State. While Jerome's objectives involved the cleansing of the last vestiges of paganism from the young institution, France avails himself of the saint's satirical methods to show the need to cleanse the French State of the remnants of the Church's influence. Although religion remains important as a historical phenomenon, France's works represent its incongruity in modern society. History is at the root of France's nostalgia for simpler times, for as a lover of history France appreciates the former role of the Church, just as Jerome valued pagan authors. Although conscious of the worth of the past, both Jerome and France visualize the future as needing to break with a past that is no longer fitting. While Jerome's vision of the future entailed abandoning paganism and embracing Christianity, France modernizes this goal by refuting all illogical belief, pagan, Christian and Revolutionary, lauding reason over illusion. Anatole France, history enthusiast, does not attempt to eliminate irrationality from the world; doing so would erase a large part of the past. Rather, in his *Etui*, he contains these precious memories of bygone eras, much as the founding fathers of the Church attempt to suppress pagan remnants in some of his stories. France, however, is torn; he leans toward rationalism, yet he retains the possibility of momentary lapses into irrational beliefs, lamenting humanity's lost innocence while lauding the merits of logic.

Notes

1. See Henri Jacoubet, *Le Genre troubadour et les origines françaises du Romantisme* (Paris: Les Belles Lettres, 1929).

2. Emile Zola explicitly labels France as a Romantic in an article titled "Les Poètes contemporains" (1878): "Le

recueil qu'il publie s'appelle *Les Noces corinthiennes*. ... Il croit nous rendre l'Antiquité. Je le nomme, parce qu'il représente toute une espèce, celle des romantiques qui ont rompu avec le Moyen Age pour inventer une poésie néoclassique, d'une vérité aussi discutable, d'ailleurs, que la poésie classique du XVIIe siècle." ["The collection he is publishing is called *Les Noces corinthiennes*. ... He thinks to give us Antiquity. I name him because he represents a whole species, that of the Romantics who broke with the Middle Ages in order to invent neoclassical poetry, whose authenticity is as questionable as that of the classical poetry of the seventeenth century."] Anatole France, *Œuvres*, ed. Marie-Claire Bancquart, 4 vols., Bibliothèque de la Pléiade (Paris: Gallimard, 1984), 1: 429, note 1. [Hereafter, references to *Œuvres* will include only the author's name, the volume number and the page number.] All translations in this chapter are by Christina Ferree Chabrier.

3. "For there is no joy but in illusion, and peace is found only in ignorance." France, "L'Humaine Tragédie," *Le Puits de sainte Claire*, 2: 645.

4. "'Jesus?' He murmured. 'Jesus of Nazareth? I do not remember.'" France, 1: 890.

5. "The end of the story stupefies the contemporary reader because it goes against his knowledge of Pilate: this knowledge exists only in relation to Jesus." France, 1: 1402.

6. In the early days of the hagiographic tradition, saints' lives served as a guide for living according to Christian dogma: "L'essentiel du discours, des sermons et des Vies a donc valeur moralisatrice; il vise à un approfondissement de la vie religieuse, en même temps qu'à l'abandon des séquelles normales du paganisme." ["The essential point of discourse, sermons and *Vitae* is moralizing; it aims to deepen religious life, at the same time aiming for the abandonment of the normal after-effects of paganism"] *Histoire de la France religieuse*, ed. Jacques Le Goff (Paris: Seuil, 1988), 1:76. The form and style of these texts evolved over centuries, however, with vernacular saints' lives appearing in the eleventh century. In addition, the lives run the gamut from strictly biographical to almost total fiction. See also Duncan Robertson, *The Medieval Saints' Lives: Spiritual Renewal and Old French Literature* (Lexington: French Forum, 1995).

7. France, 2:843. The cult of Saint Anthony is more explicitly portrayed as foolishness in "Superstitions" from *L'Histoire contemporaine*, an article appearing in *Le Figaro* on February 14, 1900. Here France deplores the Church's self-serving use of great legends: "Et voici qu'à Paris, parmi nous, des moines vendent, sous [le nom de saint Antoine], de bas miracles et des faveurs mensongères." [And now in Paris, among us, monks sell under [the name of Saint Anthony], petty miracles and false favors."] France, 3: 415. Saint Antoine also plays in the political arena in *M. Bergeret à Paris*, in a piece of propaganda: "N'infligez point, messieurs, au bon saint Antoine cette douleur imméritée de voir échouer son candidat." ["Do not inflict, sirs, on good Saint Anthony the unmerited pain of seeing his candidate fail."] France, 3: 317.

8. France, 2: 790. This vision of Saint Radegonde is again mentioned in *Le Mannequin d'osier* (1897), where France presents a definite distinction between the objectivity of science and the subjectivity of religious belief when the *voyante*, who easily replies to predictive and speculative questions, is unable to answer a question of scientific fact, the logarithm of 9 (France, 2: 900). In *L'Anneau d'améthyste* (1899), France depicts a rather more deceitful clairvoyant, "d'une intelligence lente et tardive" ["of a slow

and late intelligence"]. France, 3: 24. She nevertheless plays her role well enough to convince the faithful that she sees visions of Mary, until her foul language and promiscuity convince them otherwise. France, 3: 94.

9. See, for instance, France's article "Pourquoi sommes-nous tristes?" Here, he clearly states that faith, though once admirable, is not viable in fin-de-siècle France due to loss of naïveté: "Le plus grand mal ... c'est qu'avec la bonne ignorance la foi s'en est allée. Nous n'avons plus d'espérance et nous ne croyons plus à ce qui consolait nos pères. Cela surtout nous est pénible. Car il était doux de croire même à l'enfer." ["The worst evil is that faith has gone the way of decent ignorance. We no longer have hope and we no longer believe in that which consoled our fathers. That, above all, pains us. For it was pleasant to believe even in Hell."] France, La Vie littéraire (Paris: Calmann Lévy, 1895), 3: 8–9.

10. France, "La Pureté de M. Zola," La Vie littéraire, 2: 289. "The legends of virgin martyrs, such as they blossomed in the thirteenth century, are jewels whose dazzling richness must be tasted along with their barbarous naïveté. They are the masterpieces of a childish and marvelous art. The good people long remained bedazzled by them and it was the poor man's poetry until the sixteenth century. But Mr. Zola is strongly mistaken if he believes that today's religion retained the least memory of that."

11. "In reality, what a girl raised like Angélique learns, surrounded by piety, the odor of incense, is not at all The Golden Legend, but prayers, the everyday practice of Mass, catechism; she goes to confession, she receives communion. That is her whole life. It is inconceivable that Mr. Zola forgot all these practices." France, "La Pureté de M. Zola," 290.

12. Historian that he is, France is more understanding of past illusions than of present-day irrationality. In "L'Abbé Jérôme Coignard," his preface to Les Opinions de M. Jérôme Coignard, he states: "Je ne partage pas les croyances religieuses [de M. l'abbé Coignard] et j'estime qu'elles le décevaient, comme elles ont déçu, pour leur bonheur ou leur malheur, tant de siècles d'hommes. Mais il semble que les vieilles erreurs soient moins fâcheuses que les nouvelles, et que, puisque nous devons nous tromper, le meilleur est de s'en tenir aux illusions émoussées." ["I do not share Abbot Coignard's religious beliefs and I consider that they disappointed him, as they have disappointed, for their good fortune or misfortune, so many centuries of men. But it seems that old errors are less deplorable than new ones and that, since we must make mistakes, it is best to limit ourselves to dulled illusions."] France, 2: 213.

13. France, 1: 946.

14. "... he is ingenuous and retained the naïve faith of his childhood"; "... one of these side streets is in accordance with his heart, for bordered by pubs and hovels, in the corner of a house there is a Holy Virgin barred in her blue niche. In the evening, he goes from café to café and does his stations of beer and alcohol in a constant order: debauchery's great works require method and regularity." France, 1: 940.

15. The *arbre des fées* [fairy tree] is a conspicuous symbol of paganism in this and other works, most notably in Jeanne d'Arc.

16. "A place of pilgrimage"; "the faithful there venerated the holy memory of the saints Amic and Célestin." France, 1: 895.

17. "In the Life of Saint Paul told by Michel-Ange Marin is found the episode of the satyr who confesses to Antoine the existence of God, then flees. Saint Jerome is the first to recount these adven-

tures on which hagiographers embroidered." France, 1: 722, note 3.

18. "It came to him that Saint Jerome had had as traveling companions in the desert satyrs and centaurs who had confessed the truth." France, 1: 893.

19. René Draguet, ed., *Les Pères du désert* (Paris: Plon, 1949), 79. "... a very short man who had a hooked nose, horns in his forehead and goat hooves."

20. "A young boy barred his way. He was half dressed in an animal skin, and it was a faun rather than a boy; his gaze was piercing, he had a pug nose and a smiling face. His curly hair hid the two small horns in his stubborn forehead; ... his forked hooves were hidden in the grass." France, 1: 893.

21. "I am sent to you as an ambassador for those of my species, and we beg you all to pray for us to He who is also our God, whom we learned came for the salvation of the world, and whose name and reputation are spread throughout the earth." Draguet, 79.

22. "This day is for me as for you a holiday." France, 1: 893.

23. "He is risen." France, 1: 893.

24. "His feast day falls on September 13th, and ... as this date coincides with the autumnal equinox, the saint's day must have replaced some agricultural enchantment of the pagans. Like the rustic god whose place he took, he receives victims; he is offered cows, but they are not sacrificed. They are sold for the Church's profit." France, 3: 635.

25. "'Good hermit,' he said, 'do not exorcise me. This day is for me as for you a holiday. It would not be charitable to sadden me during Easter.'" France, 1: 893.

26. "'He is risen,' replied the faun. 'And I am very joyful for it.'" France, 1: 893.

27. "And while Célestin celebrated Mass, the 'goatfoot,' inclining his horned head to the earth, adored the sun and said: 'The earth is a large egg that you fertilize, sun, sacred sun.'" France, 1: 894.

28. France devotes two chapters of his *Vie littéraire* to Gustave Flaubert and another to the figure of Saint Anthony.

29. "In the center and in the very disk of the sun shines the face of Jesus Christ." Gustave Flaubert, *Œuvres complètes* (Paris: Seuil, 1964), 571.

30. "What a good sun! It heats you up. Ah! The good sun! What a good sun!" Flaubert, 471.

31. "We should not consider 'Saint Satyre' as a simple double of the story 'Amycus et Célestin' from the collection *L'Etui de nacre*; the latter is only the outline of the former. ... 'Saint Satyre' represents the honoring of the figures of desire, satyrs and nymphs. Then the coming of Christ slowly kills the former gods." France, 2: 1271.

32. "Small and of coarse structure; Célestin had built it with his own hands out of the debris of a temple of Venus." France, 1: 894.

33. "On the hill where Célestin had constructed the narrow chapel that Amycus decorated with mountain flowers, wood and water, today rises a church whose nave dates back to the eleventh century, and whose porch was rebuilt under Henri II, in the style of the Renaissance." France, 1: 895.

34. France explicitly marks the parallel between paganism and Christianity in *Le Mannequin d'osier*: "Les deux cultes étaient deux enfants jumeaux de Rome et de l'Orient. ... Leurs âmes étaient pareilles. Mais par le nom et le langage ils se distinguaient l'un de l'autre. Cette différence suffit à les rendre mortellement ennemis." ["The two cults were the twin children of Rome and the Orient. ... Their souls were equal. But name and language differentiated one from the other. This distinction sufficed to render them mortal enemies."] France, 2: 1000.

35. "I came to you, Father, because

you seem fairly good-natured underneath your long white beard. It seems to me that hermits are fauns weighed down by time. When I am old, I will be like you." France, 1: 894.

36. "Woe betide you, Alexandria, that worships monsters as gods! ... Beasts speak of the greatness of Jesus Christ and you give to beasts the honors and homage due only to God alone!" Draguet, 80.

37. "Incessantly vanquished and tempted by [the divinities], in the end [Célestin] himself establishes the misunderstanding that makes them enter the orthodox cult. He is taken in their graceful trap, and this mistake fills France's whole story with malice." France, 1: 1399.

38. The obvious counterexample is the abbot Jérôme Coignard, a logical yet religious character represented in *La Rôtisserie de la reine Pédauque* and *Les Opinions de M. Jérôme Coignard*. In his preface to the latter, however, France draws attention to the one illogical aspect of the abbot, his faith, by relating Christian belief with illusion and contrasting this with the rationality of ancient philosophers. In this preface, Jérôme's faith seems to be a fault: "Sa libre intelligence foulait aux pieds les croyances vulgaires et ne se rangeait point sans examen à la commune opinion, hors en ce qui touche la foi catholique, dans laquelle il fut inébranlable." ["His open intelligence trampled popular beliefs and did not go along with common opinions without examination, except in matters of Catholic faith, in which he was steadfast."] France, 2: 210. In addition, and despite France's assertion, Jérôme's faith is questionable. One critic feels that he deserves purgatory at most and is almost heretical (France, 2: 213, footnote). Indeed, the abbot's evocations of pagan antiquity surpass in number his expressions of Christian belief. Thus, the depiction of Jérôme does not disprove the illogicality of believers in religion, but strengthens the idea; the abbot is either a logical character, faulted for irrational belief in one area, or he is not a true believer and his rationality is untouched by such convictions.

39. Saint Valfroy, Walfroi or Vulfilaicus lived in the Ardennes and, according to Grégoire de Tours' *Histoire des Francs*, preached against a statue of Diane worshiped by the inhabitants of the region and even used force to break the statue. Grégoire apparently convinced Valfroy to give up this lifestyle and move into a monastery (France, 1: 902, note 1). In France's story, it is Bertauld who encounters such a statue. As in "Amycus et Célestin" France mixes elements of different legends.

40. France, 1: 897, note 1.

41. "The Italians ask of their gods only earthly possessions and tangible advantages. In this regard, despite the Asiatic terrors that invaded Europe, their religious sentiment has not changed. What they previously demanded of their gods and genies, today they expect from the Madonna and the saints." France, 3: 1001.

42. This term seems to derive from the name of the Greek god Aigipan or Ægipan. As a reward for his services, Zeus transformed this hybrid deity (part goat and part fish in some accounts, part goat and part man in others) into the constellation Capricorn. According to Littré, in nineteenth-century literature it is synonymous with *faune* or *satyre*.

43. "Because mystical nature was then revealed to Man and invisible things became visible for the glory of the Creator, one encountered nymphs, satyrs, centaurs and ægipans in forest glades." France, 1: 897.

44. France, 1: 897. "The God that I teach to you ... is the only true one. He

is unique in three persons, and his son was born of a virgin."

45. "But what you say of a divine virgin is not without truth. We know of a virgin with three visages.... She is named Diane, and her silver feet, under the pale light of the moon, skim over the thyme of the mountains. She did not consider it beneath her to receive shepherds and hunters like us in her bed of flowering hyacinths. Yet, she is still a virgin." France, 1: 897.

46. Bancquart relates France's antireligious views to the 1889 publication of Paul Bourget's *Disciple* and the differing critiques of the work. She finds France's position clearly against religion, in favor of logic: "Il sent que toute liberté d'examen serait interdite par un système qui subordonnerait l'exercice de l'intelligence à la nécessité de conserver la société dans sa formule contemporaine. C'est alors qu'il prend le parti du 'progrès.' ... Il faut donc reconnaître à l'analyse scientifique la valeur relative la plus haute chez l'homme. ... La morale ne se fonde pas sur les mœurs existantes, mais sur la lucidité" [He feels that all liberty of examination would be barred by a system that would subordinate the exercise of intelligence to the necessity of maintaining society in its contemporary structure. It is then that he takes the side of 'progress.' ... It is necessary to recognize in scientific analysis man's highest relative worth. ... Morals are not founded on existing mores, but on clear-mindedness."] Marie-Claire Bancquart, *Anatole France: un sceptique passionné* (Paris: Calmann-Lévy, 1984), 171.

47. "[Oliverie] understood that she was justly punished for having doubted heavenly power and for not going on the grace of God, as her sister Liberette had done." France, 1: 901.

48. "Because you asked for a sign in order to believe and took a stick for support, the hour of your blessed death will be delayed and the day of your glorification deferred." France, 1: 902.

49. "Liberette was born to be a great saint." France, 1: 899.

50. The naïveté attributed to the saints applies also to those who read their lives literally. Take for example the narrator in *Le Livre de mon ami*, a young boy whose attempts to emulate the saints distress his father and mother (France, 1:462–5). Although he soon abandons this practice, his earnest and literal interpretation of the lives parallels his mother's careful piety, drawing attention to the simplicity of believers and simultaneously associating religion with the lower classes. In *La Rôtisserie de la reine Pédauque*, a related work, saints and superstition again coincide when the mother maintains that applying the *Vie de sainte Marguerite* as a poultice relieves bodily pain (France, 2: 8).

51. "Less ancient." France, 4: 335.

52. "Beginning and end of all knowledge." France, 1: 904.

53. "A deadly illness." France, 1: 909.

54. "But as she was Christian and of uncommon piety, far from becoming prideful of these honors, she realized their vanity and promised herself to henceforth apply the penetration of her intelligence to resolving problems more worthy of interest, as, for example, making the sum of the numbers represented by the letters of Jesus' name and considering the marvelous properties of these numbers." France, 1: 904.

55. "Enlightened Euphrosine, love is stronger than the will; that is why it is suitable to obey it as one would a jealous master. Regarding you, I will do as it orders me, which is to take you as my wife." France, 1: 906.

56. "For the relics of Saint Iphraise healed diverse illnesses of men as well as animals." France, 3: 367. The name is apparently a dialectical variation: "... sainte Euphrosine, en parler du

Valois, sainte Iphraise" ["Saint Euphrosine, in Valois speech, Saint Iphraise"].

57. "The deacon Georges wrote with less grace than Herodotus and even Plutarch." France, 1: 912.

58. France, 1: 903, note 2.

59. France, 1: 918, note 1. France was undoubtedly familiar with many of their works. In *Le Crime de Sylvestre Bonnard*, he makes reference to Paulin Paris, when the title character evokes one of Paris' catalogues of manuscripts, calling Paris "mon savant collègue" ["my learned colleague"]. France, 1: 158. In *Le Livre de mon ami*, France refers to Gaston Paris' analysis of *Le Petit Poucet* (France, 1: 580).

60. "Happy the child who flees from the century in his robe of innocence! Men's souls are exposed to great peril in the cities, and particularly in Alexandria, because of the great number of women who are there. Women are such a danger for men that the mere thought of it gives me, even at my age, a shiver that shakes all my flesh. If there was one woman brazen enough to enter this holy house, suddenly my arm would again find its vigor in order to chase her with great blows of this crosier." France, 1: 909.

61. "Impure, and her mere footprint is a loathsome stain." France, 1: 909.

62. "What occupies and worries France ... are the relationships of intellectuals and the government with the Catholic Church." Bancquart, *Sceptique*, 217.

63. "By presenting in a series of short stories the characters of priests dangerous to the Republic." Bancquart, *Sceptique*, 218.

64. "I give you thanks, Jesus, that you gave me the strength to keep your treasure intact." France, 1: 916.

65. "'Sad Scolastica,' he said to himself, 'now that she is no more than a vain shadow, regrets the time for love and lost pleasures. The roses that come out of her and that speak for her tell us: Love, you who live. This marvel teaches us to taste the joys of life while there is still time.'" France, 1: 916.

66. France, 1: 917, note 1.

67. France, 1: 917, note 2.

68. France, 1: 914, note 1.

69. In "Oliverie et Liberette" as in "Amycus et Célestin" the evocation of nymphs and satyrs provides a subtler reminder of the sexual liberty associated with Greek and Roman beliefs.

70. "It remains only for me to explain how Saint Adjutor, who passed from this world to the next the same day as his return to Vernon, was able to throw his chains in the river to fill in the chasm. This difficulty is only too apparent. The saint came back to earth to work this miracle." France, 3: 579.

71. Visions such as the image of Claire seen by Saint Francis of Assisi in the prologue to *Le Puits de sainte Claire* (France, 2: 569) or those of Joan of Arc may also be considered as evidence of the illogicality associated with saints. Herbert Stewart says of France's *Jeanne d'Arc*: "She was a 'béguine,' and in her childhood piety she thought she heard the voices of angels. ... To Joan the 'miraculous' was quite in the order of things. It came out in evidence at her trial that her godfather, Jean Morel, believed fairies to have been driven from the village by priestly rites.... Joan's own opinion was that witchcraft was at work; and though she had never met fairies under the tree herself, she would not say that she had not seen them elsewhere." Anatole France, *The Parisian* (Freeport NY: Books for Libraries Press, 1972), 159–60.

72. "But alas, Thaïs is only a weak woman, to whom the grace of reason is refused. She tries to read the philosophers, but she does not understand them; and, whatever she does she must fall back on the puerile explanations of

the Christian myth, presented to her by an obscure deacon." Marie Lahy-Hollebecque, *Anatole France et la femme* (Paris: Baudinière, 1923), 22.

73. "Not a single time in Anatole France's whole corpus is the word intelligence applied to a woman." Lahy-Hollebecque, 20.

74. "A subtle and curiously embellished mind." France, 1: 903.

75. "[She] promised herself to henceforth apply the penetration of her intelligence to resolving problems more worthy of interest, as, for example, making the sum of the numbers represented by the letters of Jesus' name." France, 1: 904.

76. "Spread enchantments on the young men and women." France, 1: 892.

77. "In truth, his spirit was not turned toward carnal desires, and it pained him more to give up the pitcher than it did to give up women." France, 1: 919.

78. "And now, divorced from the heavenly spouse who promised me Heaven as a dowry, I became the wife of a mortal man." France, 1: 914.

79. "'Injuriosus,' she said, 'it is difficult for a man to grant such a thing to a woman. But if you make it so that we stay without stain in this world, I will give you a part of the dowry that was promised to me by my spouse and lord Jesus Christ.'" France, 1: 915.

80. France offers his reader a glimpse of the evolution of this compilation in *Le Crime de Sylvestre Bonnard* (1881). This reference to the *Golden Legend* indicates some of the main transformations of the *Vitæ*, compiled and altered by Jacobus, later adapted to suit particular regions. Sylvestre Bonnard's research on Christian Gaul leads him on a quest for a manuscript of *La Légende dorée* translated by a monk of the abbey of Saint-Germain-des-Prés. In addition to Jacobus' variations on the lives, this fourteenth-century document supposedly contains supplementary lives, added by the French monk: "Ce manuscrit, du XIVe siècle, contient, outre la traduction assez complète de l'ouvrage célèbre de Jacques de Voragine: 1° les légendes des saints Ferréol, Ferrution, Germain, Vincent et Droctovée; 2° un poème sur la *Sépulture miraculeuse de Monsieur saint Germain d'Auxerre*. Cette traduction, ces légendes et ce poème sont dus au clerc Jean Toutmouillé." [This manuscript, from the fourteenth century, contains, besides the fairly complete translation of the celebrated work of Jacobus de Voragine: 1st the legends of saints Ferréol, Ferrution, Germain, Vincent and Droctovée; 2nd a poem about the *Sépulture miraculeuse de Monsieur saint Germain d'Auxerre*. This translation, these legends and this poem are due to the scholar Jean Toutmouillé.] France, 1: 157. The sort of translation evoked in France's work alludes to a popularization of the lives. The addition of lives specifically related to the abbey of Saint-Germain-des-Prés localizes some of the saints. The suggestion of such a manuscript of the *Legend* thus reveals the importance of the saints to the establishment of regional identity.

81. "It is time for me to remember that I am not at all a hagiographer." France, 3: 591.

82. "The worst is that the children of the century, fallen into the most distressing dissoluteness, conceived a picturesque literary Christianity, which bears witness to a truly incredible mental deficiency, and finally fell into Romanticism. War and Romanticism, frightful scourges!" France, 4: 763.

83. "... Popular poetry is more subtle than science.... By a felicitous turn of its imagination, the people melted together the two Maries and thus created the marvelous model of the Madeleine. The legend consecrated it and it is the legend that inspires my little story. In this, I

believe myself to be absolutely irreproachable." "I can further invoke the authority of the scholars. Without flattering myself, on my side I have the Sorbonne. It declared, December 1st, 1521, that there is only one Marie." France, 1: 637.

84. "... History is nothing more than an art, or at the very most a false science. Who does not know today that historians preceded archeologists, as astrologers preceded astronomers, as alchemists preceded chemists, as monkeys preceded Man?" France, 1: 604.

85. "If I represented to the best of my ability the figure of the great apostle of Vimeu, it is because this figure resembles, in its essential traits, the figures of all the old evangelists of Gaul. Because of this, it merits attentive consideration by all those who are interested in the history of our country." France, 3: 591.

86. "There remain in all our heritage some bits of the goods they bequeathed to our fathers. They fought against barbarism with ferocious energy. They cleared the land; they brought to our savage ancestors the first arts of life and high hopes." France, 3: 591.

87. David S. Wiesen, *St. Jerome as a Satirist: A Study in Christian Latin Thought and Letters* (Ithaca, NY: Cornell UP, 1964).

88. France, 1: 714.

8

Unofficial and Secular Saint in Integral Nationalist Discourse: Maurice Barrès' Literary Jeanne d'Arc

Carolyn Snipes-Hoyt

Jeanne d'Arc was not yet officially a saint of the Catholic church at the end of the nineteenth century, though this historical personage had enjoyed special status as a popular cult figure once she left Vaucouleurs for Chinon to find Charles VII. Her canonization process began as a result of the efforts of Monseigneur Félix Dupanloup (1802–1878), bishop of Orléans, who first visited Jeanne's birthplace in Domremy, Lorraine, in 1869.[1] He had gone there to prepare himself for the writing of his second panegyric to be given in the Orléans cathedral as part of the yearly celebration held in that town in May to honor Jeanne's lifting of the siege in 1429. Dupanloup's visit to Jeanne's birthplace so inspired him that, when he returned to Orléans accompanied by the parish priest of Domremy, he enlisted the support of the thirteen bishops gathered in the cathedral for his sermon and set in motion the canonization process, which would not be completed until 1920, long after his death.[2] In January of 1894, the introductory brief that made her *venerable* was signed and her case was considered at the court of Pope Leo XIII in 1897.[3] These efforts to honor the medieval heroine, on the part of liberal French Catholicism in conjunction with Rome, had their counterparts in French Parliament, where a bill was first introduced by Republican Joseph Fabre in 1884 to institute a national holiday in her honor and was signed by 253 deputies from the left.[4] The two projects ran parallel, fraught with difficulties and mutual suspicion at every turn. In 1922, the national holiday was finally instituted in Jeanne's honor, two years after the canonization, thanks to the devotion of Maurice Barrès (1862–1923), who died the following year.[5]

During the period of strained relations between Church and State that went beyond the actual Separation (1905), Maurice Barrès carved out a niche for himself on both fronts of the debate surrounding Jeanne d'Arc; we can attribute this interest, in large part, to the Lorraine origins he held in common with her. Throughout his political career, Barrès exhibited enthusiasm for the basic premise of Revolutionary France: that the individual would impose a vision in the wider arena through exercise of sheer will and intelligent utilization of talents. In this regard, early ideologues of the Third Republic had recognized the value of Napoleon and Jeanne d'Arc as heroes to be presented to students in the new secular schools.[6] Consequently, Barrès and many of his generation had a special affection for Napoleon, as a figure worthy of emulation. After the turn of the twentieth century, however, Barrès could be labeled a guardian of "la vraie France" (the true France) since the events of the Dreyfus Affair convinced him of the value of traditional French institutions.[7] He staunchly defended them against the "foreign" enemy within—that is, the Jewish element.[8] He focused on his native Lorraine in his integral nationalist discourse on "la Terre et les Morts" (the earth and the dead) and in his promotion of *enracinement*, that is, the endorsement of strong connections to the land of one's birth and ancestry. Along with monarchists of the far right and the Action Française, not quite so far right, he had recourse to the figure of Jeanne d'Arc, the most famous Lorrainer.[9]

During this dynamic period of French culture, Maurice Barrès enjoyed an extraordinary double career as a writer and politician. In 1906, he experienced the unusual prestige of official recognition in both his literary and political endeavors: election to the Académie française and to Parliament, as a deputy for the 1er arrondissement in Paris.[10] In 1923, he was the last French author to be honored with a state funeral, the cortege stopping momentarily at Frémiet's equestrian statue of Jeanne d'Arc on the Rue de Rivoli, on its way to Notre-Dame cathedral in Paris.[11] Since his first vocation was literary, it is unfortunate that he never finished the play he planned to write about the heroine. Given Barrès' high visibility and influence during a period of conflict and transition, an examination of the political and literary context of the three essays Barrès did produce on Jeanne d'Arc will help elucidate the situation of this unofficial saint in French culture at the turn of the century and beyond. According to his personal literary goals, Barrès' salute to the heroine was meant to enchant and energize his reading public and, at the same time, to encapsulate his ideas on the collective conscience, which were strongly influenced by local factors he felt played an important role in forming patriotic French men and women. These essays also reveal the other side of nationalist discourse: inherent notions of xenophobia and masculine hierarchy.[12]

It could be said of Maurice Barrès, as it is of Charles Maurras, the leader of the Action Française, that he came to politics by way of aesthetics.[13] Following the lead of Maurras, Barrès appears to have made a distinction between romantic idealism—the mother of anarchy and evil—and classicism—equally ideal-driven, but standing for principles of order, including form, hierarchy and discipline, in an attempt to privilege the latter.[14] Barrès, however, admitted difficulty in shaking romantic tendencies; he was, in fact, a more charismatic figure and a more dynamic speaker than Maurras. In his first novel trilogy, *Le Culte du Moi* (1888–91), Barrès struck a chord with his reading public through his fictionalized account of a search for personal significance in a world without transcendence.[15] In the 1880s and early 1890s he was known as the "Prince de la jeunesse" for the following he commanded among the members of the youthful generation disgusted by the morass of mediocrity they perceived in a newly industrialized, profane and democratic French society. Barrès' early fiction could be subsumed under Tadié's heading "mythes de la révolte."[16] Political involvement, first as a Boulangist, was Barrès' way of rising above what they saw as the inability of the Third Republic to effect change.[17] His later use of the Jeanne d'Arc figure could be construed as yet another attempt at positive action, this time in the form of ideological discourse with attention to historical detail and literary forms of expression.

Viewed politically in the post–Revolutionary period, Barrès has been cited with Charles Péguy as the ancestral link in the French family tree of *patriotisme révolutionnaire*, which connects Jules Michelet of the nineteenth century with Charles de Gaulle and André Malraux of the twentieth, all of whom have also been associated with the *Pucelle* in one way or another.[18] Barrès' depictions of the heroine could be compared in a cross-sectional sample with others produced during the turn-of-the-century period by J.-K. Huysmans, Charles Péguy, Paul Claudel, Léon Bloy, and Anatole France, although reasons vary drastically for these writers' interest in the unofficial saint.[19] From a contemporary view, Barrès' integral nationalism and organicist explanatory strategies, both of which shaped his use of the Jeanne d'Arc figure and distinguish his discourse from some others during this period, has been called proto-fascist.[20] Barrès' deliberate move toward political conservatism might again be explained with recourse to Maurras' literary terminology: His use of Jeanne d'Arc features elements belonging to the postrevolutionary romantic current, namely, mechanical logic and the focus on the individual's often unrewarded efforts in the struggle against insurmountable forces. But these traits are found in combination with an emphasis on order and discipline derived more likely from a neo-classical aesthetics, with the accent stylistically placed on harmony, balance and serenity. A dissonance results from this juxtaposition of romantic and neo-classical aesthetics and demands interpretation.[21]

To understand the complexities of this representation, Barrès' literary Jeanne d'Arc needs first to be understood in the context of *décadance*, as a phase of French Romanticism, according to some critics, and in connection with writers such as Baudelaire, Huysmans, Mendès, and Rachilde.[22] Marie-Claire Bancquart notes that, at the beginning of his literary career, Barrès assumed a pose, similar to that of many decadent writers, attempting to shock the bourgeoisie with his immorality and his disdainful style.[23] Although he produced his texts on Jeanne d'Arc after the turn of the century, it is interesting to note the continued influence of *décadance* on his literary sensibility, even as a more mature writer. In this light, it is useful to consider Barrès' earlier representations of women, created at a time when a wave of feminism was sweeping through French society. The ethos of Barrès' first novel series was scorned, remarks Angenot. Referring to *Un Homme libre* (1889), the second novel in the *Culte du Moi* trilogy, for example, Angenot notes that women are seen as "de petits animaux qui valent le plaisir qu'elles donnent aux jeunes gens: discuter de leurs droits ou de leurs capacités congénitales est assommant et ridicule."[24] Obviously, Barrès was more concerned at that time with masculine heroism and the search for meaning in life as a masculine endeavor than with feminine heroism, virtue or individuality, certainly important elements when considering Jeanne d'Arc.

In the third novel of Barrès' first trilogy, the representation of the eponymous female character is different, however, and vaguely resembles Barrès' representation of Jeanne after the turn of the century. Bérénice, in *Le Jardin de Bérénice* (1891), fits a representational scheme that exhibits a kind of classical discipline and order, a shift noticed by other critics. First of all, Bérénice and Jeanne d'Arc are heroines in the style of Racine according to Barrès himself: "J'y reconnais les plus purs sons de l'âme."[25] In both cases, however, there is still a sincere concern for the individual, since Barrès uses the Bérénice figure to cast light on a certain "secret dans l'âme," that is, the secrets in the soul of the writer himself. Michel Mercier notes that this deeper level of the text is suggested by means of a set of spatial correspondences that frame the enigma without defining it, following symbolist strategies inherited from Baudelaire.[26] The same could be said of Barrès' Jeanne d'Arc figure in the literary essays, where the physical space is transformed from a *jardin* (a garden) or the *Musée du roi René* where Bérénice grew up, to Jeanne's childhood landscape. In one of Barrès' literary essays, "La victime des fées," the narrator himself points to the relationship he is trying to highlight between the figure of Jeanne d'Arc and the "earth" that produced her: "Ce n'est pas que je prétende expliquer une Jeanne d'Arc par sa famille, son village et sa terre. Tout ce pays, bien qu'il s'unisse avec la pensée de l'héroïne, est insuffisant à la définir et à la contenir, comme il le fut à la retenir."[27] In mentioning this problematic, Barrès shows his desire to explore creatively Taine's principle of *race, milieu, moment* and consider the case of individuals who rise above what determines them.

We must add to this representational scheme the fact that the historical Jeanne d'Arc figure is based on concrete historical information as contentious as her nineteenth-century status. In the fifteenth century, she had stood out as a result of her controversial involvement in public affairs and insistence on masculine attire, facts that were a source of dispute for many of her contemporaries and, in particular, for the judges at the Rouen Trial who condemned her to death. Moreover, details about the accusations directed at Jeanne had come to light following the first publication of the documentation from the Rouen Trial and the Rehabilitation Trial (1841–1849) by Jules Quicherat, a major event in the nineteenth-century representation of the medieval heroine. The French public became aware, for example, that Jeanne had indeed worn a soldier's armor and the clothing of a male courtier and this information was received at first with varying levels of shock and surprise.[28] Barrès' first essay on Jeanne in his 1916 collection, entitled "Domremy-la-Pucelle," in fact begins with Quicherat:

> Quicherat est allé chercher Jeanne d'Arc dans le texte des deux procès de condamnation et de réhabilitation. Depuis quatre siècles, elle était enfouie dans ces pièces de procédure. On y trouve la matérialité des faits. Les questions de ses ennemis amènent Jeanne à donner sur toute sa vie d'innombrables détails, d'une authenticité certaine.[29]

Firsthand knowledge of Jeanne's answers to her judges at Rouen had a profound effect on the nineteenth-century French public, especially when the responses were translated from the official Latin into French. Barrès quotes long passages from a French translation of the Rouen trial documentation in his essays about Jeanne, yet admits that all these facts from her life "ne nous rendent pas complètement raison de son héroïsme" and that "[i]l y a de l'inexplicable chez elle...."[30] This mystery surrounding Barrès' reconstruction of Jeanne's childhood landscape has to do with the magic she worked on her contemporaries.

It was the inhabitants of the city of Vaucouleurs in Lorraine who first recognized the powerful spiritual content of Jeanne's mission and provided the young girl with men's clothing when Robert Baudricourt sent her on her way to Chinon for an audience with Charles VII. Jeanne was revered by the general population during the two and a half years of her public life and until her death at the stake on May 30, 1431. Christine de Pisan and other poets extolled Jeanne's virtues soon after the victory at Orléans in 1429 and contemporary chronicles recounted her adventure from a number of points of view. She has remained a popular cult figure in France ever since, but the city of Orléans has honored her memory more faithfully than any other region of France, celebrating annually the lifting of the siege, with rare exceptions occurring only during periods of war.

The most notorious break with Jeanne's sustained popular acclaim in France was Voltaire's eighteenth-century epic poem, *La Pucelle d'Orléans*, ridiculing the importance she attributed to her virginity.[31] Preparations for the centenary celebration of Voltaire's death, to take place on May 30, 1878, fueled the Catholic movement to canonize Jeanne, stirring up the desire to negate the nefarious influence of the heroine's slanderer, whose death day happens to be the same.[32] Monseigneur Dupanloup, who initiated the move to canonize her, took advantage of the situation to make a call for funds to put new stained-glass windows in the cathedral at Orléans, since the originals had been destroyed during the war of 1870.[33] A group of women calling themselves the "Femmes de France" organized a demonstration that was to take place the very day of the celebration on the Place des Pyramides, where Frémiet's equestrian statue of the heroine had been erected a few years earlier.[34] The furor surrounding the centenary of Voltaire's death drew almost 20,000 pilgrims to Jeanne's birthplace in Domremy. On that occasion the project of building a basilica in her honor in the Bois-Chesnu was born. A church was to be built on the very spot where Jeanne had heard the voices of saints Michael, Catherine and Margaret, since it was thought that this would dispel any notion that they had been evil spirits, a suggestion present in the documentation from the Rouen Trial. More and more pilgrims visited the site every year—including 35,000 in 1894.[35] Conversely, Republicans became disenchanted on the whole with the project of instituting a national holiday in honor of Jeanne d'Arc as it became clear the Catholic church was claiming her as their own.[36]

All told, the attention given to Jeanne's story during the late nineteenth century made a sharp curve upward, and Barrès was swept up in many of the issues that put her at the center of political debates at that time and during the first two decades of the twentieth century. Just prior to World War I, cultural production on the heroine achieved its highest volume and variety ever, with the beatification in 1909 and the five hundredth anniversary of her birth celebrated in 1912.[37] Enthusiasm on Jeanne's behalf was generated in a number of sectors of French society during the Belle Époque: Plays were performed;[38] boy scout troops, parish gymnastic teams and feminist conferences were named after her; a colossal statue was planned for a site near Rouen; the Action Française claimed her as their icon of choice; and numerous children's books and devotional materials appeared, to mention a few examples.[39] We could add to this the complicated set of struggles that had been set in motion long before the turn of the century between the Catholic Church and Republicans in her name, and it becomes clear that the amount of discursive social space taken up by this young girl who died almost five hundred years earlier at age nineteen was considerable. Nevertheless, Jeanne's conception of France, predicated on the monarchy and the Catholic Church, had become a cause for dispute in the secular state. For staunch Catholics and more secular Republicans alike, however, the actions of this peasant maiden were problematic. She had proclaimed it her personal mission to remove the foreigner from French soil and firmly establish an unpopular crown prince on the throne of a divided France ruled by the English, insisting on her own military strategies, political insights and direct access to knowledge of God's will. Now that the facts were known, Jeanne's adventure merited a doubly ambiguous status in the annals of French history and among Church authorities. On the one hand, they had been responsible for her death at the stake, based on accusations of heresy and failure to conform to accepted norms of behavior for a woman of her standing, yet she had sworn loyalty to God, the Pope and the king of France and maintained exemplary innocence and devotion to a cause, a purity underscored by her vow of virginity.

An important factor that had contributed to the increasing attention given the medieval heroine during the later nineteenth century was the publication and dissemination of Jules Michelet's work on Jeanne. One-time professor at Collège de France and author of major serialized historical works in a romantic vein, Jules Michelet published his two chapters on the heroine in 1841, in Volume Five of *Histoire de France*, later transforming the work into a monograph that went through numerous editions with the *Bibliothèque des chemins de fer* and *Hachette*, with slight modifications. As a Republican ideologue, he found the heroine the ideal figure for the promotion of Revolutionary ideals, "la sainte de la patrie."[40] He made her the symbol of an oppressed people; in fact, the Church moved precipitately to canonize Jeanne, says Jacques Dalarun, in order to avoid being placed in the role of villain.[41] Barrès was, of course, familiar with Michelet's version of the Jeanne d'Arc story and endorsed his notion of history, praising him for his ability to revitalize the past. In particular, Barrès agreed with Michelet's method of using *milieu* to explain events.[42] However, Barrès was critical of his inclusion of certain sordid details that he felt no longer corresponded to French sensibilities.[43]

Following the defeat at Sedan and the Commune (1870–1871), Jeanne had taken on particular significance with relationship to the lost provinces, as a native of the part of Lorraine that had not been annexed by the Germans, and this is an important factor to consider with relationship to Maurice Barrès, a native Lorrainer himself. Paul Déroulède is often mentioned in conjunction with Barrès' political activities since they were together throughout the Boulangist movement of the 1880s, the Ligue des patriotes that succeeded it and until Déroulède's death in 1914. In 1875 Déroulède read a poem at the ceremony inaugurating Frémiet's armored equestrian statue of the heroine recently erected on the Place des Pyramides in Paris, referring to her as "la patronne des envahis" ("the patron saint of the invaded ones") and thus equating her with the lost provinces. The poem became part of a collection meant to instill the fighting spirit in young men, *Chants du soldat*, distributed during the 1880s to children in the new secular schools all over France under Jules Ferry. Civic representations of the heroine multiplied during the period of *statuomanie* (craze for statuary) of the 1880s, as Republicans perfected the work of nation-building and geared up to celebrate the centenary of the French Revolution.[44] Jeanne d'Arc was immortalized in the Panthéon with the introduction of three paintings by J. E. Lenepveu, joining other deities of the French nation, such as Clovis, Sainte Geneviève and Saint Denis. She became the subject of religious art as well: statues, mosaics, murals and stained-glass windows to decorate the Sacré-Coeur under construction in Montmartre, in Paris, for example, or for the basilica being built in her honor in the Bois-Chenu, near Domremy, her birthplace in Lorraine.

In his search for "discipline" after the turn of the twentieth century, in the sense of both classical aesthetics and political doctrine, Barrès began to reflect seriously on Lorraine. He developed his discourse on "La Terre et les Morts" ("The Earth and the Dead") in connection with the necessity for *enracinement* (rootedness).[45] Jeanne d'Arc, his fellow Lorrainer and early defender of France against foreign invaders, occupied his attention in this regard. Not only was she seen as an ancestor to be remembered and known for her heroism and patriotism, but she also served as an excellent example of *enracinement*, the unadulterated product of French soil. Barrès gave speeches and wrote articles about her, became involved in the effort to institute a national holiday in her honor, planned a play about her childhood, wrote a preface to Jules Baudot's play that was performed in Domremy for pilgrims visiting her birthplace in 1912 and used her story to prepare French soldiers for the ultimate sacrifice.[46]

With his literary essays, Barrès seems intent on creating, in a piece of artful writing, an image of Jeanne that would harmonize his nationalist ideals and goals, showing, as a synthesis and a set of correspondences, influences of race and milieu, building his own version of Taine's rather more mechanical deterministic principle. In these pieces on Jeanne's childhood, Barrès intentionally contemplates his native Lorraine, creating the sequel to a motif that appears in *Amori et dolori sacrum* (1903): he attempts to explore further the idea of a "Lorraine intérieure,"[47] only briefly mentioned in the earlier text. Not only does he see Jeanne d'Arc as the obvious patron saint of France, but he has become convinced that her native Lorraine is a quintessentially French plot of ground, since it divides France from Germany, linguistically and culturally, in spite of the fact that the territory, the race and the French heroine had all been called into question by this time.[48]

In order to evaluate the results of Barrès' essays on Jeanne d'Arc, specific aspects of the connection between female figure and place need to be explored further. In the model considered earlier, present in *Le Jardin de Bérénice* and the essays on Jeanne d'Arc, place outlines or delimits the enigma of the female figure, the latter serving as a trope for the narrator's inner self. But this construction could also be understood in terms of emphasis and tropological structure. In a few of Barrès' literary texts the primacy goes to place, as in the case of *La Mort de Venise*, a selection from *Amori et dolori sacrum*, where the idea of woman is nevertheless implicit, endowing the city of Venice with feminine attributes associated with a music that entices death:

> Venise chante à l'Adriatique qui la baise d'un flot débile un éternel opéra. Désespoir d'une beauté qui s'en va vers la mort. Est-ce le chant d'une vieille corruptrice ou d'une vierge sacrifiée? Au matin, parfois, dans Venise, j'entendis Iphigénie, mais les rougeurs du soir ramenaient Jézabel....[49]

Here, the female figure is not a personage in any real sense, but rather admittedly a figment of the narrator's imagination, part of a metonymical linguistic structure signifying obsession with an exotic place, a dominant theme in much of Barrès' literary writing.[50] *La Mort de Venise* is Barrès at his most romantic, self-consciously so, perhaps, in order to mark the self-willed tragic end of that current in his writing.[51] Geography is endowed with a feminine existence, specific or not, and the rhythmic prose narrative flows toward disintegration, pushed forward by the leitmotif of song. These traits characterize much of Barrès' literary writing that verges on *décadence*.

In other texts by Barrès, however, primacy goes to the female figure, as in the case of *Colette Baudoche* (1909), the story of a young French-speaking woman living in Metz. She shows great nationalistic courage in refusing to marry a Prussian professor who falls in love with her and her "superior" culture. In this case, the female figure is allowed a concrete textual existence and her identity is specifically tied to a location, occupied Lorraine, in a more stable linguistic configuration. The figures of Colette Baudoche and Jeanne d'Arc are closely linked, in fact, since both are ideological representations of female figures, meant to communicate positive ideas related to *enracinement*, or connection to a precise location, and integral nationalist dogma in general. They are Barrès' attempt at discipline and order, classical paradigmatic representations meant to convey a sense of balance and serenity as opposed to the more syntagmatic and metonymical representation leading to dissolution and chaos, as seen in *La Mort de Venise*. In both *Colette Baudoche* and the Jeanne d'Arc essays, the female figure is defined, to a large extent, through her landscape, and the reverse is true as well: The French landscape produces these women. In *Colette Baudoche*, the reader learns that "Bien que privées d'une beauté souveraine, les filles du pays messin, nettes et lumineuses, s'accordent avec les prairies, les collines, le ciel et la rivière."[52] In the case of Jeanne, there is a distinct effort to show the harmony between the feminine figure and the environment where she spent the first years of her life, with an emphasis on the combination of cultural influences present in the Lorraine region: "Les diverses puissances religieuses éparses dans cette vallé meusienne, à la fois celtique, latine et catholique, Jeanne les ramasse et les accorde."[53]

In the essays on Jeanne and in *Colette Baudoche*, in fact, there is blatant recourse to organicist explanatory logic, whereby details signify a whole that has a different quality from the sum of its parts, according to the synecdochic and paradigmatic configuration of nationalist discourse. The female figure helps to define Frenchness in the symbolic code, through the connections established with her geographic and racial origins. For Barrès, Alsace and Lorraine take on a particular meaning as a point where what it means to be French meets the "other" at the elevation called Sion-Vaudémont—Barrès' "Sainte colline nationale"[54]—and at Sainte-Odile in Alsace.

What impresses Barrès is that the Gallo-Romans have stood firm in this part of France against the Germanic peoples over the centuries, holding onto their culture and language: "Sainte-Odile d'Alsace et Sion de Lorraine ... symbolisent les vicissitudes de la résistance latine à la pensée germanique."[55] Lorrainers and Alsatians have shown their willingness to fight for this identity. As a signifier for the region of Lorraine, "la sainte figure de la vierge lorraine"[56] evokes then at once a collective identity and impenetrable autonomy, this latter a characteristic of the allegorical representation of virgins as vessels without leaks. Barrès gives his readers to understand that both the collective and the autonomous are necessary ways of viewing and defining the individual within society and, in particular, viewing French allegiances during the pre–World War I years.

In keeping with this chauvinistic discourse, the figures of both Colette Baudoche and Jeanne d'Arc face Germany and all things German, in a Manichean opposition. During the late 1890s and early 1900s, the evocation of the name of Jeanne d'Arc had appeared as the counterbalance to the hated Jew, sometimes personified as Alfred Dreyfus during the course of the successive Dreyfus Affairs, as many scholars of the far right have indicated. For example, on May 19, 1896, Catholic students demonstrated around Frémiet's statue in the Place des Pyramides, crying "Vive Jeanne d'Arc et vive le Roi!" Afterward they ran to the offices of the *Peuple français*, Abbé Garnier's newspaper, and cried out "Mort aux Juifs!" Garnier replied, exclaiming "Vive Jeanne d'Arc! Vive la France aux Français."[57] An outspoken antidreyfusard and anti–Semite during the fin-de-siècle period, Barrès contemplated the Jewish Captain Alfred Dreyfus at the Rennes Trial during which he was demoted and wrote, "Ce déraciné se sent mal à l'aise dans un des carreaux de notre vieux jardin français.... Que Dreyfus est capable de trahir, je le conclus de sa race."[58] Barrès' discursive violence wills the innocent man dead, a treacherous Judas who must give himself over to his fate: "Seule, dans un bois décrié, une branche d'arbre se tend vers lui. Pour qu'il s'y pende."[59]

After the Agadir crisis, Barrès and other anti–Semites began to concentrate on the enemy across the Rhine, and attention was drawn away from the enemy within. Germany sent the *Panther* to Agadir, on the Atlantic coast of Morocco, after a failure in negotiations that had been under way for some time concerning the Franco-German exploitation of that country. This was an effort on the part of the Germans to convince the French government to offer compensation for losses suffered there. The news from Agadir in July of 1911 caused no immediate panic, notes Weber, but many historians agree that it was the first general mobilization of French patriotism. In fact, as Weber explains, the French had refused in general to see Germany as an actual enemy to combat until this time.[60] In the written texts of the speeches Barrès gave once the war with Germany had actually begun, in 1914 and 1915, and included in *Autour de Jeanne d'Arc*, the Germans are vilified openly. The saintly and innocent figure of the heroine offsets the negative German value, as she had been used earlier with regard to the Jewish element. In "La fête nationale de Jeanne d'Arc" (December 22, 1914), for example, Barrès suggests that the Germans have revered disloyalty and cruelty, and he accuses them of crushing the weak to enslave them, while the French, in the knightly Jeanne d'Arc, possess a model of "héroïsme généreux" ("noble heroism").[61] In the four texts of speeches that appear in *Autour de Jeanne d'Arc*, Barrès depicts a monstrous and ferocious Germany. While the Germans gather before the altars of Thor, he admonishes the French: "Etudiez Jeanne d'Arc, méditez sa vie, sa mort, sa verve charmante, sa chevalerie, son génie mystérieux, son sacrifice."[62]

The strong Manichean contrast set forth in *Autour de Jeanne d'Arc*, delineating German monstrosity and French humanity, had circulated as a trope in the *Revanche* rhetoric of the last decades of the nineteenth century.[63] But attitudes among the educated had softened. As a child of eight, Barrès had witnessed the entry of Prussian soldiers into his native Charmes, in Lorraine; in the intervening years, however, Richard Wagner, in addition to German philosophers and writers such as Schopenhauer, Goethe and Nietzsche, had had a profound effect on Barrès and his generation. Performances of such compelling plots as *Tristan und Isolde* obsessed Barrès at least until World War I.[64] Wagner's artistic project—the notion of the *Gesamtkunstwerk*, the power, the national myth, the emphasis on primitive impulses, the individual and the collective conscience—continued to fascinate Barrès throughout his career, as biographers have pointed out. Barrès had seen in Wagner's use of myth the possibility for an *éthique nouvelle* (a new ethic) capable of replacing the Christian one as a source of collective memories.[65] However, Barrès drew the line at Nietzsche, whose superman he considered unchristian and inhumane. At the end of the text of his May speech in 1914, given at Place des Pyramides in Paris, he pleads with his audience to consider Jeanne as a heroine who rises above the normal cut of humanity and yet is worthy of admiration, in comparison to the diabolical Nietzschean superman that has, for him, come to characterize the entire German nation: "Cette personne surhumaine, toute pleine de pitié divine, nous devons l'opposer à l'indigne surhomme, d'une félicité diabolique, où se complaît aujourd'hui la Germanie."[66]

Contemplation of this German invention led Barrès to focus on positive aspects of the various currents that, for him, work together to define the French character and distinguish it from all others. They are related to its Celtic, Latin and Christian origins. Barrès makes it clear to his readers that he has found the French figure that will illustrate positive elements of the national psyche and successfully combat the force of Germanic myth, hoping no doubt, with this discovery and elaboration, to bring power of Wagnerian proportions to his political vision. The ideals "la sainte figure de la vierge lorraine" represents are the best the West has to offer, he notes, "la loi d'amour et de justice," which is "la loi qui toujours a prêché de limiter et d'adoucir les droits de la Force."[67] Barrès wishes to insist on the notion that the French are civilized and the Germans are not, thereby endorsing conformity to certain *doxa* viewed as peculiar to French culture and worthy of promotion in the paradigm of Nation.

Additionally, Barrès knows it is important to emphasize that Jeanne d'Arc, as a continuation of a tradition of feminine allegorical figures representing virtues, was not only pure, but French and feminine, thus fully supporting divisions between the sexes and respecting family values. This text exhibits an effort to answer Freemason opponents of the national holiday in Jeanne's honor, like Louis Martin, whose accusations made Jeanne a "Walkyrie hommasse" ("a mannish Walkyrie"), "crétine" ("idiot") and "cabotine"("show off"). [68] As a pure and innocent virgin, the Jeanne d'Arc of legend and history aided Barrès and other ideologues in surmounting the degeneracy associated with women that threatened to infect Western European civilization. The image of the prostitute had dominated in French culture during the last quarter of the nineteenth century and had served as the vehicle for masculine fears of uncontrolled feminine sexual freedom, the spread of syphilis, degeneracy, and low birthrates. The masculine hierarchy was faced with the challenging task of ensuring the cooperation of women in order to maintain the purity of the race.[69] In *La mort de Venise* the Barrésian narrator shows his fascination with the disintegrating city of Venice, calling her "une vieille corruptrice," a Siren wooing him to lose himself in her attractions, and hesitates momentarily as to whether he should call her a "vierge sacrifiée."[70] As a virgin and martyr, Jeanne would be better suited than the city of Venice for the label of "vierge sacrifiée," most readers would conclude, if he had mentioned the medieval heroine in this text, where Lorraine is equated with true values. As a virgin willing to be sacrificed for her country, Jeanne could more likely be associated with Iphigenia than the disintegrating Venice. Jeanne's image was, in fact, to prove useful to Barrès as an illustration of the coherence of integral nationalism, as a trope for the inviolable and the geographic rootedness he wanted to promote as part of a paradigm that emphasized regional identities, where the local was privileged as essential to membership in a larger group.

In the essays on Jeanne d'Arc, the precise geographic connection was reinforced through the tourist brochure style of the narrator, who beckons the reader to make the acquaintance of the heroine in her humble and unique surroundings. The narrator-tourist guide takes his reading public on a visit of the area: "... je voudrais que vous vinssiez dans ce pays de Domremy ... Nous nous y acheminerons derrière une longue suite de visiteurs...."[71] The fact that Barrès places emphasis in this text on Jeanne's uncorrupted purity and equates her with a specific region makes her an appropriate signifier in this geographical scheme whose purpose is to identify members of the social group, while excluding other sectors of the population. The Catholic component of belonging is indicated when the tourist guide–narrator shows the reader the church where Jeanne worshiped: "Nous mettrons nos doigts dans la cuve de granit où elle prenait l'eau bénite; nous vénérerons la sainte Marguérite de pierre ... qui a vu Jeanne agenouillée."[72] Catholicism is one of the traditional French institutions that Barrès began supporting prominently in the wake of the Dreyfus Affair and after the turn of the century. He is said to have undergone a conversion experience during this period, like a number of his contemporaries— Huysmans, Claudel and Péguy, for example.

Nevertheless, the pre–Christian element in Lorraine identity figures prominently in these essays. Following Jules Michelet, Barrès sheds a positive light on the details from the trial documentation about Jeanne's alleged participation in pre–Christian May Day rituals, including the invocation of fairies around an oak tree: *l'Arbre des Dames les Fées*, in *le Bois-Chenu*.[73] His strategy is reminiscent of Wagner in its romanticization of pagan ancestors and practices and in its evocation of a foggy atmosphere suggesting the mythical past. The details from Jeanne's trial documentation are given life in Barrès' text "Domremy-la-Pucelle," where the narrator conjures the heroine's childhood home in Lorraine: "A Domremy, nous sommes enveloppés dans la vapeur de mystère où Jeanne se forme."[74] The *Beau mai* (May tree) of the trial documentation figures in this text as part of the décor, as do the *gui celtique* (Celtic mistletoe) and *fontaines fées* (fairy fountains) or "[f]ontaines druidiques." ("fountains of the Druids")[75] Jeanne herself is called "cette fée dont nous avons fait une sainte."[76] In the essay entitled "La victime des fées," there is mention as well of "Merlin, le roi des enchanteurs," who was supposed to have predicted Jeanne's mission.[77]

The reader-tourist is told what conclusions to draw, rather than shown the surroundings, and allowed to develop a personal relationship with them, a practice that contributes to the ideological intent of these essays. The narrator admonishes the reader, for example, not to see Jeanne as the heroine of an idyll and not to tie a blue ribbon around her neck as one sees on the virgins in the Place Saint Sulpice in Paris.[78] He speaks with deprecation to those who would sweeten and sentimentalize her story. Selections from Jeanne's testimony from the Rouen trial are quoted, providing an authentic note that echoes throughout the essays. Jeanne identifies herself and her family, commenting innocently on her involvement in the pagan rituals of the May Day celebrations that had been, and still were, problematic for the Church. Barrès ends "La victime des fées" with a long sentence subtly pointing to the irony of the present situation, where the nuns of Saint Theresa occupy the very site where Jeanne heard her voices:

> Toutes les messes de la basilique, toutes les prières que
> murmurent sans trêve, de jour et de nuit, les religieuses de
> Sainte-Thérèse, installées là, dans leur Carmel (et qui boivent
> aujourd'hui l'eau de la fontaine druidique), ne sont pas de trop
> pour châtier les présences mystérieuses qui compromirent Jeanne,
> et dont les stériles menées ont servi de prétexte pour allumer
> le bûcher de l'enfant qui, sans les connaître, leur apportait des
> couronnes.[79]

It is important that the voices Jeanne heard really came from the saints and God in order for her candidacy for sainthood to be successful, yet Barrès wishes to show the innocence of rural pre-Christian practices and uphold them as part of French identity. This view stands in direct opposition to Voltaire, known for his mockery of medieval superstition.

The modern tourists visiting Jeanne's birthplace are supposed to breathe in the local atmosphere, weighed down with the history of a people; that *brouillard* (fog) is meant to produce a dissolving action that strangely runs counter to the defining and concentrating movements that elsewhere are associated with establishing local and national identity: "Les villages s'enfoncent dans la brume, le coeur se perd dans le ravissement."[80] Jeanne is "La victime des fées," according to the title of the third of these essays, in both a negative and a positive sense. Her ecclesiastical judges in Rouen wished to show her guilt in this regard, yet within Barrès' integral nationalist paradigm, Jeanne is an ancestor, and the pagan element of her background adds something of the delightfully primitive in Wagnerian legends: "Ces brouillards du paganisme local sont admis à baiser les pieds nus de la Jeannette quand elle court, dans les prairies de la Meuse."[81] The imagery of mist conveys a sense of the way the collective conscience is formed and affects behavior.

The pagan Celtic element is placed almost on par with the other major components of what Barrès sees as defining the French people; he considered it a religion in its own right. Barrès had noted in *Mes Cahiers*, that Jeanne unifies religious fervor from three sources—the Roman, the Celtic and the Christian.[82] The idea would be repeated in the essay "Domremy-la-Pucelle": "Les diverses puissances religieuses ..., à la fois celtique, latine et catholique, Jeanne les ramasse et les accorde."[83] The three major components of the French national character would still be evident to the contemporary tourist to this region, the narrator insists in "La victime des fées." Jeanne's education took place, "au milieu des fontaines druidiques, des vestiges latins et des vieilles églises chrétiennes," three concrete details that work together ("c'est un beau concert") and signify a whole that is conceptual: the French nation.[84]

Barrès highlights the Gallo-Roman period in Lorraine history in the essay entitled "L'enfant dans la prairie," where the Latin influences are considered in combination with the Christian and are responsible for the "love" and "justice" he cites as the major contribution France can make to the world—"le rêve généreux de la France Eternelle." He writes about the family of Baccius whose virgin daughter Libaire resisted Emperor Julian the Apostate's advances out of loyalty to her Christian religion. Barrès suggests that Jeanne might very well have heard this story as a child, since there was a shrine near Domremy containing a small statue of Saint Libaire. Barrès makes reference to other women in Lorraine. In particular, he directs attention to Michelet's mention of some peculiarities of the Lorraine situation in his account of Jeanne d'Arc in *Histoire de France* (1842); this is a region where daughters took their mothers' surnames and where the abbesses of Remiremont had presided over a feudal court. Barrès credits Michelet with recognizing the important role that women have played in public life in Lorraine.[85]

Curiously, the message that comes across to the reader concerning women in this collection of texts about Jeanne d'Arc is one of a clearly defined feminine role within a masculine hierarchy. Although Barrès concedes the predisposition of the Lorraine nation to recognize the right of virgins to guide and save its people, this active feminine role is not the example put forward in his speech to the "jeunes filles de Paris." In 1915, these women submitted a letter to Barrès, President of the *Ligue des patriotes*, requesting that they be allowed to lay flowers at the statue of Jeanne d'Arc on the Place des Pyramides instead of the masculine members of the Ligue, who were at the front, and they were invited to do so. In the speech Barrès gave at the ceremony, he encouraged them to pray and care for the wounded, quoting Jeanne d'Arc in the trial documentation with regard to the latter: "Les femmes prieront, les hommes batailleront, Dieu vaincra!"[86] Although the historical Jeanne wore armor and rode a horse into battle, it is her concern for wounded soldiers, both French and English, that is very often mentioned during this period of high production on the heroine, to the exclusion of all else.

This nurturing role recommended for women during the war comes at the end of a period of heightened feminist activity that ended in disappointment. One of the most radical French feminists, Madeleine Pelletier, scandalized Parisian society at the turn of the century with her masculine clothing and with her demands for the vote (not granted until 1944) and the right to hold public office.[87] Even mainstream feminists had long deplored inequalities that made married women minors and subject to much higher penalties than men for breaches of the marriage contract. In this speech entitled "Jeanne d'Arc et les jeunes filles de Paris," Barrès addresses an audience of educated women and women employed in tertiary positions. They have included their professions and occupations with their signatures, but the political leader shows no sensitivity to their special status or concerns.

As a political gesture, then, Barrès' portrait of Jeanne d'Arc more effectively serves the interests of Catholic French men than those of young French women, non-Catholics living in France, or people of other ethnic origins. In the three essays about Jeanne's childhood, Barrès sees the necessity of including "des faits locaux"[88] for his integral nationalist purposes. He creates an atmosphere and a heroine meant to entice the reader. As tourists embarking on a secular pilgrimage, the readers find themselves nevertheless at the mercy of their tour guide. The Barrésian narrator includes certain nostalgic and romanticized details of Jeanne's childhood that further his purposes, while omitting the crass and the vulgar, or simply the real. His Jeanne is pious and innocent, but also *surhumaine*, that is, not accountable to the mores of her social equals. This figure is set off against the Nietzschean superman, but strangely resembles him in her extreme sense of her individual difference. She was "une enfant qui souffrait" because of the orders she received that went against the customs of her country and against her parents' wishes.[89] This aspect of Jeanne's portrait is perhaps an indication of the depth of Barrès' convictions concerning the strength of the individual, man or woman, in spite of the notion of the French national character he hoped to promote.

Nevertheless, in the texts of the speeches that follow the essays on her childhood, Barrès is able to focus on Jeanne's fighting spirit when it is necessary to spur young male soldiers on to fight courageously, as one would refer to the amulet depicting a virgin warrior goddess such as Athena. In "Le combat éternel de Jeanne d'Arc," for example, he extolls the bravery of the men on the front and places the example of the heroine before his audience. Even in this context, Barrès entirely skirts the facts of Jeanne's soldier life and the question of her military expertise and concentrates instead on her martyrdom for her country. This figure finds its place within the nationalist scheme and is tailored to fit the circumstances. Jeanne's example provides an incentive and a justification for the loss of life in a just cause and provides a rallying point for all French political factions. Barrès shows optimism that the national holiday will for this reason finally be instituted in honor of Jeanne d'Arc. All nations will recognize France's role in the promotion of justice and humanity and she will serve as an appropriate symbol of this vocation, "l'étendard au-dessus des peuples unis pour le triomphe de la civilisation!"[90] All the same, the silences of the text reveal that Jeanne could not be considered a woman who refused to spend her life at the family hearth and chose instead to become involved in public affairs.

In his literary Jeanne d'Arc, Barrès then subsumes the heroine under the heading *vierge sacrifiée*, similar to Iphigenia, the heroine of classical tragedy who gives her life for her country and her family. She honored a set of values and affiliations that Barrès wished to encourage to provide order and discipline in a secular France. Barrès imbues Jeanne's image with details meant both to capture his readers' imaginations and inspire their enthusiasm. Unfortunately, this trope falls short of displaying the alluring qualities of the dissolute woman that obsessed the artistic Barrès, incurably romantic and decadent until his death. Earlier, Barrès had lauded the virgins depicted in decadent literature, but it was their propensity for depravity that he found so irresistible in Mendès and others.[91] These negative images of women are set aside and refused entry into the symbolic code of Barrès' monologic ideological writing since they disintegrate social distinctions and threaten to absorb the masculine subject, destroying his capacity to act.[92]

Barrès showed great admiration for Jeanne d'Arc and attempted to portray her in such a way as to endear her to his countrymen and inspire their patriotism. Although he carried out his project by amalgamating his literary and political goals, her image could not compete in his artistic self with the powerful dissolving effect of Richard Wagner's plots and music, or decadent literature, a fatal attraction most often at odds with the incompatible desire for distinction and effectiveness in the world outside the self. Perhaps we could say that Barrès' literary Jeanne truly wears "le visage sans éclat de [sa] terre natale" mentioned in the preface to *La Mort de Venise*, that is unable to compete in his imagination with the irresistible dissolution of Venice, "la vieille corruptrice."[93]

Notes

1. The spelling I use for this town has been preferred traditionally, as I understand it, by the inhabitants of Domremy, that is, without the accent aigu. Please note, for example, Pierre Marot's title for a book sold in Jeanne's birthplace, as a souvenir for tourists: *Jeanne la bonne Lorraine à Domremy* (Colmar-Ingersheim: S.A.E.P, 1980). See also, Georges Boulanger, "En pélerinage à Domremy," in *Le Pays lorrain et le pays messin. Revue mensuelle illustrée. Littérature, beaux-arts, histoire, traditions populaires*, 9 (Nancy, 1912), 635-36. This author, not the more famous General Boulanger, recommended this spelling in 1912 in order to demonstrate local interests against the encroachment of Parisian bourgeois society.

2. Marot, 98.

3. Jacques Dalarun, "Le troisième procès de Jeanne d'Arc," in *Images de Jeanne d'Arc. Actes du Colloque de Rouen 25-26-27 mai 1999*, ed. Jean Maurice and Daniel Couty (Paris: PUF, 2000): 54.

4. Gerd Krumeich, *Jeanne d'Arc à travers l'histoire*, trans. Josie Mély, Marie-Hélène Pateau and Lisette Rosenfeld (Paris: Albin Michel, 1993), 211-16. The bill did not become law at that time, and Fabre reintroduced it in 1894, again without success.

5. In the intervening years, some others had tried to reactivate the bill originally introduced by Fabre. For example, in 1897, the "Femmes de France" (a group of women from all social classes) submitted a petition requesting that the Chamber of Deputies ratify at its earliest convenience the law voted by the Senate to institute a national holiday in honor of Jeanne d'Arc. In March of 1898, shortly after Emile Zola's dramatic intervention in the Dreyfus Affair with the publication of "J'Accuse...!", Deputy François Césaire de Mahy addressed the Chamber, pleading the cause of the "Femmes de France" and stating that it was a question of France's honor (Krumeich 203, 225). In 1912 Deputy Georges Berry reintroduced the bill more successfully. Maurice Barrès was officially appointed to the commission of eleven established at that time by the nationalist cabinet of Poincaré to study the question. See Philippe Contamine, "Jeanne d'Arc dans la mémoire des droites," in *Histoire des droites en France, 2.Cultures*, ed. Jean-François Sirinelli (Paris: Gallimard, 1992): 425-26.

6. Mona Ozouf notes the importance of patriotism in the curriculum. An article in *L'École* (Feb. 2 1884) recommends young students be taught to sing the "l'Hymne national, la Chanson de Roland, l'Hymne à Jeanne d'Arc" so that, after the horrors of Sedan, the *Revanche* can take place. See Mona Ozouf, *L'École, l'Église et la République (1871-1914)* (Paris: Cana/Jean Offredo, 1982), 113. In his novel *Les Déracinés* (1897), Maurice Barrès includes a chapter entitled "Au tombeau de Napoléon" in which the young students from Nancy swear on the tomb of Napoleon that they will be men, that they will conquer the city, that glory and power will be theirs. See Zeev Sternhell, *Maurice Barrès et le nationalisme français* (Paris: Armand Colin/FNSP, 1972), 117.

7. See Krumeich, 206.

8. About the same time, his father's death in 1898 and his mother's in 1901 played an important role in shaping his ideas on "la Terre et les Morts" and *enracinement*, according to Georges Tronquart, *La Lorraine de Barrès. Mythe ou réalité?* (Nancy: Publications Université de Nancy, 1980), 55; and Marie-Claire Bancquart in *Les Écrivains et l'histoire d'après Maurice Barrès, Léon Bloy, Anatole France, Charles Péguy* (Paris: Nizet, 1966), 331.

9. The Action Française was founded in 1899 by men influenced by Charles

Maurras' 1898 apologia for the forgery of Colonel Henry, according to Eugen Weber, who notes that it was born of the confusion of the Dreyfus affair, "an attempt to work out the broad lines of the French recovery." It started as a patriotic republican movement, formed by supporters of the traditional institutions of French society (i.e., the Church and the Army) in the wake of Zola's intervention in the Dreyfus Affair. During 1899 the Waldeck-Rousseau government was suppressing conspiracies to overthrow the regime and the highly implicated Ligue de la Patrie française was therefore deteriorating. The Action Française turned from a Republican movement, with many members from the Ligue, to a royalist one, as Weber explains: "the most *sui generis* and the most successful neo-royalist movement of the twentieth century." See Eugen Weber, Action Française. Royalism and Reaction in Twentieth-Century France (Stanford CA: Stanford Univ. Press, 1962), 17–18, 20.

Martha Hanna notes that the Action Française preferred Jeanne d'Arc to the Republican Marianne, because of her "unimpeachable virtue." See Martha Hanna, "Iconology and Ideology: Images of Joan of Arc in the Idiom of the Action Française, 1908–1931," *French Historical Studies* 14.2 (1985): 216. The royalist and Catholic reactionaries of the Action Française of the pre–World War I period, and others, were concerned about signs of the decline of France, in particular, low birthrates and, often implicitly, the rise in sexually transmitted diseases due to widespread prostitution, factors involving women that were given as a partial explanation for the defeat at Sedan and the loss of Alsace-Lorraine (Weber, 13). The Action Française therefore studiously refused the libertarianism associated with the revolutionary Marianne and found that Jeanne d'Arc suited its royalist and Catholic goals.

10. Previously, he had served as Nancy's Boulangist deputy from 1889 to 1892, running unsuccessful campaigns for the same office during the remainder of the 1890s, while continuing both his political and literary writing.

11. Yves Chiron, *Maurice Barrès. Le Prince de la jeunesse* (Paris: Perrin, 1986), 384–85. As will become evident in this paper, Frémiet's statue of Jeanne d'Arc, an early monument reflecting a *Revanche* sentiment, was erected in 1874 in the Place des Pyramides. It became an important landmark in Paris during the fin-de-siècle period, the focus of many public statements and demonstrations.

12. Barrès' ultimate set of three carefully crafted literary essays depicting Jeanne are devoted to her childhood in Lorraine and bear the titles: "Domremy-la-Pucelle," "L'enfant dans la prairie," and "La victime des fées." In English, these would be "Domremy-the-Maid," "The Child in the Meadow," and "The Victim of the Fairies." The second and third essays first appeared in print in 1912 in the *Écho de Paris* (January 5 and 6, respectively), a nationalist paper, with the heading "Jubilé de Jeanne d'Arc," to honor the five hundredth anniversary of the heroine's birth. Once the war had begun, Barrès published all three essays as a monograph with Champion, entitled *Autour de Jeanne d'Arc* (1916), in order to raise funds for the wounded. This work, which forms the basis of this study, consists of a reprinting, with only slight revision, of the three above-mentioned essays and includes four other pieces, the texts of speeches given by Maurice Barrès from the end of 1914 to May of 1915: "La fête nationale" ("The National Holiday"), "Le culte de Jeanne d'Arc" ("Joan of Arc Worship"), "Les jeunes filles de Paris" ("The Young Ladies of Paris") and "Le combat éternel" ("The Eternal Bat-

tle"). The essays were published again posthumously as a section in *Le Mystère en pleine lumière* (Plon, 1926), with very few modifications.

All references to *Autour de Jeanne d'Arc* (Paris: Champion, 1916) will be cited simply as AJA and a page number. This system will also be used for references to texts included in *Maurice Barrès. Romans et voyages*, ed. Vital Rambaud (Paris: Robert Laffont, 1994); references to *Amori et dolori sacrum* will be indicated as ADS; references to *Amities françaises*, AF; and references to *Colette Baudoche*, CB. Translations into English of passages from these works and other sources are by Carolyn Snipes-Hoyt.

13. Jonathan Fishbane remarks that Barrès' "artificial world" of literary creation "offered him a means to overcome his own obsessive introspection, his own low point in energy, and this led him into the world of action." He adds that "Barrès the nationalist was really Barrès the aesthete transfigured." See "From Decadence to Nationalism in the Early Writings of Maurice Barrès," *Nineteenth-Century French Studies* 13:4 (1985): 266.

14. Weber 1962, 77.

15. Zeev Sternhell, *Maurice Barrès et le nationalisme français* (Paris: Armand Colin/FNSP, 1972), 49.

16. "Myths of revolt." See Jean-Yves Tadié, *Introduction à la vie littéraire du XIXe siècle* (Paris: Bordas, 1970), 124–25.

17. For a discussion of Boulangism, see Marc Angenot, 1889: *Un état du discours social* (Longueil, PQ: Le Préambule, 1989). In chapter 33, entitled "La propagande boulangiste," Angenot defines this phenomenon not as a political party, but as a loose coalition of heterogenous forces and diverse personalities that developed around a program based on propaganda and the image of a leader who promised "une République honnête," an honest republic (714). The popular leader, Georges Boulanger cut an impressive figure on horseback wearing his military uniform. Barrès and others supplied the ideas that made up the Boulangist platform, advocating the elimination of the Senate and the President; instead, the new government would feature a "strong" executive power and popular referendum (719). The Boulangists and others complained about parliamentary government of the Third Republic, which they saw as in the control of the bourgeoisie (721). General Boulanger fled France at the last minute when his followers were ready to bring off a coup d'état in 1889.

18. See Janine Mossuz-Lavau, *André Malraux et le gaullisme*, 2nd ed. (Paris: FNSP, 1982), 136. What follows is a list of these writers' connections to Jeanne d'Arc. Jules Michelet's work on Jeanne d'Arc will be mentioned later in this study. Native of Orléans and contemporary of Barrès, Charles Péguy paid tribute to the heroine with originality in attempting to interiorize her experience, to see her from a religious point of view, but at the same time, to bring her down from her pedestal. The subject of his first dramatic work, a trilogy, was *Joan of Arc* (1887). Often called his "socialist" Jeanne d'Arc, it was read by only a few. Thirteen years later, after his adult conversion experience, he produced another play, his "Catholic" Jeanne: *Mystère de la charité de Jeanne d'Arc* (1910). In other of Péguy's works, Jeanne appears as a secondary character, for example, in the poem *Tapisserie de sainte Geneviève et Jeanne d'Arc* (1912). See Jean Bastaire, "Appendice: Jeanne à travers la littérature," in *Pour Jeanne d'Arc. Petit traité d'incarnation* (Paris: Éditions du Cerf, 1979), 136–38. As Minister of Culture for the Gaullist regime, André Malraux gave two speeches on Jeanne d'Arc, making explicit comparisons between the two occupations of France, the one by the English in the fifteenth century and the

other by the Germans during World War II (see Mossuz-Lavau, 178). Malraux also initiated the founding of the Centre Jeanne d'Arc in Orléans. See Michel Winock, "Jeanne d'Arc," in *Les Lieux de mémoire. Les France, III. De l'archive à l'emblème*, 3, ed. Pierre Nora (Paris: Gallimard, 1992), 674. As for Charles de Gaulle's personal connection to Jeanne d'Arc, a parallel has been drawn between him and the heroine, for his leading role in the *Résistance*. He has been caricatured as Jeanne d'Arc in drawings, such as one by Jean Effel entitled *Le Général de Gaulle en Jeanne d'Arc* (1959). See Françoise Meltzer, *For Fear of the Fire. Joan of Arc and the Limits of Subjectivity* (Chicago: University of Chicago Press, 2001), 15 and Fig. 9.

19. Marie-Claire Bancquart classifies Léon Bloy and Charles Péguy as "ceux qui croyaient au Ciel" (believers) and Maurice Barrès and Anatole France as "ceux qui ne croyaient pas au Ciel" ("non-believers"). Charles Péguy's works are mentioned in footnote 18 (*supra*); in 1915 Léon Bloy published *Jeanne d'Arc et l'Allemagne* (Crès and Mercure de France); Jeanne appears in Paul Claudel's *L'Annonce faite à Marie*, first performed in 1912, but she is also the subject of his oratorio entitled *Jeanne d'Arc au bûcher* (first performed in 1939); Anatole France wrote a biography of the heroine, entitled *Vie de Jeanne d'Arc* (2 volumes), patterned after Renan's rational look at the Christ figure in *Vie de Jésus*. It was published with Calmann-Lévy in 1908, revised in 1909, and reprinted in over thirty-eight editions. Barrès was familiar with France's manuscript, which he had begun writing before the turn of the century. For information on the preceding items, see Nadia Margolis, *Joan of Arc in History, Literature, and Film* (New York/London: Garland, 1990), items #422 (France), #1214 (Péguy), #1264 (Bloy), #1277 (Claudel), #1309–21 (Péguy). In the novel *Là-bas* (1891), J.-K. Huysmans' narrator evokes Jeanne d'Arc and Gilles de Rais, the infamous young nobleman from the Vendée region of France who fought alongside the heroine and was burned at the stake in October of 1440 for the sexual assault and murder of dozens of children.

20. The case for proto-facism is made convincingly by Zeev Sternhell in *Maurice Barrès et le nationalisme français* and other works. Other historians who have considered the use of the Jeanne d'Arc figure by the political right include the following: Philippe Contamine (essay cited *supra*); Michel Winock, "Jeanne d'Arc et les Juifs," in *Nationalisme, antisémitisme et fascisme en France* (Paris: Seuil, 1982): 145–56; Nadia Margolis, "The 'Joan Phenomenon' and the French Right," in *Fresh Verdicts on Joan of Arc*, ed. Bonnie Wheeler and Charles T. Wood (New York/London: Garland, 1996): 265–87; and Martha Hanna (essay cited *supra*). All of the above implicate Barrès, directly or tangentially.

21. In this paper I use Hayden White's useful insights, from *Metahistory*, in describing the surface and deeper levels of historical writing. Surface levels include explanation by emplotment, formal argument and ideological implication. I will have recourse as well to White's notions on deeper levels, where the writing of history is considered a "poetic act" and tropes help to explain linguistic patterns and are connected to surface manifestations. See Hayden White, *Metahistory. The Historical Imagination in Nineteenth-Century Europe* (Baltimore/London: The John Hopkins Univ. Press, 1973), ix–xii and 1–42.

22. Sternhell, 42–45.

23. Bancquart, 25.

24. "Little animals who are worth no more than the pleasure they provide for young men: to discuss their rights or

their intellectual capacity is deadly boring and ridiculous." Angenot, 842.

25. "I recognize there the purest notes of the soul." AF, 178–79. Barrès named his heroine in Le Jardin de Bérénice (1891) after Racine's eponymous heroine. Barrès adds to this list of young French women known for their purity of soul Bernadette Soubirous of Lourdes.

26. Michel Mercier, "Préface," Le Jardin de Bérénice, Maurice Barrès (Paris: Flammarion, 1988), 19.

27. "It is not that I pretend to be able to explain a Joan of Arc in terms of her family, her village and the earth that produced her. This entire land, although it may be in harmony with the heroine's thought, could only insufficiently define or contain her, just as it was incapable of holding her prisoner." AJA, 37.

28. In order to soften the effect of this fascinating, yet startling information, Ingres depicted, in his now-famous oil painting, the heroine in full armor standing with her banner at the coronation of Charles VII in the cathedral at Reims, but added strips of skirt to float down over her metal-clad legs. Both the Rouen and the Rehabilitation trials, transcribed in official Latin, were presented by Jules Quicherat, with introduction, notes, and annexes in French, between 1841 and 1849. Joseph Fabre, who first introduced the bill to institute a national holiday in Jeanne's honor, is noted also for translations into French of both Jeanne's Rouen Trial (1884) and the Rehabilitation Trial (1888). (See Winock 1992, 685).

29. "Quicherat went looking for Joan of Arc within the texts of the condemnation and rehabilitation trial documentation. For four centuries she has been buried in the paper of these proceedings. The materiality of facts is to be found there. The questions posed by her enemies led Joan to give innumerable details from her life, all of indisputable authenticity." AJA, 11.

30. "All these facts from her life fall short of explaining her heroism. There is something inexplicable about her...." AJA, 11.

31. Margolis 1990, #1163.

32. Dalarun, 61.

33. Krumeich, 207.

34. Winock 1992, 696.

35. Winock 1992, 692.

36. Krumeich, 221.

37. In his essay entitled "Jeanne d'Arc dans la mémoire des droites," Philippe Contamine compares Jeanne's représentation during World War II and, more recently, by Jean-Marie Le Pen's Front national, with the representation of Jeanne during this turn-of-the-twentieth-century period: "Elle demeure certes un point de ralliement, elle relève du décor rituel où se déploie l'extrême droite, mais elle ne bénéficie plus, en dépit des apparences, de cette extraordinaire ferveur, de cette intensité d'attention et d'espérance que l'on constate à la fin du XIXe et au début du XXe siècle. Elle ne fait plus guère des 'passions françaises.'" ["She remains most certainly a rallying point, a part of the ritual decor deployed by the extreme right, but she no longer benefits from the extraordinary fervor, the intensity of attention and hope that is evident at the end of the nineteenth century and at the beginning of the twentieth, in spite of appearances. She hardly serves to stimulate 'French passions' anymore."] (Contamine, 400).

38. At age 65, Sarah Bernhardt was cast in the role of Jeanne d'Arc in Le Procès de Jeanne (1909), a play attributed to Moreau. In 1890, she had successfully played the title role in Jules Barbier's Jeanne d'Arc (1873), put to music by Gounod (see Winock 1992, 678).

39. See my doctoral dissertation entitled "Les constructions multiples d'une femme: Jeanne d'Arc fête son cinq centième anniversaire" (Univ. of Alberta 1998) for examples of some events that

took place in the year 1912, in addition to the continuing battle for the institution of a national holiday in honor of Joan and the canonization process: Plans were still under way for a monumental statue of the heroine to be erected in Rouen, as evident in an article by Henry Jouin, "La fête de Jeanne d'Arc, fête nationale," in *Jehanne la Pucelle. Revue documentaire paraissant chaque mois. Organe du Comité de la Statue monumentale de Jeanne d'Arc*, 3 (Paris: Desclée, de Brouwer et Cie, 1912); an illustrated prayer book entitled Missel de Jeanne d'Arc appeared, illus. Jos Girard (Limoges: Paul Mellotté, 1912); children's books published in 1912 included Comtesse d'Houdetot, *Le page de Jehanne*, illus. Édouard Zier (Paris: Hachette, 1912) and Frantz Funck-Brentano, *Jeanne d'Arc*, illus. O.D.V. Guillonnet (Paris: C. Boivin, 1912). James F. McMillan reports on feminist activities that used the heroine's name just after the turn of the twentieth century in *France and Women 1789–1914. Gender, Society and Politics* (Routledge, 2000), 204: "[Marie] Maugeret sought to rally all Catholic women beneath the banner of Joan of Arc rather than of Marianne. [She] therefore launched a *Fédération Jeanne d'Arc* with the aim of staging an annual conference dedicated to Joan, the first of which was held in 1904. ... In 1906 at the third *Congrès Jeanne d'Arc* she went further, devoting the last day of the proceedings to 'women and politics.'"

40. "Saint of the Fatherland." Margolis 1990, #463–68, #538.

41. Dalarun, 55.

42. Bancquart, 32.

43. One of the "matériaux parfois bien grossiers" Barrès refers to in Michelet's chapters on the heroine in *Histoire de France* might be the mention of Jeanne's abnormal menstrual cycle. Parenthetically, Barrès adds to his remark about Michelet's biography of Jeanne, "et qu'eût-ce été, Seigneur, s'il l'eût composée dans sa vieillesse extraordinaire!" "And what would it have been, good Lord, if he had written [his version of Joan's story] during his extraordinary old age!" AJA, 32.

44. Krumeich, 209–10.

45. The first novel in Barrès's second novel series, *Le Roman de l'énergie nationale* (1897–1902), bears the title *Les Déracinés* (The Uprooted Ones). The vocabulary of vegetation coincides with the organicist explanatory mode characteristic of his integral nationalist period.

46. Jeanne is the subject of two short chapters in a collection of soldier stories from the front, intended to inspire the fighters with courage and to keep up the moral of loved ones at home as well. This work bears the title *L'Âme française et la guerre. Les saints de la France* (Emile-Paul Frères, 1915).

47. ADS, 48.

48. In 1802 German dramatist Friedrich Schiller had written a play about the heroine, entitled *Die Jungfrau von Orleans*. This monumental literary achievement had served as an early nineteenth-century challenge to French dramatists, poets and historians to reclaim Jeanne d'Arc with a major work of their own. Barrès and others lamented that by the end of the century this goal had not been reached. A true French talent, Victor Hugo, had not produced a masterpiece about the heroine, for example, nor had any other, since Voltaire's attempt was not considered worthy.

A major issue during the fin-de-siècle period was of course the retrieval of Alsace-Lorraine from the Germans, who annexed the region in 1871. But, on another level, scholars in France and Germany were disputing the racial, territorial and linguistic implications of certain medieval documents that lay at the source of these questions. Alsace-Lorraine might have remained a separate kingdom called *Lotharingia*—the Middle Kingdom—named after Charlemagne's grandson Lothar, who received it from his father in the ninth century. Charlemagne's other two grandsons, Louis the German and Charles the Bald, each received an entitlement as well, from their father Louis the Pious, the former *Germania* and the latter *Francia*. They documented their agreement not to side with Lothar against the other in the *Oaths of Strasbourg* (842 A.D.), written in two vernacular languages (Romance and Rhenish Franconian German) and Latin. During the period between the defeat at Sedan and World War I, medieval studies were just taking shape in France in order, literally, to keep the Germans from annexing their past, as Barrès suggests (AJA, 60). French scholars found the possibility unsettling, for example, that the root of the word *français* was Germanic (*franc*) with a Romance ending and that Charlemagne's Frankish warriors, the *Francs de France* of *La Chanson de Roland*, might have been German, disguised as French. See Howard Bloch, "The First Document and the Birth of Medieval Studies," in *A New History of French Literature*, ed. Denis Hollier (Cambridge MA: Harvard Univ. Press, 1989), 6–13.

49. "Venice sings to the Adriatic who in turn greets it with a kiss, the gentle incoming tide of an eternal opera. This is the despair of a beauty that is giving itself up to death. Is it the song of an aged depraved woman or of a virgin about to be sacrificed? In the morning, sometimes, in Venice, I hear Iphigenia, but the red evening sunset brings back Jezabel." ADS, 47.

50. Ida-Marie Frandon has amply illustrated Barrès' fascination with the Orient, showing the influence of a woman in this regard, the poet Anna de Noailles, with whom he had a liaison. See Frandon's extensive study on Barrèsian exoticism: *L'Orient de Maurice Barrès* (Geneva: Droz, 1952).

51. See Catherine Perry, "Reconfiguring Wagner's Tristan: Political Aesthetics in the Works of Maurice Barrès," *French Forum*, no. 3 (Sept. 1998): 317–35.

52. "Though deprived of sovereign beauty, the clean and luminous girls of the Metz area match the prairies, hills, sky and river." CB, 347. Saint Colette of Corbie (d. 1447) may have been an inspiration for the first name of Barrès' fictitious Colette Baudoche. Known for founding eighteen convents and many other accomplishments, Colette of Corbie actually met Jeanne d'Arc and shared many excellent qualities, according to Barrès. AF, 165.

53. "The various, but scattered, religious powers present in the Meuse valley, simultaneously Celtic, Latin and Catholic, are gathered and harmonized by Joan of Arc." AJA, 20.

54. "The sacred national hill." ADS, 101.

55. "Sainte-Odile in Alsace and Sion in Lorraine ... symbolize the vicissitudes of Latin resistance to German thought." ADS, 101.

56. "The holy figure of the Lorraine virgin." AJA, 59.

57. "Long live Joan of Arc and long live the King!" "Death to the Jews!" "Long live Joan of Arc! Long live France for the French." Contamine, 412.

58. "This uprooted individual feels ill at ease on the tiled floor of this old French garden.... I conclude from his race that Dreyfus is capable of treachery." Maurice Barrès, *Scènes et doctrines du nationalisme*, Vol. 1 (Paris: Plon, 1925), 161.

59. "Alone, in a disparaged wood, the branch of a tree reaches out toward him. So that he may hang himself." Barrès, *Scènes et doctrines*, 144.

60. Eugen Weber, *The Nationalist Revival in France 1905/1914* (Berkeley/Los

Angeles: Univ. of California Press, 1959), 93, 95.

61. AJA, 48.

62. "Study Joan of Arc, meditate her life, her death, her charming verve, her knightly behavior, her mysterious genius, her sacrifice." AJA, 60.

63. Even the budding genre of science fiction is testimony to this revanchiste paradigm. In *Les 500 millions de la Bégum* (1879), Jules Verne creates a French character, the peaceful, erudite French Dr. Sarrasin, who wishes to turn the city he has inherited into a model city, *France-ville*. His German antagonist, Herr Schultze, creates a city of steel (*la Cité de l'Acier*), characterized by its well-hidden technological wonders and wealth and by its machine-driven efficiency, but lack of human warmth.

64. Sternhell, 44–45.

65. In *Du sang, de la volupté et de la mort* (1894), Barrès writes, "Que fondent Gundry, Tannhauser, Tristan, héros déchirants de Wagner? Les lois de l'Individu. Une seule loi vaut: celle que nous arrachons de notre coeur sincère. ... Le prophète de Bayreuth est venu à son heure pour discipliner ceux qui n'entendent plus les dogmes ni les codes. Allons à Wahnfried, sur la tombe de Wagner, honorer les pressentiments d'une éthique nouvelle" (quoted in Sternhell, 45). ["What is the function of Wagner's agonizing heros—Gundry, Tannhauser, Tristan? They establish the laws of the Individual. One single law is valid, the one that is plucked from our own sincere hearts.... The moment has come for the prophet of Bayreuth to discipline those who listen to neither dogma nor codes. Let's us go to Wahnfried, to Wagner's tomb, to pay our respects to the premonitions of a new ethic."] But later, as Catherine Perry notes, "Barrès comes to recognize that Wagnerian drama celebrates self-abdication by merging individual identity with a mythical collectivity." She cites Wagner's *Tristan und Isolde* as particularly important for Barrès in exemplifying the difficulty of achieving and preserving individual identity (324). Perry also notices the way Barrès juxtaposes Venice and Lorraine in *La Mort de Venise*, a contrast that she connects to the author's changing views on the individual (325–28).

66. "We are supposed to contrast this superhuman being, full of divine pity, with the unworthy superman, whose devilish bliss is Germany's pleasure at present." AJA, 74.

67. "The law of love and justice ... the law that has always stated that those who hold all the power must limit and soften the rights of Force." AJA, 58–59.

68. Contamine, 413.

69. Alain Corbin, *Les Filles de noce. Misère sexuelle et prostitution (19e siècle)*, (Paris: Flammarion, 1982), 45–47, 386–89.

70. "An old depraved woman" or "a virgin about to be sacrificed." ADS, 47.

71. "I would like for you to come to the country of Domremy.... We will follow a long line of visitors...." AJA, 12.

72. "We will put our fingers in the granite basin where she got holy water; we will venerate the stone statue of Saint Margaret ... who saw Joan kneeling down." AJA, 15.

73. AJA, 28.

74. "In Domremy, we are enveloped in the mysterious vapor in which Joan was formed." AJA, 20.

75. AJA, 15, 20.

76. "This fairy that we have transformed into a saint." AJA, 20.

77. "Merlin, the king of sorcerers." AJA, 38.

78. AJA, 16–17.

79. "All the masses at the Basilica, all the prayers murmured without pause, day and night, by the nuns of Saint Theresa who live there, in their Carmel (and who, today, drink the water from

the druidic fountain), are not in excess of what is needed to chastise the mysterious presences that compromised Joan, and whose sterile goings-on served as a pretext for lighting the stake of the child who, without knowing them, brought them garlands of flowers." AJA, 40.

80. "The villages are buried in the fog; the heart loses itself in raptures." AJA, 21.

81. "These mists of local paganism are allowed to kiss Joan's bare feet when she runs, in the meadows of the Meuse." AJA, 38.

82. Maurice Barrès, Mes Cahiers, Vol. VI (Paris: Plon, 1933), 254.

83. "The various religious powers ..., simultaneously Celtic, Latin and Catholic, Joan gathers them together and harmonizes them." (Cited supra.) AJA, 20.

84. Her education took place "among druidic fountains, Latin ruins and ancient Christian churches"; "a beautiful chorus" that together signifies the French nation. AJA, 39.

85. AJA, 32. In his Cahiers, Barrès occasionally mentions in one breath Louise Michel and Jeanne d'Arc, both formidable women from Lorraine. See, for example, Maurice Barrès, Mes Cahiers, Vol. 10 (Paris: Plon, 1936), 238.

86. "The women will pray; the men will go to battle, and God will be victorious!" AJA, 67.

87. McMillan, 208–11.

88. AJA, 12. This could be translated as "local color."

89. She was "a child who suffered." AJA, 74.

90. She is "the banner raised above all peoples united for the triumph of civilization!"AJA, 74.

91. See Sternhell, 44.

92. See Fishbane, 266.

93. "Joan of Arc truly wears the lackluster face of [his] native country." ADS, 13, 47. I would like thank Paul Robards for his invaluable assistance in locating library materials. Thanks also go to Eric Cahm for reading an earlier draft of this paper and giving suggestions.

Conclusion

Elizabeth Emery

> Je m'étonne que l'Eglise n'ait pas songé plus tôt à nous prendre Jeanne d'Arc. Il y a dans l'héroïne nationale une figure légendaire dont le catholicisme doit tirer un excellent parti. M. Dupanloup, qui combat avec autant d'intelligence que d'âpreté, a certainement compris l'éclat d'une pareille béatification.... Mais faire simplement une sainte de Jeanne d'Arc, ce serait une pauvre besogne; il doit s'agir surtout de faire d'une vérité une légende. Quand la généreuse fille sera une sainte dûment reconnue, la grandeur réelle de ses victoires disparaîtra pour les fidèles devant les rêveries de sa nature ardente. On nous prend une héroïne, on nous rendra une sainte Thérèse ... justement à l'heure où le miracle s'analyse et s'explique. M. Dupanloup va chercher une légende dans le passé, il choisit la légende la plus populaire, et il va en souffleter la science; c'est là le coup d'audace.... Mais, avant que l'Eglise lui décerne la palme des vierges et des martyres, je voudrais en parler comme d'une simple fille de la terre, comme d'une robuste campagnarde, en qui tout un âge de fièvre mystique et guerrière se résuma. Jeanne est une époque, une époque de foi et d'hallucination, d'évanouissement extatique et de furie héroïque.[1]
> —Emile Zola, 1869

Emile Zola's fervent secular and nationalist response to Joan of Arc's canonization process, published in the newspaper *Le Rappel*, highlights many of the issues at play in the treatment of medieval saints at the end of the nineteenth century in France. It touches on nearly every topic treated in this volume, from interest in an allegedly picturesque historical period and scientific curiosity about mystical visions to the Church's relationship to saints and questions of national heritage.

Zola's depiction of Joan as the ultimate representative of an idealized Middle Ages—"Joan is an era, an era of faith and hallucination, ecstatic fainting and heroic fury"—clearly points to the artistic possibilities latent in her story. Like saints Julian, Antoine and Genevieve discussed in the essays of Rori Bloom, Madhuri Mukherjee, Barbara Larson and Christina Ferree Chabrier, her legend allowed artists to paint colorful tableaux dedicated to the mystical visions and seemingly outrageous violence of the Middle Ages. The pleasure Gustave Flaubert, Henri de Rivière, Gustave Moreau or Anatole France took in adapting medieval saints' lives in their works stemmed from this Romantic appreciation for the local color of an exotic historical period, but also from a fascination for the works of medieval art on display in fin-de-siècle France, notably stained glass, painting, books of hours and tapestry.[2] The public was similarly attracted to the saints as curiosities, reverential relics of the Middle Ages: the words *simple, naive, primitive, candid* and *pure* were those most associated both with saints and with the art of the Middle Ages.[3] Saints thus became figures of predilection for evoking the medieval period. Like the individual panels of stained-glass windows so admired by fin-de-siècle artists in museums, saints were removed from their larger context and placed on display. Vignettes or puppets estranged from their original signification, they became nonthreatening figures for a largely secular Parisian public.

Vestiges of the past, saints nonetheless invited eminently modern adaptations. Henri Rivière created his pre-cinematic shadow theater using state of the art technology, while Odilon Redon incorporated new scientific observations about cells in his depictions of Saint Anthony's visions. Using positivist methodologies, even the Catholic Church attempted to develop new methods for evaluating the historical veracity of saints' lives, while Gustave Flaubert and Anatole France used *vitae* as a pretext for questioning belief in modern France.

If saints seemed exotic for the late nineteenth century, it was, in part, because France had become a primarily secular country in which mystical visions took place more often in psychiatric hospitals or in remote rural locales than in every day life.[4] The representations of Saint Anthony by Flaubert and Redon sought, as Barbara Larson's essay demonstrates, to probe the links between nature, temptation, religious thought and visions, questioning these relationships and their effect on mysticism. Similarly, the fascination of Naturalist writers Zola and Huysmans with mystics originated in their scientific curiosity about the physical causes of visions (or hallucinations). It is for this reason that Zola reacted so strongly to reports of Joan's canonization process; he felt that insisting on the religious aspects of Joan's life would repudiate the findings of scientists, who had convincingly attributed her visions to physiological causes.

Such scientific interest, however, often developed into much more. At a time captivated by mysticism and the occult, exploration of medieval visions led to new hybrids. Redon, for example, reconciled the two through the study of theosophy, which, as Barbara Larson has shown, tended to mix a variety of different religions with the discoveries of Darwin and aspects of evolutionary theory. At the other extreme, Huysmans became a Catholic oblate as a result of his Naturalist exploration of medieval mysticism. Science and faith merge in Huysmans' often gruesome representations of Lydwine's physical torments; they are redeemed as "vicarious suffering," a superior form of religious sacrifice capable of saving sinners.

Such macabre visions were indisputably magnetic, appealing to a broad spectrum of the public seduced and appalled by the seemingly paranormal in a society haunted by fears about madness and disease.[5] In his newspaper reports about the official Salons of 1875, 1876, 1879 and 1896, Zola was astounded by the sheer number of religious paintings on display (two to three hundred in 1875 alone): "Chez nous la peinture religieuse est devenue objet de commerce. Il y a des modèles dont les peintres ne se départissent point: les saintes-vierges sont dessinées de chic, fixées une fois pour toutes; les saints de bois, les crucifixions sont colorés d'après des recettes invariables."[6] A veritable "industry," artists produced images of saints in styles as far removed from those of medieval *Primitifs* as possible, said Zola. They appeared on the market to fulfill the needs of the new churches being constructed and the garish esthetic tastes of their parishioners.[7] Portraits of Joan of Arc were particularly loathesome, he argued, because they failed to capture her two sides: simple country girl and ecstatic visionary.[8]

As medieval saints were appropriated by the public as exotic literary and artistic themes and as the scientific establishment contested the legitimacy of their visions, the Church renewed its efforts to reposition saints within historical and religious frameworks. It is the attempt to wrest Joan from the popular claims on her as patriot and hero that most irritates Zola in his 1869 article. As Elizabeth Emery and C. J. T. Talar have shown, a number of religious orders began publicity campaigns to remind readers of the religious inspiration responsible for mystical visions and pilgrimages in the Middle Ages; so, too, Dupanloup had chosen to re-emphasize Joan's dedication to God and the importance she had placed on following the voices of her saints.

Zola's disgust with this technique is palpable; by validating the religious inspiration behind Joan's actions, he felt that the Church negated her true accomplishments as patriot and warrior. Dupanloup was stealing a historical figure by creating a saint; he was transforming a hero owned by the nation into a mere legend. As a staunch Republican, Zola echoes the century-long claim (instigated by Jules Michelet) that Joan is the ultimate representative of the French nation, a figure who foreshadowed the rise of the people in the French Revolution:

> Elle est le peuple aussi. C'est là ce qui la dresse debout au-dessus des âges. Elle est le peuple se levant d'indignation, d'un coin de la patrie avilie, et se ruant à la défense du sol, quand les armées des rois n'ont plus de sang ni de courage. Elle est la patrie éternellement jeune trouvant des femmes pour la défendre, le jour où les hommes manquent. ... elle sauva la France, elle aurait sauvé la liberté, si l'heure de la liberté avait sonné. L'histoire voit en elle une des plus hautes personnifications d'un peuple et d'un siècle: la religion n'y peut voir qu'un mensonge.[9]

Twenty years before Barrès, Zola linked Joan, in this article, to the earth, to her peasant origins, and to the French notion of *patrimoine*, of national heritage. Like Anatole France and Barrès, who were nostalgic for saints' lives as an example of the disappearing folklore and traditions of the French countryside, Zola names Joan of Arc as a crucial figure for understanding the French people. The maid from Lorraine, like Genevieve of Paris, is inextricable from the geographical space with which she had become associated. This tendency to link saints to the countryside occurred throughout Europe at this time as rural towns united in celebrating their local traditions. The increased popularity of both pilgrimages and tourist travel prompted small towns and communes to blend old legends with local history, thus leading to increased association between saints, tourism, local identity and regional devotional practices.[10]

Such collaborations notwithstanding, disputes over the patriotic or religious signification of saints took place often between Republicans and Catholics; the 1905 separation of Church and State can be considered their apogee. Anatole France's use of saints to mock superstitious or seeming irrational behavior is a notable example. Yet the drive to assess the importance of saints' lives also took place within the Church itself. C. J. T. Talar's essay evaluates the ways in which the historical school of Delehaye called into question the authenticity of hagiographical texts, thereby undermining the validity of the legends on which cults of many saints had been based. Adopting the historical and positivistic methods practiced in the fin de siècle prompted reconsideration of saints' lives and provoked questions about the role they should play, even within the modern Church.

For late nineteenth-century France, then, hagiographies were truly an enigma. Every essay in this volume has explored this theme in one way or another: Saints' lives were vestiges of a nearly forgotten era, testaments to a former belief system and fascinating for nineteenth-century readers, secular or devout. But they also puzzled readers no longer familiar with the genre. They struggled to understand hagiography, to define it, and to give it a purpose in their own time.

We began this volume by asking why an increasingly secular French society would have experienced such widespread fascination for the saints, religious figures *par excellence*. What did a saint represent for this period of shifting political allegiances and de-Christianization? What was a saint's origin? Did saints really exist? Did stories about them have valid uses in modern society? And if so, how could one write a saint's life in the modern world? These were some of the questions asked by Huysmans in *En Route*, as his character Durtal reflected on modern and medieval hagiography: If medieval hagiography is defined by its profound religious belief, is it even possible to attempt to imitate hagiographical models without falling into cheap imitation, turning a figure like Joan of Arc into an actress? How, in a period marked by individualism, secular beliefs and materialism, could one write a hagiography?[11] Is a saint's life legend, history or hagiography?

Zola's defense of Joan of Arc provides privileged insight into the process of hagiographical construction at the end of the nineteenth century, while responding to many of the issues raised in this volume. For him, Joan is a valuable part of French history, representing a critical moment in the people's support of the nation. Accordingly, what most troubles him in Dupanloup's embrace of Joan for the Church is the question of historical truth: "L'histoire voit en elle une des plus hautes personnifications d'un peuple et d'un siècle: la religion n'y peut voir qu'un mensonge." Zola sees in Joan of Arc a historical reality (she is a character from history, not yet a saint) and does not want her to be turned into what he considers a "lie," a legend. For him, as for Anatole France, saints' lives are fairy tales, colorful and fanciful elements of popular belief that function purely as fantasy in modern society.[12]

In outlining the process of rewriting that will take place as Dupanloup, a powerful bishop, chooses to reinterpret a well-known figure, Zola reveals one of the fundamental motivations for Republican interest in the saints: competition over national legends. Occurring just before the end of the Second Empire (1869), when France had not yet become a Republic, the Church's new version of Joan of Arc's life poses a threat to one of the few existing Republican symbols. Indeed, Zola insinuates that hagiography—the very process of examining a historical figure's life—is marked by narrative extrapolation. Any new interpretation of the basic facts will, inherently, change the truth of preexisting stories, overwriting them with the new.[13]

In his insistence on the dangers of competing versions of a saint's life, Zola foreshadows the works of scholars such as Hayden White, Victor Turner, and Pierre Nora, who have argued for the power of narrative in interpreting historical events or symbolic figures.[14] In *Les Lieux de mémoire*, for example, Nora defines a site or realm of memory as people, places, things or events that have been "consecrated" as part of the national heritage. Yet the very process of creating these new sites of memory, he argues, inherently replaces true memories of the past with the newly constructed ones.[15] By adding yet another legend to those already associated with Joan, Zola fears that the Church will be able to claim her for its own beliefs, thus causing the French to forget their original memory (Zola's patriotic version, itself a post–Revolutionary construct) and weaken the national myth.[16] Eventually, the historical Joan will be forgotten entirely, replaced by the new legends about her: fairy tale heroine, patriot warrior, simple French countrywoman, illuminated mystic, saint.[17] Zola instinctively realized that Dupanloup was working as would a medieval hagiographer, that is to say that he was more interested in portraying a good model of Christian faith than in analyzing the historical details of her adventure.[18] In the Middle Ages, saints' lives were loosely based on saints' biographies, but they tended to skimp on historical reality, borrowing instead from other saints' lives, Biblical stories or parables.[19]

But was Zola's worry necessary? Did one version of Joan of Arc have to replace the other? In the late nineteenth century, different groups tended to claim and propagate their own version of a particular saint, focusing alternately on legend, historical elements, fears of the occult or faith. Yet these competing narratives did not detract from the saints; paradoxically, they grew in popularity, leading to many publications about them in the early years of the twentieth century. Sometimes, as in the case of Delehaye, these were saints treated in the Catholic context, but as often as not, they were the fairy tale saints of theater and cabaret, children's books and opera.[20] Saints appreciated by some for their Christian virtues and godliness (Sainte Geneviève and Saint Michel, for example) were revered by others as national heroes. The subject of sublime works of art, they were also legendary heroes or figures of superior moral virtue, medical anomalies whose abilities bemused scientists, blessed figures capable of accomplishing miracles or symbols of French achievement. All could evoke parallels with modern-day situations, from the eremitical writer dedicated to his craft to the hysterical medical subject, devout Catholic or actor. This profusion of conflicting stories about the saints was akin to what happened in the late Middle Ages: As specific saints went in and out of fashion, their images were used as adornment for churches and as talismans against sickness, all through a semi-feudal system based on allegiance and protection. As new attitudes to the saints' images emerged, the old ones still thrived.[21]

Though Huysmans questioned whether it was still possible to write hagiographies in the medieval vein, the essays in this volume seem to argue that not only was it possible, it was widely done. In fact, the disparate and competing narratives about saints' lives discussed here, while generally without the reverential style and religious commitment valued by Huysmans, strikingly resemble the medieval practice of *translatio* outlined in Laurie Postlewate's essay. Lacking the religious intent of *vitae*, these authors, artists and thinkers remained nonetheless very close to medieval hagiographers' relationship to saints: They tended to subordinate accurate biographical sketches of saints to other purposes, often personal, pedagogical or moral: obtaining favors from God, shoring up a local church, encouraging soldiers. In defining hagiography, Thomas Head reminds us that saints' lives "tell us at least as much about the author and about those who used the text— their ideals and practices, their concerns and aspirations—as it does about the saints who are their subjects."[22] Not surprisingly, the same could be said of the multiple and often self-serving uses to which the nineteenth century put them: Saints' lives reveal, among other things, nostalgia for the past and fears about modernization, contamination and disappearing belief systems.

Although we have focused on saints' lives in this volume, the turn of the century's tendency to rewrite legendary figures of French history for personal or political purposes—a process that we could call neo-hagiography—was not limited to the saints. In the first years of the Third Republic as the government finally distanced itself from the monarchy and the Church, France experienced a crisis of identity. Old figures, from Charlemagne and Clovis to the Ancien Régime itself, were called into question once again and reinterpreted to legitimize the fledgling Republic.[23] Anne Thiesse has proposed that it is such construction of new narratives that builds the nation; it cannot exist until such fictions have been created. It is, in fact, precisely the moment when the collective accepts the new stories about its common identity that the nation can move forward toward constituting itself.[24] The late nineteenth century was a period particularly rich in such narrative creation; one has only to look at the entries contained in Pierre Nora's *Les Lieux de mémoire* (itself a venerable *Golden Legend* comprised of the myths of nation formulated in the Third Republic) to understand this phenomenon. As Nora put it, "The holy nation thus acquired a holy history; through the nation our memory continued to rest upon a sacred foundation."[25]

If we take at face value Rosemonde Sanson's assertion that patriotism was the only common religion of late nineteenth-century France, we can extrapolate that the fin-de-siècle process of appropriating history and rewriting it for particular national or political purposes paralleled the sanctifying goals of medieval hagiographers.[26] Often as not, the creation of such new nationalist narrative involved transforming the old national symbols—king, Church, State—and repositioning them in a way that supported the new regime. The medieval period, for example, once seen as inherently tied to the Ancien Régime, was lauded in government documents and official discourse as a period that had validated the *liberté, égalité, fraternité* of the Republic and which had set in place many of the laws and traditions in practice today.[27] Zola's defense of Joan as a manifestation of *le peuple* is supremely characteristic of this tendency.

As the Third Republic asserted itself, it built a new image by reclaiming old models and rewriting them, thus eliding offending elements such as religion and king and replacing them with the cult of nation. This is the same process that Zola had criticized in the saint-building project of the Church, but in reverse: While the Church added religious significations to Joan's story, the Republic took them away. As a result, figures like Roland, who is deeply committed to God and king in *La Chanson de Roland*, became, in late nineteenth-century representations, "La France faite homme," France incarnate.[28] After the separation of Church and State, rewriting the lives of leading French historical figures including Charlemagne, Clovis, Voltaire, Rousseau and Diderot took place in a similar vein to that which occurred in the medieval composition of saints' lives. Eschewing particular biographical details, such as relationship to king and court, Voltaire, Rousseau and Diderot became the patron saints of the French Revolution. Valuing them primarily for their contributions to the nation allowed a changing France to maintain its old legends, while grafting new ones upon them.

The neo-hagiographical impulse that appropriated the saints for a variety of secular uses in the nineteenth century was also behind the new myths of nation that flourished during the Third Republic as an increasingly secular state sought to divest itself of the political powers of the Church. In the end, it was the Republic that won the discursive battle to claim national figures: Its narrative inventions took treasured aspects of communal life and transformed them into national icons. Appropriating even the hagiographical process itself, Republicans built a canon for the secular saints of nationalism, the new religion of the twentieth century.

Notes

1. "I am astonished that the Church did not consider taking Joan of Arc from us earlier. There is in this national heroine a legendary figure that Catholicism will put to good use. Mr. Dupanloup, who fights with as much intelligence as ferocity, has certainly understood the scandal of such a beatification.... But simply making Joan of Arc a saint would be poor work; above all, it is necessary to turn truth into legend. When the generous girl is a duly recognized saint, the real greatness of her victories will disappear for the faithful, overwhelmed by reveries about her passionate nature. They take a heroine from us and give back a Saint Teresa ... particularly at the moment when we are analyzing and explaining miracles. Mr. Dupanloup seeks a legend in the past, he chooses the most popular legend, and he is going to use it to slap science; this is a daring strike.... But before the Church gives her the palm leaf of virgins and martyrs, I would like to speak of her as a simple girl of the land, as a robust countrywoman in whom an entire age of mystical and warlike fever were condensed. Joan is an era, an era of faith and hallucination, ecstatic fainting and heroic fury." "Une Nouvelle sainte," *Le Rappel*, 15 May 1869. Reprinted in *Oeuvres complètes*, 15 vols. (Paris: Cercle du livre précieux, 1968), 13: 229–31. For more about Dupanloup's project and the canonization process itself, see Carolyn Snipes-Hoyt's essay in Part 4 of this volume.

2. For more about the late nineteenth-century fascination for medieval art, see Elizabeth Emery and Laura Morowitz, *Consuming the Past: The Medieval Revival in Fin-de-siècle France* (London: Ashgate Press, 2003).

3. See Chapter 2 of Emery and Morowitz. The words were applied equally to those modern artists, such as Flaubert, Henri de Rivière, or Carlos Schwabe (illustrator of Zola's *Rêve*), who imitated medieval art or techniques in their modern works.

4. See, for example, Cristina Mazzoni's discussion of medical studies of hysteria at the Salpêtrière Hospital and throughout Europe in *Saint Hysteria: Neurosis, Mysticism, and Gender in European Culture* (Ithaca, NY: Cornell University Press, 1996). George Didi-Huberman chronicles the pictorial legacy of these experiments in *Invention de l'hystérie: Charcot et l'iconographie photographique de la Salpêtrière* (Paris: Macula, 1982). Sandra Zimdars-Swartz traces Marian apparitions in *Encountering Mary from La Salette to Medjugorje* (Princeton: Princeton University Press, 1991), while Suzanne Kaufman describes rural cults of the saints in "Miracles, Medicine and the Spectacle of Lourdes: Popular Religion and Modernity in Fin-de-Siècle France" (Ph.D. dissertation, Rutgers, The State University of New Jersey, 1996).

5. On the fears of madness as linked to disease, see Robert A. Nye, *Crime, Madness, and Politics in Modern France: The Medical Concept of National Decline* (Princeton: Princeton University Press, 1984); Cristina Mazzoni, *Saint Hysteria*; Janet Beizer, *Ventriloquized Bodies: Narratives of Hysteria in Nineteenth-Century*

France (Ithaca: Cornell University Press, 1994); and Barbara Spackman, *Decadent Genealogies: The Rhetoric of Sickness from Baudelaire to D'Annunzio* (Ithaca: Cornell University Press, 1989).

6. "In France religious painting has become commercial. There are models that painters can't leave alone: saint-virgins are drawn smartly, fixed once and for all; saints in wood, crucifixions colored in according to unchanging recipes." "Lettres de Paris, nouvelles artistiques et littéraires, salon de 1879." Originally printed in *Le Voltaire*, 18–22 June 1880 and reprinted in *Oeuvres complètes*, 12: 1005–22.

7. See "Lettres de Paris, une expo, le salon de 1875." Originally printed in *Le messager de l'Europe*, June 1875. Retranslated from Russian and republished in *Oeuvres complètes*, 12:920–42.

8. In speaking of Monchablon's portrait of Joan, he states: "... cette Jeanne d'Arc, cette grosse fille montée sur un cheval caracolant, est la figure la plus vulgaire qu'on puisse concevoir. Il faut constater par ailleurs que Jeanne d'Arc n'a rien inspiré de bon jusqu'ici à aucun artiste de France.... Cette fille forte et douce, cette étonnante créature, comme jaillie du rêve d'un poète, ne se prête pas à notre art." "Lettres de Paris," *Le Messager* (June 1876), 954. Reprinted in *Oeuvres complètes*, 12: 954. This negative opinion changed after he saw Bastien-Lepage's painting. Apart from the physical representation of Joan's vision, which he disliked, Zola thought that the painter had captured the essence of Joan's experience (see Fig. 3.17 and Elizabeth Emery's discussion of Zola's reaction to the painting in this volume). Zola had always been fascinated by Joan of Arc and once planned to write a poem about her. See especially his correspondence from 1858 to 1867. *Correspondance*, ed. B. H. Bakker et al. (Montreal and Paris: Les Presses de l'Université de Montréal and Editions du Centre National de la Recherche Scientifique, 1978–1995), 1:320.

9. "She is the people, too. It is this that makes her stand out across the ages. She is the people rising in indignation from a degraded corner of the homeland and throwing themselves into defending the land when the king's armies have run out of blood and courage. She is the homeland ever young, finding women to defend it, the day when men lack ... she saved France, she would have saved liberty if the hour of liberty had come. History sees in her one of the highest personifications of a people and a century: religion can see in her only a lie," 231. For more about the battles between Republicans and the Church over Joan of Arc, see Carolyn Snipes-Hoyt's contribution to this volume. The relationship between Michelet and Joan of Arc has long been studied. A few good sources include Jacques Seebacher, "Le Peuple de Jeanne," *L'Information littéraire* 27 (1995): 62–66; Suzanne Guerlac and Paul Viallencix, "Michelet and the Legend of Joan," *Clio* 6 (1997): 193–203; Simone Fraisse, "Michelet ou l'évangéliste de Jeanne," *Amitié de Charles Péguy: Bulletin d'Informations et de Recherches* 21:82 (April–June 1998): 70–74.

10. Publications such as *Le Pèlerin*, discussed in Elizabeth Emery's essay, linked the two traditions, as had hagiographical accounts in general (see C. J. T. Talar's discussion of Saint Cecilia's legend). Many of the articles published in the journal include testimonials from pilgrimage planners attempting to draw tourists to their towns. A 16 August 1873 article, entitled "Pèlerinages de la semaine," for example, focuses on the Belgian town of Notre-Dame de Walcourt (near the French and Belgian border). The article presents the history and origin of the pilgrimage, inspired by fourteenth-century events. Subsequent issues

trace the pilgrimage to the late nineteenth century. Today, the city's web site continues this pilgrim/tourist tradition: "Walcourt vaut le détour." For more about the marketing and celebration of local pilgrimages, see Michael R. Marrus, "Cultures on the Move: Pilgrims and Pilgrimages in Nineteenth-Century France." *Stanford French Review* 1 (1977): 205–20.

11. "Comment arriver à exprimer aujourd'hui le suc dolent et le blanc parfum des très anciennes traductions de la *Légende dorée* de Voragine? Comment lier en une candide gerbe ces fleurs plaintives que les moines cultivèrent dans les pourpris des cloîtres, alors que l'hagiographie était la soeur de l'art barbare et charmant des enlumineurs et des verriers, de l'ardente et de la chaste peinture des Primitifs?" This is the citation that opens Elizabeth Emery's essay.

12. See his preparatory manuscripts for *Le Rêve* in which he repeatedly categorizes the *Légende dorée* as "vieilles histoires" and "légendes," insisting on the "crédulité" of those of believed them and linking them to the imagination. Bibliothèque Nationale de France ms. NAF10324, fols. 35, 193 and ms. NAF10323, fol. 22, 35, 59. Christina Ferree Chabrier discusses this tendency with regard to Anatole France in Part 4 of this volume.

13. See Christina Ferree Chabrier's essay, in which she posits that, for Anatole France, too, "History is no more than the art of storytelling under the guise of truth."

14. In *Metahistory*, White argues that a historical work is "a verbal structure in the form of a narrative prose discourse that purports to be a model, or icon, of past structures and processes in the interest of *explaining what they were by representing* them." *Metahistory: The Historical Imagination in Nineteenth-Century Europe* (Baltimore: Johns Hopkins Press, 1973).

Placing similar emphasis on the importance of verbal structures, Victor Turner has proposed that a symbol's distinguishing characteristic is its semantic flexibility. Because its meaning is not fixed, individuals may transform a symbol's accepted sense by bringing new associations to it or by "including it in a complex of purely private fantasies." Given enough visibility, the individual can reformulate the symbol. "Symbolic Studies." *Annual Review of Anthropology* (1975): 145–161, 150–151, 154.

15. Nora introduced the term *lieu de mémoire* in the eponymous seven-volume work he directed from 1984–1992 (*Les Lieux de Mémoire*. Paris: Gallimard). It has now entered major dictionaries such as *Le Grand Robert de la langue française*. For a definition, see Nora's preface to the English edition, in which he defines the term (*Realms of Memory*. New York: Columbia University Press, 1992), xv–xxiv. See also his article "Between Memory and History: *Les Lieux de Mémoire*," *Representations* 26 (Spring 1989): 7–25.

16. Arguments about the conflicts between history and memory are integral to nearly any discussion of the importance of historical research in the present and have been explored by a number of post nineteenth-century thinkers including Maurice Halbwachs, Pierre Nora and Paul Ricoeur. More recently, scholars such as Jörn Rüsen and Patrick Geary have attempted to see more symbiotic relationships between memory and history. See, for example, Halbwach's classic *The Collective Memory* (New York: Harper and Row, 1950); Paul Ricoeur's "Gedächtnis—Vergessen—Geschichte," in K. E. Müller and J. Rüsen, eds, *Ihistorische Sinnbildung. Problemstellungen, Zeitkonzepte, Wahrnehmungshorizonte, Darstellungsstrategien* (Reinbek: Rowohlt, 1997), 433–54; or Patrick Geary's *Phantoms of Remembrance. Memory and Oblivion at the End of the First*

Millennium (Princeton: Princeton University Press, 1994).

17. In fact, by her rehabilitation trial in 1450, twenty years after her death, the "real" Joan had already become a legend. In his 1869 article, Zola did anticipate the flood of new interpretations of her life that would result from the canonization process. By World War I, Joan of Arc had been adopted for innumerable causes and by groups from all over the political and religious spectrum. For more about the Jewish Joan, the anti-Semitic Joan, the patriotic Joan, the anti-German Joan or the mystical Joan, see Michel Winock.

18. Although most scholars of hagiography have argued that the goal of a saint's life was not necessarily to relate the facts (historical accuracy by today's standards), a number of medieval scholars have recently shown the ways in which the medieval conception of truth relied on what was commonly accepted as history in the Middle Ages. As such, hagiographers did try to represent hagiography as history. See Suzanne Fleischman, "On the Representation of History and Fiction in the Middle Ages," *History and Theory. Studies in the Philosophy of History*, 22 (1983): 278–310; Felice Lifshitz, "Beyond Positivism and Genre: 'Hagiographical' Texts as Historical Narrative," *Viator* 24 (1994): 95–113.

19. See Thomas Head, "Hagiography" for more about the stylistic borrowings of many hagiographers. André Vauchez underlines the fact that such techniques result from the hagiographical genre itself, which is less concerned with the individual saint, than with "blurring the individual's traits and transforming his or her lifetime into a fragment of eternity." *Sainthood in the Later Middle Ages*. Trans. Jean Birrell (Cambridge: Cambridge University Press, 1997). This conflict between legend and history is at the heart of issues discussed in C. J. T. Talar's contribution to this volume.

20. See Introduction, nn. 15 and 16; Chapter 4, nn. 15, 16 and 31; and Chapter 8, n. 39.

21. Eamon Duffy, *The Stripping of the Altars: Traditional Religion in England 1400–1500* (New Haven: Yale University Press, 1992), 168. His entire chapter on the saints provides a wealth of information about the ways in which saintly images were used, 164–205.

22. "Hagiography," in the *Online Reference Book for Medieval Studies* (http://the-orb.net/encyclop/religion/hagiography/hagio.htm). See also Laurie Postlewate's essay in this volume for examples of the different ways saints' lives were used in the Middle Ages.

23. See Mona Ozouf, *L'École, l'Église et la République (1871-1914)* (Paris: Cana/Jean Offredo, 1982); Christian Amalvi, *De l'art et de la manière d'accommoder les héros de l'histoire de France: essais de mythologie nationale* (Paris: Albin Michel, 1988); Emery, "'The 'Truth' About the Middle Ages: *La Revue des Deux Mondes* and Late Nineteenth-Century French Medievalism," in *The Quest for the "Real" Middle Ages*, Clare A. Simmons, ed. (London: Frank Cass, 2001), 99–114.

24. "La nation naît d'un postulat et d'une invention. Mais elle ne vit que par l'adhésion collective à cette fiction." See *La Création des identités nationales. Europe XVIIIe–XXe siècles* (Paris: Seuil, 1999), 14, 11–12.

25. See p. 11 of "Between Memory and History."

26. See p. 461 of Rosemonde Sanson, "La Fête de Jeanne d'Arc en 1894: Controverse et Célébration." *Revue d'histoire moderne et contemporaine* 20 (1973): 444–63.

27. See Chapter 1 of Emery and Morowitz, *Consuming the Past*.

28. The term is Léon Gautier's, but similar terms were common in the period

following the Franco-Prussian war. See *La Chanson de Roland* (Tours: Alfred Mame et fils, éditeurs, 1872), vii. For a discussion of Roland as moral and patriotic figure after the war see Almavi. Harry Redman, Jr. extensively discusses the use of Roland in nineteenth-century literature, *The Roland Legend in Nineteenth-Century French Literature* (Lexington: University of Kentucky Press, 1991).

Select Bibliography of Secondary Sources

Aigrain, René. *L'hagiographie: ses sources, ses méthodes, son histoire.* Mayenne: Bloud & Gay, 1953.
Amalvi, Christian. *De l'art et de la manière d'accommoder les héros de l'histoire de France: essais de mythologie nationale.* Paris: Albin Michel, 1988.
Aykanian, Nancy. "Flaubert's 'Medieval Trifle': 'La Légende de saint Julien l'Hospitalier.'" *Romance-Review* 6:1 (Fall 1996): 69–84.
Bart, B. F., and R. F. Cook. *The Legendary Sources of Flaubert's "Saint Julien."* Toronto: University of Toronto Press, 1977.
Beizer, Janet. *Ventriloquized Bodies: Narratives of Hysteria in Nineteenth-Century France.* Ithaca: Cornell University Press, 1994.
Bellemin-Noël, Jean. *Le Quatrième Conte de Gustave Flaubert.* Paris: Presses Universitaires de France, 1990, p. 77.
Berta, Michel. "Les 'Trois villes' d'Emile Zola et la tradition hagiographique des premières 'vitae' aux 'Trois Contes' de Gustave Flaubert." Ph.D. dissertation. Queens University, Canada, 1990.
Biasi, Pierre-Marc. "Le Palimpseste hagiographique: L'Appropriation ludique des sources édifiantes dans la rédaction de 'La Légende de saint Julien l'Hospitalier.'" *La Revue des Lettres Modernes* 777–781 (1986): 69–124.
Bibliothèque Nationale de France. Dossier "*Le Rêve* de Zola dans tous ses états." http://gallica.bnf.fr/Zola/.
Blumenfeld-Kosinski, Renate, and Timea Szell, eds. *Images of Sainthood in Medieval Europe.* Ithaca: Cornell University Press, 1991.
Cabanès, Jean-Louis. "Rêver La Légende dorée." *Les Cahiers Naturalistes* 76 (2002): 25–47.
Cate, Phillip, and Mary Shaw, eds. *The Spirit of Montmartre: Cabarets, Humor, and the Avant-Garde, 1875–1905.* New Brunswick NJ: Jane Voorhees Zimmerli Art Museum, Rutgers, The State University of New Jersey, 1996.
Chelini, Jean. *Les Chemins de Dieu: histoire des pèlerinages chrétiens des origines à nos jours.* Paris: Hachette, 1982.

Colin, Pierre. *L'audace et le soupçon: La crise de modernisme dans le catholicisme français (1893-1914)*. Paris: Desclée de Brouwer, 1997.

Contamine, Philippe. "Jeanne d'Arc dans la mémoire des droites." In *Histoire des droites en France. 2. Cultures*, ed. Jean-François Sirinelli. Paris: Gallimard, 1992.

Corbin, Alain. *Les filles de noce: misère sexuelle et prostitution*. Paris: Flammarion, 1982.

Coustet, Robert. "Odilon Redon miraculé." *Revue de l'art* (1993): 83–85.

Curtis, Sarah. *Educating the Faithful: Religion, Schooling, and Society in Nineteenth-Century France*. DeKalb: Northern Illinois University Press, 2000.

Dakyns, Janine. *The Middle Ages in French Literature: 1851–1900*. London: Oxford University Press, 1973.

Daly, Gabriel. *Transcendence and Immanence: A Study in Catholic Modernism and Integralism*. Oxford: Clarendon Press, 1980.

Debray-Genette, Raymonde. "'La Légende de Saint Julien l'Hospitalier': forme simple et forme savante." In *Essais sur Flaubert*, ed. Charles Carlut. Paris: Nizet, 1979.

Delehaye, Hippolyte. *L'Oeuvre des Bollandistes à travers trois siècles, 1615–1915*. Bruxelles: Société des Bollandistes, 1959.

Devlin, Judith. *The Superstitious Mind: French Peasants and the Supernatural in the Nineteenth Century*. New Haven: Yale University Press, 1987.

Didi-Huberman, George. *Invention de l'hystérie: Charcot et l'iconographie photographique de la Salpêtrière*. Paris: Macula, 1982.

Driskel, Michael Paul. *Representing Belief: Religion, Art, and Society in Nineteenth-Century France*. University Park: Pennsylvania State University Press, 1992.

Dubois, Jacques, and Jean-Loup Lemaitre. *Sources et méthodes de l'hagiographie médiévale*. Paris: Editions du Cerf, 1993.

Duchartre, Pierre-Louis, and René Saulnier. *L'Imagerie parisienne, l'imagerie de la rue Saint-Jacques*. Paris: Gründ, 1944.

Dunn-Lardeau, Brenda, ed. *Entre la lumière et les Ténèbres: Aspects du Moyen Age et de la Renaissance dans la Culture des XIXe et XXe Siècles*. Paris: Champion, 1999.

Emery, Elizabeth. *Romancing the Cathedral: Gothic Architecture in Fin-de-siècle French Culture*. Albany: State University of New York Press, 2001.

____, and Laura Morowitz. *Consuming the Past: The Medieval Revival in Fin-de-siècle France*. London: Ashgate Press, 2003.

Fleischman, Suzanne. "On the Representation of History and Fiction in the Middle Ages." *History and Theory* 22 (1983): 278–310.

Fleith, Barbara, and Franco Morenzoni, eds. *De la sainteté à l'hagiographie: genèse et usage de la Légende dorée*. Genève: Droz, 2001.

Goldstein, Jan. "The Uses of Male Hysteria: Medical and Literary Discourse in Nineteenth-Century France." *Representations* 34 (Spring 1991): 135.

Gordon, Rae Beth. *Ornament, Fantasy, and Desire in Nineteenth-Century French Literature*. Princeton: Princeton University Press, 1992.

Griffiths, Richard. *The Reactionary Revolution: The Catholic Revival in French Literature 1870–1914*. London: Constable, 1966.

Gugelot, Frédéric. *La Conversion des intellectuels au Catholicisme en France 1885–1935*. Paris: CNRS Editions, 1998.

Hanna, Martha. "Iconology and Ideology: Images of Joan of Arc in the Idiom of the Action Française, 1908–1931." *French Historical Studies* 14.2 (1985): 215–39.

Harris, Ruth. *Lourdes: Body and Spirit in the Secular Age*. New York: Viking, 1999.

Head, Thomas. "Hagiography." In *Medieval France: An Encyclopedia*, ed. William Kibler and Grover Zinn. New York: Garland, 1995, pp. 433–37.

―――, ed. *Medieval Hagiography: An Anthology*. New York: Routledge, 2001.

Heffernan, Thomas. *Sacred Biography: Saints and Their Biographers in the Middle Ages*. New York: Oxford University Press, 1988.

Hill, Harvey. *The Politics of Modernism: Alfred Loisy and the Scientific Study of Religion*. Washington DC: Catholic University of America Press, 2002.

Hindman, Sandra, Michael Camille, Nina Rowe, and Rowan Watson. *Manuscript Illumination in the Modern Age*. Evanston IL: Mary and Leigh Block Museum of Art, 2001.

Hollywood, Amy M. *Sensible Ecstasy: Mysticism, Sexual Difference, and the Demands of History*. Chicago: University of Chicago Press, 2002.

Jeanne, Paul. *Les Théâtres d'Ombres à Montmartre de 1887 à 1923*. Paris: Les Editions des presses modernes au Palais-Royal, 1937.

Jodock, Darrell, ed. *Catholicism Contending with Modernity: Roman Catholic Modernism and Anti-Modernism in Historical Context*. Cambridge: Cambridge University Press, 2000.

Jonas, Raymond. *France and the Cult of the Sacred Heart: An Epic Tale for Modern Times*. Berkeley: University of California Press, 2000.

―――. "Sacred Tourism and Secular Pilgrimage: Montmartre and the Basilica of the Sacré-Coeur." In *Montmartre and the Making of Mass Culture*, ed. Gabriel Weisberg. New Brunswick NJ: Rutgers University Press, 2001, pp. 94–119.

Kaufman, Suzanne. "Miracles, Medicine and the Spectacle of Lourdes: Popular Religion and Modernity in Fin-de-siècle France." Ph.D. dissertation, Rutgers University, 1996.

Krumeich, Gerd. *Jeanne d'Arc à travers l'histoire*. Trans. Josie Mély, Marie-Hélène Pateau and Lisette Rosenfeld. Paris: Albin Michel, 1993.

Kselman, Thomas A. *Miracles and Prophecies in Nineteenth-Century France*. New Brunswick NJ: Rutgers University Press, 1983.

Lajoux, Alexandra Reed. "From Emma to Félicité: The Use of Hagiography in the Works of Gustave Flaubert." *Studies in Medievalism* 2:2 (Spring 1983): 35–50.

Lapp, John C. "Art and Hallucination in Flaubert." *French Studies* 10 (1956): 311–22.

Léal, Barry. "Reflexions on Sainthood: Flaubert's Tentation de Saint Antoine." *AUMLA* 72 (Nov. 1989): 252–260.

Lehmann, Gérard. "*La Légende de Saint Julien l'Hospitalier*": Essai sur l'imaginaire flaubertien. Odense: Odense University Press, 1999.

Lifshitz, Felice. "Beyond Positivism and Genre: 'Hagiographical' Texts as Historical Narrative." *Viator* 24 (1994): 95–113.

Lowrie, Joyce O. *The Violent Mystique: Thematics of Retribution and Expiation in Balzac, Barbey d'Aurevilly, Bloy and Huysmans*. Geneva: Droz, 1974.

Mâle, Emile. *The Gothic Image: Religious Art in France of the Thirteenth Century*. Trans. Dora Nussey. New York: Harper and Row, 1972.

Margolis, Nadia. "The 'Joan Phenomenon' and the French Right." In *Fresh Verdicts on Joan of Arc*, ed. Bonnie Wheeler and Charles T. Wood. New York: Garland, 1996, pp. 265–87.

Marrus, Michael R. "Cultures on the Move: Pilgrims and Pilgrimages in Nineteenth-Century France." *Stanford French Review* 1 (1977): 205–20.

Mayeski, Marie Anne. "New Voices in the Tradition: Medieval Hagiography Revisited." *Theological Studies* 63, no. 4 (December 2002): 690–710.

Mazzoni, Cristina. *Saint Hysteria: Neurosis, Mysticism, and Gender in European Culture*. Ithaca: Cornell University Press, 1996.

Morgan, Naomi. "La légende de Saint Julien l'hospitalier ou la vision à travers la vitre." *Image [&] Narrative, The Online Magazine of the Visual Narrative* 3 (August 2001).

Mrosovsky, Kitty. Introduction to *The Temptation of Saint Anthony*, by Gustave Flaubert. Ithaca: Cornell University Press, 1980.

Neefs, Jacques. "L'Exposition littéraire des religions: *La Tentation de Saint Antoine*, 1874." *Revue d'Histoire Littéraire de la France* 81:4–5 (1981): 637–47.

Nye, Robert A. *Crime, Madness, and Politics in Modern France: The Medical Concept of National Decline*. Princeton: Princeton University Press, 1984.

Oberthur, Mariel. *Cafés and Cabarets of Montmartre*. Salt Lake City UT: Gibbs M. Smith, 1984.

Ozouf, Mona. *L'École, l'église et la République (1871-1914)*. Paris: Cana/Jean Offredo, 1982.

Peeters, Paul. *L'Oeuvre des Bollandistes*. Bruxelles: Palais des Académies, 1961.

Pirotte, J. *Les Images de dévotion, témoins de la mentalité d'une époque, 1840-1965*. Louvain-la-Neuve: Publications du centre belge d'histoire rurale, 1974.

Reames, Sherry L. *The Legenda Aurea: A Reexamination of Its Paradoxical History*. Madison: University of Wisconsin Press, 1985.

Reff, Theodore. "Cezanne, Flaubert, Saint Anthony and the Queen of Sheba." *The Art Bulletin* 44 (Spring 1962): 113–25.

Reventlow, Henning Graf, and William Farmer, eds. *Biblical Studies and the Shifting of Paradigms, 1850-1914*. Sheffield: Sheffield Academic Press, 1995.

Richards, Sylvie. "The Historical Figure as Palimpsest: Flaubert's *La Tentation de Saint Antoine*." *French-Literature-Series* 8 (1981): 85–93.

Ridoux, Charles. *L'évolution des études médiévales en France de 1860 à 1914*. Paris: Champion, 2001.

Robertson, Duncan. *The Medieval Saints' Lives: Spiritual Renewal and Old French Literature*. Lexington KY: French Forum, 1995.

Rosenbaum-Dondaine, Catherine. *L'Image de piété en France, 1814-1914*. Paris: Musée-Galerie de la SEITA, 1984.

____. "Un siècle et demi de petite imagerie de piété (après 1814)." *Revue de la Bibliothèque nationale* 6 (1982).

Ryan, William Granger. Introduction to *The Golden Legend: Readings on the Saints*, by Jacobus de Voragine. Princeton: Princeton University Press, 1993, pp. xvi–xvii.

Schwartz, Vanessa. *Spectacular Realities: Early Mass Culture in Fin-de-siècle Paris*. Berkeley: University of California Press, 1988.

Seginger, Gisèle. "L'Artiste, le saint: Les Tentations de Saint Antoine." *Romantisme* 17:55 (1987): 79–90.

Seybolt, Robert F. "The *Legenda aurea*, Bible, and *Historia scholastica*." *Speculum* 21 (1946): 339–42.

Seznec, Jean. *Nouvelles Etudes sur la Tentation de Saint-Antoine*. Ed. F. Saxl. Studies of the Warburg Institute. London: University of London, 1949, p. 61.

Spackman, Barbara. *Decadent Genealogies: The Rhetoric of Sickness from Baudelaire to D'Annunzio*. Ithaca: Cornell University Press, 1989.

Sternhell, Zeev. *Maurice Barrès et le nationalisme français*. Paris: Armand Colin/FNSP, 1972.

Sticca, Sandro, ed. *Saints: Studies in Hagiography*. Binghamton NY: Center for Medieval and Renaissance Studies, 1996.

Sumption, Jonathan. *Pilgrimage: An Image of Mediaeval Religion*. Totowa NJ: Rowman and Littlefield, 1975.

Talar, C. J. T. "(Anti)hagiography and Mysticism in the Work of J.-K. Huysmans." *Excavatio* IX (1997): 73–83.

____. "A Naturalistic Hagiography: J.-K. Huysmans' *Sainte Lydwine de Schiedam*." In *Sanctity and Secularity during the Modernist Period*, ed. L. Barmann and C. J. T. Talar. Brussels: Société des Bollandistes, 1999, pp. 151–81.

____. "Pious Legend and 'Pious Fraud': Albert Houtin (1867–1926) and the Controversy over the Apostolic Origins of the Churches of France," in *Sanctity and Secularity During the Modernist Period*, ed. L. Barmann and C. J. T. Talar. Brussels: Société des Bollandistes, 1999: 47–65.

Thompson, Anne B. "Shaping a Saint's Life: Frideswide of Oxford," *Medium Aevum* 63, no. 1 (1994) 34–52.

Todorov, Tzvetan. *Introduction à la littérature fantastique*. Paris: Seuil, 1970.

Tronquart, Georges. *La Lorraine de Barrès: Mythe ou réalité?* Nancy: Publications Université de Nancy, 1980.

Vauchez, André. *La sainteté en Occident aux derniers siècles du Moyen Age d'après les procès de canonisation et les documents hagiographiques*. Rome: Ecole française de Rome, 1988.

Vircondelet, Alain. *Le monde merveilleux des images pieuses*. Paris: Hermé, 1988.

Vitz, Evelyn Birge. "The Impact of Christian Doctrine on Medieval Literature."

In *The New History of French Literature*, ed. Denis Hollier. Cambridge: Harvard University Press, 1989: 13–18.

Weber, Eugen. *Action Française: Royalism and Reaction in Twentieth-Century France*. Stanford CA: Stanford University Press, 1962.

———. *The Nationalist Revival in France 1905–1914*. Berkeley: University of California Press, 1959.

Whiting, Steven Moore. "Music on Montmartre." In *The Spirit of Montmartre: Cabarets, Humor and the Avant-garde, 1875–1905*, ed. Phillip Dennis Cate and Mary Shaw. New Brunswick NJ: Rutgers University Press, 1996, pp. 14–88.

Wilson, Steven, ed. *Saints and Their Cults*. Cambridge: Cambridge University Press, 1983.

Winock, Michel. "Jeanne d'Arc et les Juifs." In *Nationalisme, antisémitisme et fascisme en France*. Paris: Seuil, 1982, pp. 145–56.

———. "Joan of Arc." In *Realms of Memory: The Construction of the French Past*. Vol 3. Trans. Arthur Goldhammer. New York: Columbia University Press, 1997, pp. 433–82.

Ziegler, Robert. "Interpretation as Awakening from Zola's *Le Rêve*." *Nineteenth Century French Studies* 21 (Fall 1992): 130–41.

Zimdars-Swartz, Sandra. *Encountering Mary from La Salette to Medjugorje*. Princeton: Princeton University Press, 1991.

About the Contributors

Rori Bloom is an assistant professor of French at the University of Florida. A specialist in eighteenth-century French literature, she is the author of articles on Sade, Casanova and Prevost.

Christina Ferree Chabrier currently teaches French at Duke University. Her research interests include literature of the Belle Epoque, aesthetics and medievalism. She is particularly fascinated by works that are surprising, shocking or subversive.

Elizabeth Emery, associate professor of French at Montclair State University, teaches French language, literature, and culture. She is the author of *Romancing the Cathedral: Gothic Architecture in Fin-de-siècle French Culture* (Albany: State University of New York Press, 2001) and co-author (with Laura Morowitz) of *Consuming the Past: The Medieval Revival in Fin-de-siècle France* (London: Ashgate, 2003). The North American editor of *Romance Studies* and associate editor of *Excavatio*, she has published essays about medievalism and nineteenth- and twentieth-century literature in journals including *The French Review*, *Prose Studies*, *Modern Language Studies*, *Les Cahiers Naturalistes*, *French Literature Series*, *Excavatio*, and *The Year's Work in Medievalism*.

Barbara Larson is a fine arts professor at Syracuse University. Her book *The Dark Side of Nature: Science, Society and the Fantastic in the Work of Odilon Redon* will be published by Pennsylvania State University Press in 2005. Dr. Larson's articles on science and art at the fin de siècle have appeared in exhibition catalogues such as *L'âme au corps: arts et sciences, 1793-1893* (Réunion des musées nationaux, Gallimard/Electa, 1993), *Lost Paradise: Symbolist Europe* (Montreal Museum of Fine Arts, 1995), and *Cosmos* (Montreal Museum of Fine Arts, 1999), in journals including *Nineteenth-Century Art Worldwide* and *Excavatio*, and in the forthcoming book *In Sickness and in Health: Disease as a Metaphor in Art and Popular Wisdom* (University of Delaware Press, 2004).

Madhuri Mukherjee is an assistant professor at the William Paterson University of New Jersey. She specializes in nineteenth- and twentieth-century French poetry and theater and also teaches courses in Asian Studies. She is particularly familiar with turn of the century avant-garde movements and has annotated and catalogued the Schimmel Rare Book Library of nineteenth-century books and periodicals located in the Zimmerli Art Museum at Rutgers University. She has published articles in *Paul Claudel Papers*, presented numerous conference papers in her field, and is currently working on a book manuscript entitled *Symbolist Orientalisms*, an analysis of the theatricalization of poetry as it relates to a latent orientalist thrust in French literary movements.

Laurie Postlewate is a senior lecturer in French at Barnard College of Columbia University, where she teaches pre-modern literature and culture. She is the author of articles on medieval hagiography and Anglo-Norman literature, and is the editor of a forthcoming volume of essays on performance in the Middle Ages and Renaissance.

Carolyn Snipes-Hoyt is an assistant professor of French at Pacific Union College. She wrote her Ph.D. dissertation on Joan of Arc in pre–World War I French society and has published articles related to that research in journals such as the *French Review* and *Excavatio*. She has presented numerous conference papers on the representation of Joan of Arc and other medieval figures during the fin-de-siècle period.

C. J. T. Talar is professor of systematic theology at the University of St. Thomas School of Theology. He is the author of *(Re)Reading, Reception and Rhetoric* (Peter Lang, 1999) and co-editor with Lawrence Barmann of *Sanctity and Secularity during the Modernist Period* (Société des Bollandistes/Subsidia Hagiographica, 1999). His research interests center on nineteenth-century Catholicism, primarily in France, and he has published in such journals as *Louvain Studies, Catholic Historical Review, US Catholic Historian, Literature & Theology, Excavatio, Journal for the History of Modern Theology,* and *Greyfriars Review*.

Index

A Rebours 50, 57, 80, 127
Acta Sanctorum 4, 133, 142, 143, 159
Action Française 196–197, 201, 213, 214
Acts of the Martyrs 147–148
Adjutor, Saint 181, 192
Agatha, Saint 85
Agnes, Saint 85, 87, 91, 97, 104–105, 113, 133
Albert of Jerusalem, Saint 143
Alexis, Saint 125, 129, 135, 137
Alzon, Emmanuel d' 100
Amic, Saint 164, 167–172, 178, 180, 183, 186–190, 192
Ammonaria 60–61, 64, 73
Amori et dolori sacrum 203, 215
Analecta Bollandiana 4, 153, 159
Anthony, Saint 5, 8, 13, 25–44, 47–81, 90, 92–93, 100, 166–168, 170, 187–189, 224
Anthony of Padua, Saint 166
Anticlericalism 2, 7, 49, 150, 179
Apollo 34
Aquinas, Saint Thomas 105
Assumptionist Order 99–106, 114
Athanasius, Saint 48, 79
Attila the Hun 37, 40
Auriol, George 28

Bailly, Edmond 74
Bailly, Father Vincent de Paul 102–103, 115–116
Balthasar 184–185
Balzac, Honoré 24, 68, 135
Baptist, Saint John the 13–14
Barbe, Saint 85, 100, 110, 170, 175
Barbey d'Aurevilly, Jules 57, 109, 135

Barrès, Maurice 195–221, 226; Amori et dolori sacrum 203, 215; Colette Baudoche 204, 205, 215, 219; Le Culte du moi 197–198; Un Homme libre 198; Le Jardin de Bérénice 198, 203, 217; La Mort de Venise 203–204, 207, 212, 220; "La Terre et les Morts" 196, 202, 213
Barthes, Roland 17, 23
Basilisk 173
Bastien-Lepage, Jules 94–95
Baudelaire, Charles 198–199, 232
Baudrillart, Jean 106, 108
Belief 3, 7, 8, 17, 71–73, 84, 89, 90, 100, 101, 107, 114, 115, 134, 137, 166, 167, 170, 173–174, 177, 179–180, 182, 185–187, 190, 224, 227, 229
Bernadette Soubirous, Saint 4, 98, 217
Bernard, Saint 105
Bernhardt, Sarah 217
Berthet, Adolphe 119
Berthold, Saint 143, 172–174, 190
The Bible 3, 4, 9, 87, 173, 180, 181; see also New Testament; Old Testament
Blanc, Claudius 38
Bloy, Léon 100, 126, 135, 197, 213, 216
Bollandists 4, 9, 7, 106, 115, 133, 139–159
Bonaventure, Saint 105, 134
Bosch, Hieronymus 48–49, 68
Bouasse family 102, 115
Bouilhet, Louis 43
Boulangist movement 197, 202, 213–215
Boullan, Abbé 126, 135
Bourget, Paul 111
Bozon, Nicole 123, 130, 131, 134, 137

245

Bremond, Henri 151, 159
Bridget, Saint 98, 135
Broussolle, Abbé J.C. 108, 116
Brugman, Jan 122, 133
Bruneau, Alfred 94–95, 108, 112–113
Brunet, Gustave 5, 87–88, 108–109
Buddhism 34, 74, 75
Buffon 68

Cabanis, Pierre 64
Callot, Jacques 49–50, 57, 65, 67
Caran d'Ache 32
Carmelites 143
Cathedral 1, 8, 20, 41, 84–85, 91, 93, 107–108, 110, 120, 195, 196, 200, 217, 246
La Cathédrale 120
Catherine of Alexandria, Saint 95, 121, 133, 200
Catherine of Siena, Saint 98
Catholic Church 1–10, 72, 84, 99–116, 119–138, 139–159, 163–195, 200–202, 208–209, 224, 231
Catholic Revival 8, 99–115
Cecilia, Saint 85, 139–159
Célestin, Saint 164, 167–172, 178, 180–183, 186, 188–190, 192
Cells 71, 81
Celtic 143, 207–210, 219, 221
Chantal, Saint 151, 159
Charcot, Jean-Martin 59, 64, 80, 97, 98, 231, 246
Charlemagne 229, 230
Charles the Bald 219
Charles VII 195, 200, 217
Charpentier, Georges 112
Chat Noir 1–2, 25–44, 51, 76, 79, 84, 84, 111, 112
Chateaubriand, François-René de 88
Childéric 37
Children 3, 14, 38, 87, 91, 103, 105, 116, 189, 193, 202, 216
Chimera ii, 50, 65, 67, 72–73, 75
Christ 16, 72, 85, 89, 99, 103, 109, 116, 126, 128–129, 136, 137, 140, 156, 165, 167–171, 175–177, 179, 183, 185, 189, 190, 193, 216
Christian faith 3, 7, 19, 119–138, 141, 174–180, 185, 228
Christina, Saint 85
Christine de Pisan 200

Church and State, separation of 2, 7, 144, 150, 167, 186, 196, 226, 230
Claudel, Paul 100, 197, 208, 216
Clavaud, Armand 68
Clovis 37, 202, 229, 230
Colette, Saint 127–128, 136
Colette Baudoche 204, 205, 215, 219
Compostela, Santiago de 48
La Conquête de Plassans 98–99, 114
Contagion 5, 7
Cornély, Saint 168
Creation 14, 28, 47, 93, 102, 133, 145, 215, 230
Creuzer, Friedrich 43
Le Crime de Sylvèstre Bonnard 87–88, 109, 192–193
Le Culte du moi 197–198
Cuvier, 68
Cybèle 63
Cyprian of Antioch 145
Cyprian of Carthage 145

Darwin, Charles 225
Daux, C. 51
Death 21, 37, 52, 57, 61–63, 65, 72, 73, 75, 82, 91, 94, 109, 126, 128, 137, 151, 152, 155–157, 167, 169, 175, 191, 195, 199, 200–203, 212–213, 219, 220, 234
Decadence 49, 100, 127, 128, 186, 198, 212, 232
De Gaulle, Charles 197, 216
Delaroche, Paul 49
Delehaye, Hippolyte 9, 139–159, 226, 228, 246; Légendes hagiographiques 139–159
Deman, Edmond 52, 79, 81
Denis, Maurice 93
Denis of Paris, Saint 141, 202
Denis Piramus 119–120, 133
Denys the Areopagite, Saint 105, 141
Déroulède, Paul 202
Derrida, Jacques 14, 22
Destrée, Jules 67, 80
Devil 32, 33, 52, 65, 72, 76, 77, 137, 167, 169
Diderot, Denis 230
Les Dieux ont soif 163
Doin, Jean 71, 81
Domremy 195–221
Dorothy, Saint 85, 100

Dream 1, 8, 18, 23, 65, 80, 83–118, 210, 223, 232
Droctovée, Saint 193
Du Camp, Maxime 43
Duchesne, Louis 139–159
Dupanloup, Bishop Félix 116, 195, 200, 223, 225–228, 231
Dupuytren Museum 67

Ecole critique 139–159
Ecole légendaire 139–159
Edmund, Saint 119, 120, 133
L'Education sentimentale 17, 23, 43
Egypt 48
Elizabeth of Hungary, Saint 98
En Route 10, 83–84, 92, 105, 107, 109, 112, 115–116, 120, 227
Ensor, James 52
Esquirol, Jean Etienne 64, 98
L'Etui de nacre 163–194
Eudel, Paul 28, 42
Euphrosine (Iphraise), Saint 164, 175–179, 182, 191–192
Evolution 48, 67, 68, 141, 193
Expiatory suffering 126

Fabre, Joseph 195, 213, 217
Faith 3, 7, 17, 19, 22, 37, 40, 49, 71, 84, 88–92, 99–106, 108, 116, 130, 134, 136–137, 141, 144, 148, 151–152, 156, 159, 163–194, 224–225, 228, 231
Fantastic 14, 16–18, 47–48, 65, 79, 148, 164
Faust 34, 50, 76
La Faute de l'abbé Mouret 98–99
Feminist 201, 211, 218
Femme fatale 51–63
Femmes de France 200, 213
Ferréol, Saint 193
Ferrution, Saint 193
Ferry, Jules 202
Flaubert, Gustave 5, 8, 13–24, 25–44, 47–81, 92–93, 98, 112, 114, 169, 172, 189, 224, 231; L'Education sentimentale 17, 23, 43; La Légende de Saint Julien l'Hospitalier 8, 13–23, 84, 90, 92–93, 100, 111, 112; Madame Bovary 13, 43; Salammbô 43, 98; La Tentation de Saint Antoine 5, 8, 13, 25–44, 47–81, 90, 92–93, 100, 166–168, 170, 187–189, 224; Trois contes 8, 13–23, 84, 90, 92–93, 100, 111, 112
Foligno, Angela di 105
Fourcauld, Louis de 100
Fra Angelico 103
Fra Lippi 103
Fragerolle, Georges 32
France, Anatole 7, 64, 87, 106, 108–109, 116, 163–194, 197, 213, 216, 224, 226, 227, 233; Balthasar 184–185; Le Crime de Sylvèstre Bonnard 87–88, 109, 192–193; Les Dieux ont soif 163; L'Etui de nacre 163–194; L'Ile des pingouins 163–164; La Légende de sainte Radegonde 163; Le Lys rouge 116; Le Mannequin d'osier 187, 189; L'Orme du Mail 116, 166; Pierre Nozière 168, 181, 184, 185; Le Puits de sainte Claire 169, 187, 192; La Révolte des anges 184; La Rôtisserie de la reine Pédauque 190, 191; Les Sept Femmes de la Barbe-bleue 175; Sur la pierre blanche 172; Thaïs 64, 164, 167, 169, 178, 182, 192; La Vie de Jeanne d'Arc 164, 216
Francis of Assisi, Saint 80, 192
Françoise Romaine, Saint 127–128
Franco-Prussian War 49, 235
Freemasonry 136, 207
French Revolution 2, 143, 164, 182, 186, 196, 198, 201–202, 214, 226, 228, 230
Freud, Sigmund 16, 52
Froc-Robert 102, 115
Funck-Brentano, Frantz 218

Gabriel, Saint 15
Gallet, Louis 94
Gambetta, Léon 2
Gauguin, Paul 61
Genet, Jean 13
Genevieve, Saint 25–44, 85, 87, 90, 93, 100, 202, 215, 224, 226, 228
Genre troubadour 163, 186
George, Saint 91, 97, 110
Gériolles, A. de 109, 111
Gerlac, Jan 122, 133
Germain d'Auxerre, Saint, 37–40, 112, 193
Germany 9, 43, 140, 152, 205, 206, 218–220, 234
Gertrude, Saint 98

Gilles, Saint 124, 134
Giotto 103
Gluttony 47
Gnosticism 73
God 3, 18, 22, 34, 39, 40, 77, 84, 85, 90–91, 98, 109, 110, 113, 115, 121, 127, 130, 134, 136, 137, 157, 172, 174, 180, 188–190, 191, 201, 209, 221, 226, 229, 230
Goddesses 57, 63, 211
Gods 34, 65, 68, 74, 76, 109, 174, 189–190,
Goethe, Johann Wolfgang von 50, 206
Golden Calf 32
Golden Legend 3, 6, 9, 14, 44, 48, 83–116, 188, 193, 230
Gounod, Charles 32, 34, 217
Grasset, Eugène 30
Greek 3, 16, 57, 105, 143, 190, 192
Gregory the Great 124
Grisar, L'Affaire 149–150, 159
Grünewald, Matthias 58–59, 68, 77
Guéranger, Dom Prosper 115, 139–159

Hagiography 3, 5, 7, 8, 9, 14, 17, 31, 84, 88–92, 99–106, 229, 234
Hallucination 17, 23, 52, 77, 80, 98, 224, 231
Hannah 15
Haydn 32, 34
Hébert, Marcel 154, 159
Hegel, Georg Wilhelm Friedrich 98
Helen of Troy 56, 63, 72
Hello, Ernest 84, 109
Hennequin, Emile 48
Herbert, Michel 26, 41
Hérodias 13, 14
Hinduism 34, 43
Holy cards 6, 9, 101–102
Holy Family 16
Un Homme libre 198
Houtin, Albert 156
Hugo, Victor 68, 88, 101, 110, 113, 134, 163, 218
Huns 37–40
Huret, Jules 5, 111, 112
Huysmans, J.-K. 6, 8, 10, 50, 57, 59, 79, 80, 83–84, 89–90, 92, 100–109, 112, 113, 116, 119–138, 197, 198, 208, 216, 225, 227, 229; *A Rebours* 50, 57, 80, 127; *La Cathédrale* 120; Des Esseintes,

Jean Floressas 57, 59, 127; Durtal 10, 84, 90, 107, 227; *En Route* 10, 83–84, 92, 105, 107, 109, 112, 115–116, 120, 227; *Là-Bas* 107, 120, 216; *Marthe* 57; *Sainte Lydwine de Schiedam* 8, 119–138
Hypnos 65
Hysteria 3, 7, 64, 65, 80, 97, 99 114, 122, 231

L'Ile des pingouins 163–164
Imbert-Gourbeyre, Antonin 114
Index, The Roman 143, 151, 155, 156, 159
Iphigenia 207, 212, 219
Iphraise (Euphrosine), Saint 164, 175–179, 182, 191–192
Isis 63, 74

Jacobus de Voragine 3–5, 48, 83–116, 184, 193, 233
Japonisme 27, 41
Le Jardin de Bérénice 198, 203, 217
Jeanniot 87
Jerome, Saint 167–170, 178, 185–186, 188, 189, 194
Jesus Christ 6, 15, 77, 85, 91, 110, 121, 125, 128, 130, 135–138, 140, 143, 155, 156, 165, 169, 170, 176, 180, 182–183, 187, 189, 190, 192, 193, 216
Jews 136, 165, 196, 205, 206, 219, 234
Joan of Arc 7, 94–95, 97, 98, 100, 113, 164, 182, 188, 192, 195–221, 223–235
Jouy, Jules 28
Julian, Emperor 210
Julian, Saint 8, 13–23, 84, 88, 90, 92–93, 100, 111, 112, 210, 224
Juliana, Saint 121

Kempis, Thomas à 122, 133
Khnopff, Fernand 52, 65
Knouphis 73

Là-Bas 107, 120, 216
Langlois, H. E. 21
Larousse, Pierre 2
Launoy, Jean de 140, 142, 155
Laurent, Saint 132, 138
La Légende de Saint Julien l'Hospitalier 8, 13–23, 84, 90, 92–93, 100, 111, 112
La Légende de sainte Radegonde 163
Légendes hagiographiques 139–159

Legends 1–9, 13–23, 33, 37, 41, 44, 48, 63, 83–118, 139–159, 163–194, 207, 209, 224, 226, 223–235
Legrand du Saulle, Henri 98, 114
Lemaître, Jules 25, 27, 31, 34, 36, 41, 43, 44, 99, 107, 108
Lenepveu, Jules-Eugène 202
Leo XIII, Pope 195
Lepers 16, 18–21, 23
Le Poittevin, Alfred 76
Libaire, Saint 210
Liberette, Saint 164, 171–174, 180, 182, 191, 192
Lieux de mémoire 216, 228, 230–233
Ligue des patriotes 202, 210
Loisy, Bishop Alfred 149–159
Longis, Saint 181
Lorrain, Jean 1–8, 114, 213
Lorraine region 195–221, 226
Lourdes 4, 10, 98, 114, 217, 231
Luke, Saint 155
Lunel 30
Lust 47–49, 51–63, 136, 183
Lydwina, Saint i, 7, 8, 119–138, 225
Le Lys rouge 116

Madame Bovary 13, 43
Madness 5, 48, 64–65, 97–99, 114, 119, 225, 231
Maël, Saint 164
Maeterlinck, Maurice 93, 112
Maison de la Bonne Presse 103, 116
Mâle, Emile 87, 89–90, 109–110
Mallarmé, Stéphane 61, 111, 112, 113
Malraux, André 197, 215, 216
Mandyn, Jan 48–49, 67
Manichean 205–206
Le Mannequin d'osier 187, 189
Margaret, Saint 95, 123, 131, 137, 200, 220
Marianne (Symbol of French Republic) 214, 218
Marie de France 15, 23
Marthe 57
Marthe, Saint 130
Martin, Louis 207
Martyrs 13, 52, 63, 64, 77, 85, 140, 143–159, 166, 175, 188, 207, 212, 223, 231
Mary Magdalene 123, 184, 193
Mary the Egyptian, Saint 131
Matthew, Saint 155

Maupassant, Guy de 92
Maurras, Charles 197, 214
Maury, Alfred 5, 10, 112
Maximus, Saint 151–153
Mendès, Catulle 198, 212
Mérovée 37
Meyer, Paul 178
Michael, Saint 95, 200
Michel, Louise 221
Michelet, Jules 68, 71, 197, 201–202, 208, 210, 215, 218, 226, 232
Microscope 71, 81
The Middle Ages 3–10, 15, 19, 21, 36, 43, 87–91, 97, 102, 106, 107–110, 113, 115, 116, 119–138, 147, 163–164, 177, 182, 187, 224–225, 228–229, 234
Miracles 4, 10, 37, 48, 65, 83, 85, 89–90, 93, 98, 102, 107, 110, 111, 113, 114, 122–123, 134, 137, 142, 146, 152, 175, 177–178, 181–182, 187, 192, 223, 229, 231
Misogyny 7, 51–63, 97, 114, 178–183, 198, 204–207, 210–212
Le Missel de Jeanne d'Arc 218
Monarchy 2, 201, 229
Monks 49, 52, 61, 65, 77, 83, 106, 111, 128–129, 136–137, 148, 176, 187, 193, 233
Monsters 56, 65–72, 79, 81, 190
Montaigne, Michel Eyquem de 67
Montmartre 25–44, 79, 202
Moréas, Jean 2, 112
Moreau, Gustave 95, 224
Morot, Aimé-Nicolas 49
La Mort de Venise 203–204, 207, 212, 220
Moses 73
Music 3, 5, 12, 25–44, 79, 80, 94–97, 111, 113, 159, 203, 212, 217
Mystery plays 1–2, 7, 26, 31, 36–42, 93, 215
Mysticism 1, 3, 4, 68, 72, 74, 80, 92, 94, 95, 97–99, 106, 112–114, 135, 156, 224, 225, 231

Napoleon Bonaparte 4, 30, 143, 196, 213
Nationalism 184–186, 197, 207, 215, 231
Naturalism 5, 68, 71, 84, 87, 91–93, 95, 98, 99, 100, 122, 127, 225

Nebuchadnezzar 63
New Testament 15, 155
Nicholas, Saint 87, 121, 122, 134, 175, 178
Nietzsche, Friedrich 206, 211
Noah 15, 31, 137
Nodier, Charles 163
Notre-Dame-de-Lorette 38
Notre-Dame de Paris 108, 113, 178, 183, 196

Oannes 68, 72
Occult 72–74, 126, 225, 228
Odile, Saint 204–205, 219
Oedipus 16, 23
Old French 119–138, 187, 219
Old Testament 15, 155; Adam 15, 22, 23, 27; Eve 74; Eden 44, 74; Genesis, Story of 15, 21, 47, 111; Sarah 15, 217
Oliverie, Saint 164, 171–175, 180, 182, 191, 192
Onoflette, The Blessed 181
Onuphre, Saint 176, 179
Opera 3, 6, 50, 87, 94–97, 101, 103, 108, 112, 133, 219, 228
Ophites 73
Orientalism 15, 19, 34, 52, 63, 65, 143
Orléans 37, 195, 200, 215–216
L'Orme du Mail 116, 166
Osiris 63

Pagan traditions 14, 16, 47, 73, 74, 158, 166–174, 180–181, 185, 186, 190, 208–210
Papebroch, Daniel 142–143, 156
Paris, Gaston 116, 178, 192
Paris, Paulin 178, 192
Patriotism 7, 202, 205, 212–213, 230
Patron saints 37, 202–203, 230
Paul, Saint 134, 167, 178, 188
Péguy, Charles 100, 197, 208, 213, 215, 216, 232
Le Pèlerin 2, 102, 103, 105, 115–116, 232
Pelletier, Madeleine 211
Picard, Edmond 52
Pierre Nozière 168, 181, 184, 185
Pilgrimage 4, 9, 10, 48, 98, 102, 114, 115, 167, 188, 211, 225–226, 232–233
Pinel, Philippe 98
Plague 37, 47–48, 120
Pontius Pilate 165

Pouchet, Georges 67, 72
Prendergast 22, 24
The Primitives (painters) 1, 7, 80, 83–84, 92, 106–107, 111, 225, 223
Prostitutes 52, 56–57, 61, 63, 207
Protestants 110, 129, 136, 139, 140
Le Puits de sainte Claire 169, 187, 192
Puppets 2, 25–44, 49, 79, 90, 101, 224

Quicherat, Jules 199, 217

Rachilde (Marguerite Eymery) 198
Radegonde, Saint 163, 166, 187
Raphaël 103
Redon, Odilon 5, 47–81, 93, 113, 114, 224, 225
Relics 4, 106, 123, 127, 177, 191, 224
Republicans in France 2, 5, 49, 72, 181, 195, 201, 214, 226–228
Restoration 2
Le Rêve 2, 6, 83–116, 166, 233
La Révolte des anges 184
Ribadeneira 8
Rivière, Henri 5, 25–44, 51, 76, 90, 93, 114, 204, 224, 231
Romans 146, 149, 150, 151, 185, 186, 205, 210
Romanticism 52, 68, 71, 89, 98, 109, 163, 184, 186–187, 193, 198, 197–198, 201, 204, 208, 211–212, 224
Rops, Félicien 52–53, 59, 114
Rossi, Giovanni Battista de 152–54
Rosweyde, Héribert 142, 144
La Rôtisserie de la reine Pédauque 190, 191
Rouen 20–21, 79, 93, 199–201, 209, 213, 217–218
Rougon-Macquart series 84, 99, 107, 108
Rousseau, Jean-Jacques 230
Roze, J.-M. 105, 108
Rutebeuf 131–132, 138

Saba, Queen of 186
Sabatier, Paul 150, 159
Saint-Hilaire, Geoffroy 67, 68, 81
Saint-Sulpice 36, 44, 103
Saint-Victor, Hugues and Richard 105
Sainte Lydwine de Schiedam 8, 119–138
Salammbô 43, 98
La Salette 4, 98, 114, 231
Salis, Rodolphe 25–44

Salons (Painting), Paris 10, 51, 61, 113, 225, 232
La Salpêtrière hospital 59, 64, 80, 98, 101, 114, 231
Sand, George 9, 79–81
Sartre, Jean-Paul 13
Schiller, Friedrich 218
Schoengauer, Martin 48
Schools 2, 8, 74, 140, 196, 202, 226
Schopenhauer, Arthur 206
Schwabe, Carlos 95–97, 112, 113, 231
Schweitzer, Albert 155
Scolastica, Saint 164, 179–183, 192
Sculptures 85, 108, 110
Second Empire 2, 8, 49, 228
Les Sept Femmes de la Barbe-bleue 175
Serpent 18, 23, 63, 67, 72–74, 173
Sérusier, Paul 93
Shadow theater 2–3, 25–44, 51, 76, 79, 84, 90, 112, 224
Sheba, Queen of 33–34, 52, 61, 72, 79
Sickness 5, 7, 37, 44, 47–48, 57–59, 65, 80, 100, 120, 207, 229, 232
Simond, Charles 111
Simorg-Anka 52
Sivry, Charles de 30
Skepticism 2, 122, 140, 163, 174–175, 181
Smedt, Charles de 149, 156, 158
Société des Anciens Textes Français 116, 120
Solanges, Saint 97
Solesmes 141, 147, 155
Somm, Hnery 28, 30
Sphinx 50, 65–67
Stained glass 1, 4–5, 8, 13–23, 27, 32, 36, 39–40, 88, 92, 95, 110–111, 224
Suffering 61, 64, 80, 120, 121, 125–128, 130, 131, 133, 135–136, 138, 225
Superstition 7, 170, 181, 191, 209
Sur la pierre blanche 172
Symbolism 4, 27, 35, 50, 52, 65, 91–95, 105, 95, 110–113, 199
Syphilis 48–49, 57–59, 80, 152, 157, 207

Taine, Hippolyte 98, 199, 203,
Tapestries 19, 21, 88, 224
Tassaert 49
La Tentation de Saint Antoine 5, 8, 13, 25–44, 47–81, 90, 92–93, 100, 166–168, 170, 187–189, 224

Teresa, Saint 64, 80, 98, 105, 209, 220, 223, 231
La Terre 84
"La Terre et les Morts" 196, 202, 213
Thaïs 64, 164, 167, 169, 178, 182, 192
Thaïs, Saint 64, 164, 167, 169, 178, 182, 192
Theater 1–2, 7, 25–44, 84, 93, 101, 112–113, 224, 228
Theosophy 74, 225
Third Republic 2–3, 8, 64, 196–197, 215, 229–230
Tiburtius 151, 153
Tillemont, Sébastien le Nain de 140–142, 155
Tinchant, Albert 30, 32
Todorov, Tzvetan 17–19, 23
Tourism 208–210, 213, 226, 232–233
Translations of saints' lives 5, 9, 42, 84, 87, 88, 91, 103, 105, 106, 108, 109, 112–113, 120, 123, 143, 155–157, 159, 193, 199, 221
Tristan und Isolde 206, 219, 220
Trois contes 8, 13–23, 84, 90, 92–93, 100, 111, 112
Tyrrell, George 141, 142, 156

Uruboros 74

Valerian, Saint 151, 153
Valfroy (or Vulfilaicus or Walfroi), Saint 172, 190
Vatican 144, 149, 150
Verlaine, Paul 27, 50, 113
Verne, Jules 220
Veronica, Saint 141
La Vie de Jeanne d'Arc 164, 216
La Vie des saints 4–5, 8, 97, 102–105, 115–116
Villiers de l'Isle-Adam, Philippe-Auguste-Mathias 27
Vincent, Saint 193
Virgin Mary 15, 98, 99, 103, 114, 120, 125, 188, 231
Virgins, 85, 91, 100, 134, 151, 155, 174, 179, 183, 188, 191, 200, 201, 205, 207, 209, 210–212, 219–220, 231, 232
Visions 5, 7, 13–23, 39, 47–81, 83–118, 126–128, 130, 134, 136, 144, 146, 151, 154, 159, 166, 169, 185–187, 188, 192, 224–225, 232

Vitae 3, 7, 50, 121, 187, 224, 229
Voltaire 113, 209, 230, 232

Wace 121, 125, 134, 135
Wagner, Richard 32, 34, 94–95, 11, 112, 113, 206–209, 212, 219–220; Odin 34; *Tristan und Isolde* 206, 219, 220; Walkyries 34, 207
Wellhausen, Julius 155
Weyden, Rogier van der 84
White, Hayden 216, 228

World War I 42, 201, 205, 206, 214, 219, 234
Wyzewa, Teodor de 105, 109, 113

Zacchaeus 141
Zola, Emile 5, 10, 83–116, 122, 127, 166, 186, 188, 223–235; *La Conquête de Plassans* 98–99, 114; *La Faute de l'abbé Mouret* 98–99; *Le Rêve* 2, 6, 83–116, 166, 233; *Rougon-Macquart* series 84, 99, 107, 108; *La Terre* 84

www.ingramcontent.com/pod-product-compliance
Lightning Source LLC
Chambersburg PA
CBHW051216300426
44116CB00006B/602